W9-ADB-871

Contemporary Italian Sociology

A Reader

This book is published as part of the joint publishing agreement established in 1977 between the Fondation de la Maison des Sciences de l'Homme and the Press Syndicate of the University of Cambridge. Titles published under this arrangement may appear in any European language or, in the case of volumes of collected essays, in several languages.

New books will appear either as individual titles or in one of the series which the Maison des Sciences de l'Homme and the Cambridge University Press have jointly agreed to publish. All books published jointly by the Maison des Sciences de l'Homme and the Cambridge University Press will be distributed by the Press throughout the world.

Cet ouvrage est publié dans le cadre de l'accord de co-édition passé en 1977 entre la Fondation de la Maison des Sciences de l'Homme et le Press Syndicate de l'Université de Cambridge. Toutes les langues européennes sont admises pour les titres couverts par cet accord, et les ouvrages collectifs peuvent paraître en plusieures langues.

Les ouvrages paraissent soit isolément, soit dans l'une des séries que la Maison des Sciences de l'Homme et Cambridge Press ont convenu de publier ensemble. La distribution dans le monde entier des titres ainsi publiés conjointement par les deux établissements est assurée par Cambridge University Press.

Contemporary Italian Sociology

A Reader

Edited, translated and with an introduction by
DIANA PINTO
Research Fellow, Institut d'Histoire du Temps Present, Paris

CAMBRIDGE UNIVERSITY PRESS
Cambridge
London   New York   New Rochelle   Melbourne   Sydney

EDITIONS DE LA MAISON DES SCIENCES DE L'HOMME
Paris

CAMBRIDGE UNIVERSITY PRESS
Cambridge, New York, Melbourne, Madrid, Cape Town,
Singapore, São Paulo, Delhi, Tokyo, Mexico City

Cambridge University Press
The Edinburgh Building, Cambridge CB2 8RU, UK

Published in the United States of America by
Cambridge University Press, New York

www.cambridge.org
Information on this title: www.cambridge.org/9780521281911

© Maison des Sciences de l'Homme and Cambridge University Press 1981

This publication is in copyright. Subject to statutory exception
and to the provisions of relevant collective licensing agreements,
no reproduction of any part may take place without the written
permission of Cambridge University Press.

First published 1981
Re-issued 2013

A catalogue record for this publication is available from the British Library

ISBN 978-0-521-23738-3 Hardback
ISBN 978-0-521-28191-1 Paperback

Cambridge University Press has no responsibility for the persistence or
accuracy of URLs for external or third-party internet websites referred to in
this publication, and does not guarantee that any content on such websites is,
or will remain, accurate or appropriate. Information regarding prices, travel
timetables, and other factual information given in this work is correct at
the time of first printing but Cambridge University Press does not guarantee
the accuracy of such information thereafter.

MILSTEIN
H+M
22
.I55
C66
1981

Contents

Preface   *page* vii
Acknowledgements   ix
Biographical Notes on the Authors   xi
Introduction, by Diana Pinto   1

Part I The Labour Market

1 Internal Migrations and the Capitalist Labour Market   33
  Massimo Paci
2 The Mansholt Plan and the Mezzogiorno   47
  Enrico Pugliese
3 From Capital to Periphery   66
  Franco Ferrarotti
4 Some Hypotheses on Education in Italy   78
  Marzio Barbagli
5 Education and Internal Migrations   90
  Marzio Barbagli

Part II Social Classes

6 Middle Strata in the Mechanisms of Consensus   101
  Alessandro Pizzorno
7 Uneven Development and Social Disaggregation: Notes
  for an Analysis of Classes in the South   124
  Carlo Donolo

Part III Social Actors and Politics

8 The Trade Union Movement, Social and Economic Crisis
  and Historical Compromise   159
  Emilio Reyneri
9 Ten Hypotheses for the Analysis of New Movements   173
  Alberto Melucci

Part IV Dualism, the Welfare State and Market Economy

10 A Case of Welfare Capitalism: Italian Society   195
      Laura Balbo
11 Class Structure in Italian Society   206
      Massimo Paci

Part V Appendix

12 From Sociological Research to the Enquiry   223
      Vittorio Capecchi

Index   231

Preface

In preparing an anthology of contemporary Italian sociology for an English-speaking public I have set myself a double task: first, of presenting a series of sociological reflections on Italy in the 1970s, and more importantly of stressing that this largely unknown scholarship is central (or should be) to the concerns of the international social science community. The problems Italy has had to confront in the last decade, as I stress in the Introduction, are pertinent to all national experiences, whether in the most 'advanced' or the 'less developed' parts of the world. This anthology, therefore, is not didactic in the conventional sense of the term and must carry its own justification for international 'centrality'.

I should first say a word about what the anthology does *not* purport to achieve. It does not provide an overall 'sampler' of Italian sociological scholarship. Many sociological areas in which Italian research is largely derivative or simply on a par with other traditions have been omitted (e.g. the sociology of organizations, mass media, polling, social psychology). More specialized fields such as the sociology of religion or of the theatre have also not been included. Italian work in social theory, whether as a reflection of the 'old masters' such as Mosca and Pareto, or as a more contemporary reflection on the state (one thinks here of the work of Norberto Bobbio), is also left out because it belongs more properly to the realm of philosophy and jurisprudence.

This anthology in effect carries a 'thesis': namely, that in analysing the social and economic imbalances of Italian society in the 1970s Italian sociologists have touched upon the crucial social problems which are both the consequence and the residue of a modernization strategy which pervaded *all* countries in the postwar period. Indeed, in my opinion, one can speak of Italy as 'metaphor' in the study of far larger social, economic and political settings, and it is with this criterion in mind that I have chosen the twelve texts in this anthology, even when they seemed uniquely concerned with the most specific of Italian issues.

The compilation of anthologies often involves difficult choices, the weighing of comparative advantages and painful decisions on what to leave out. I feel I owe the reader one explanation: the work of Francesco

Preface

Alberoni, one of Italy's foremost sociologists, does not appear here. His theoretical analyses of the 'nascent state' and of collective movements span time periods and geographical areas far beyond contemporary Italy and could not be treated with justice in this book. Furthermore, his full-scale work *Movimento e Istituzione,* which contains his key ideas, is forthcoming in English translation from Columbia University Press. The English-speaking reader will therefore have access to Alberoni's work without my having to distort it to fit this anthology's analytical scheme.

In preparing this anthology I have naturally incurred many debts; the first is to all the Italian sociologists whose opinions and ideas have fed, shaped and reshaped my vision of the field. Needless to say, all the errors and omissions are mine, as is the final 'slant' given to the anthology.

Two persons have been particularly encouraging during the long preparatory phase of the anthology: Clemens Heller of the Maison des Sciences de l'Homme, who originally suggested the idea for the anthology and who subsequently financed several research trips to Italy where I was able to meet sociologists from all parts of the country, especially, thanks to the Italian Social Science Council, in Catania, Sicily, and who also financed a great portion of the final typing of the anthology manuscript. Suzanne Berger gave a critical reading of the introduction at a time when I was no longer sure 'Italian sociology' could ever really be 'explained'. Patricia Williams and Susan Allen-Mills of Cambridge University Press must also be thanked for their patience and for their trust in the final product.

D.P.

Acknowledgements

The editor and publisher wish to thank the following authors, journals and publishing houses for having given permission to translate and to reproduce the texts in this anthology:

1. The journal *Problemi del Socialismo* of the Fondazione Lelio e Lisli Basso–Isocco for Massimo Paci's 'Migrazioni interne e mercato capitalistico del lavoro', *Problemi del Socialismo,* no. 48 (September–October 1970), pp. 671–87.

2. The journal *Inchiesta* for Enrico Pugliese's 'Piano Mansholt e Mezzogiorno', *Inchiesta* (Winter 1972), pp. 11–20.

3. Franco Ferrarotti for permission to translate portions of his book, *Roma da capitale a periferia* (Bari 1974), pp. 6–13, 27–38.

4. The publishing house Il Mulino for excerpts from Marzio Barbagli's book *Disoccupazione intellettuale e sistema scolastico in Italia* (Bologna 1974): 'Alcune ipotesi sull'educazione in Italia'; and 'Educazione e Migrazioni interne', pp. 11–27, 465–78.

5. The Agnelli Foundation which sponsored the conference for which the paper was written and the publishing house Garzanti for the use of Alessandro Pizzorno's 'I ceti medi nei meccanismi di consenso' in F. L. Cavazza and S. R. Graubard (eds.), *Il caso italiano,* 2 vols (Milan 1974), pp. 315–37.

6. Carlo Donolo and the *Quaderni Piacentini* for the use of 'Sviluppo ineguale e disgregazione sociale nel Mezzogiorno', *Quaderni Piacentini,* no. 47 (July 1972), pp. 101–29.

7. The journal *Il Mulino* for the use of Emilio Reyneri's 'Movimento sindacale, crisi socio-economica e compromesso storico', *Il Mulino* (July–August 1977), pp. 501–13.

8. Alberto Melucci and the *Quaderni Piacentini* for the use of Melucci's 'Dieci ipotesi per l'analisi dei nuovi movimenti', *Quaderni Piacentini,* no. 65–6 (February 1978), pp. 3–19.

9. The journal *Inchiesta* for Laura Balbo's 'Un caso di capitalismo assistenziale: la società italiana', *Inchiesta* (July–August 1977), pp. 11–16.

10. The *Archives Européennes de Sociologie* for the reproduction of Massimo Paci's 'Class Structure in Italian Society', *Archives Européennes de So-*

ciologie, xx (1979), 40–55. This is the only text which has not been newly translated for this anthology.

11. The publishing house Il Mulino for excerpts from Vittorio Capecchi's article, 'Dalla ricerca sociologica all'inchiesta' in P. Rossi (ed.), *Ricerca sociologica e ruolo del sociologo* (Bologna 1972), pp. 108–20.

Biographical Notes on the Authors

BALBO, Laura: born in 1933, Associate Professor of Urban Sociology at the University of Milan. Her main sociological interests centre on the links between the family, the state and society. She is the author (with G. Chiaretti and G. Massironi) of *L'Inferma Scienza* (Bologna 1975); *Stato di famiglia* (Milan 1977); and most recently has edited with R. Zehar, *Interferenze: lo stato, la vita familiare, la vita privata* (Milan 1979).

BARBAGLI, Marzio: born in 1938, Professor of Sociology at the Faculty of Education of the University of Bologna. He has carried out research on Italy's educational system, writing with M. Dei, *Le vestali della classe media* (Bologna 1969), and *Disoccupazione intellettuale e sistema scolastico in Italia* (Bologna 1973). He is currently interested in changes in family structure in Italy in the period 1880–1950, and is also carrying out empirical research on the organizational structures of the militants in the Italian Communist Party.

CAPECCHI, Vittorio: Professor of Sociology at the Faculty of Education of the University of Bologna, editor of the journal *Inchiesta,* Director of the Bureau of Studies of the Metal Workers' Union (FIOM) for Emilia Romagna, editor of the journal *Quality and Quantity.* Capecchi's most recent work has focused on sociological analyses of production in the context of his trade union activities.

DONOLO, Carlo: Professor of Political Sociology at the University of Salerno, trained in jurisprudence in the Normal School of Pisa and in social sciences at the Institut für Sozial Forschung in Frankfurt. Author of numerous articles on the student movement, the state, politics and the Frankfurt School, he has written *Mutamento o transizione?* (Bologna 1977), and edited, among other works, *Classi sociali e politica nel Mezzogiorno* (Turin 1978). He continues to be interested in social classes and the link between politics and the state, particularly in the South.

Biographical notes

FERRAROTTI, Franco: born in 1925, Professor of Sociology at the University of Rome, editor of *La Critica Sociologica*. He is the author of several works, the most recent of which are *Roma da capitale a periferia* (Bari 1970); *Max Weber e il destino della ragione* (Bari 1972); and, most recently, *Alle origini della violenza* (Milan 1979). Ferrarotti and his team of researchers are currently completing a major sociological study of the city of Rome, its class divisions and productive activities.

MELUCCI, Alberto: born in 1943, Associate Professor of Political Sociology at the University of Milan. He has a doctorate from the Ecole Pratique des Hautes Etudes where he worked under Alain Touraine. He has written the following books: *Lotte sociali e mutamento* (Milan 1974); *Classe dominante e industrializzazione* (Milan 1974); and *Sistema politico partiti e movimenti sociali* (Milan 1977); he also edited *Movimenti di rivolta* (Milan 1976). He is currently working on the theoretical implications of individual and collective identity and on the new type of mobilization of women's, youth and ecological collective movements, while also analysing the problem of collective violence and terrorism.

PACI, Massimo: born in 1936, Professor of Economic Sociology at the University of Urbino (Ancona). His interests include the sociology of the labour market and of the family. He has written (with B. Contini), *Difesa del suolo e sviluppo dell'agricoltura* (Bologna 1972); *Mercato del lavoro e classi sociali in Italia* (Bologna 1973); *Immagine della società e coscienza di classe* (Padova 1969); *Famiglia e mercato del lavoro in un'economia periferica* (Bologna 1980); he has edited *Capitalismo e classi sociali in Italia* (Bologna 1978). His 'Education and the Capitalist Labour Market' appeared in J. Karabel and A. H. Halsey (eds.), *Power and Ideology in Education* (New York 1977).

PIZZORNO, Alessandro: born in 1924, Krupp Foundation Professor of European Studies at Harvard University, former director of the Department of Sociology of the University of Milan. He has written extensively in the realm of industrial and political sociology. Among his works is *Comunità e razionalizzazione* (Turin 1960). He was the editor and research director of a six-volume study on Italian industrial struggles of the late 1960s, *Lotte operaie e sindacato in Italia 1968–1972* (Bologna 1975–8), and the editor with C. Crouch of *The Resurgence of Class Conflict in Western Europe since 1968* (London 1978). He is currently working on the problems of political representation and the state.

PUGLIESE, Enrico: born in 1942, Associate Professor of Economic Sociology at the University of Salerno and researcher at the Centre for Economic and Agrarian Studies at Portici. He has worked on the problems of the Italian South and on the role of agriculture in the labour market. In addition to numerous articles he has co-authored with G. Mottura, *Agricoltura, Mezzogiorno e mercato del lavoro* (Bologna 1975); he has edited with A. Graziani, *Investimenti e disoccupazione nel Mezzogiorno* (Bologna 1979). His most recent work in English is 'Capitalism in Agriculture' in F. Buttel and H. Newby (eds.), *The Rural Sociology of Advanced Societies* (Allanhead Osmun 1980). He is a frequent contributor to the journal *Inchiesta*.

REYNERI, Emilio: born in 1943, Associate Professor of labour sociology at the University of Catania and director of the Centre for Research on Work Problems of the ISVI (Instituto di Formazione e Ricerca sui Problemi Sociali dello Sviluppo). His principal interests are in the sociology of work and industrial relations, industrial democracy and trade unionism. Most recently he has been working on the impact of migration in the European and Southern labour market, analysing the latter as a subsidized economy. He has written (with M. Regini) *Lotte operaie e organizzazione del lavoro* (Padova 1971); (with M. Regini and I. Regalia) 'Labour Conflicts and Industrial Relations in Italy' in C. Crouch and A. Pizzorno (eds.), *The Resurgence of Class Conflict in Western Europe since 1968* (London 1978); *La catena migratoria* (Bologna 1979). A recent contribution in English is his 'Migration and Sending Area as a Subsidized System in Sicily', *Mediterranean Studies*, ii (1979), no. 3.

Introduction

Diana Pinto

Perched on top of the international North–South divide, and often referred to as the 'last of the first and the first of the last', Italy provides ideal terrain for a sociological understanding of the interpenetration of the logic of modernization and the logic of backwardness. This interpenetration also exists elsewhere, of course, and is the outcome of the encounter of advanced urban industrial settings and the more traditional agrarian, artisanal and commercial components of society. It is in Italy, however, with its chronic division between North and South, that the convergence has been most dramatic.

In the last decade Italy has had to confront the economic crises, social conflicts and political tensions linked to the industrial growth, sectorial reconversion and international competition of the most advanced countries, along with the social dislocation, increased economic dependence and peripheral roles of the underdeveloped countries. One example will suffice: during the economic crisis of the 1970s, Italy was unable (like France or Germany) to send her *gastarbeiters* home because they were her own citizens, Southern workers (uncomfortably) 'home' in the North.

Seen as the 'sick man' of Europe, Italy has been studied most recently as a special case among Western democracies and advanced industrial nations. Indeed its very claim to membership in the 'club' has been at times reconsidered by Italians and non-Italians alike. Even non-experts have a vision of Italy in the last decade as a country besieged by intense working-class militancy and strikes, social struggles in agrarian and urban environments, a worsening economic situation, heavy unemployment, rising middle-class fears, violence, youthful anomie and, most recently, the scourage of terrorism. Italy's political instability and ungovernability and its weak state, when coupled with the 'problem' of the Communist Party's entry into the government, have also contributed to the general international attention paid to the country in recent years.

Contemporary anxiety over Italy's political, social and economic problems has only matched in intensity the exaltation which similar observers had expressed only a decade earlier when contemplating Italy's 'eco-

1

nomic miracle' and her rapid entrance into the ranks of advanced industrial societies. There is a difference, however. For most of the early
1960s the Italian case was seen as an example of economic growth, modernization, social mobility and cultural brilliance. Studies of the country
abounded in English as proof that the Western democratic (and the
'American') model of development, with all of its social correlates, could
work and be exported.[1] Significantly, the most recent studies of Italy's
crisis, internal imbalances, social dislocation and economic dualisms have
been mainly in Italian, even when the experts writing them have been
American or European. The two major collections which analyse the
Italian crisis, *Il caso italiano* (edited by F. L. Cavazza and S. Graubard)
and *La crisi italiana* (edited by L. Graziano and S. Tarrow), have not been
translated or presented in their complete form in to English even
though they were the product of transatlantic cooperation.[2] The implicit
assumption is easy to perceive: when Italy was doing well she could be
pointed out as an example of Western strength and success; when she
was doing badly, the *specificity* of her 'case' had to be stressed so as not to
bring into question the entire Western frame of reference. The desire to
stress the uniqueness of Italy's development also found eager allies in
the ranks of young Italian leftist intellectuals, bent on showing that because of her 'special' conditions Italy could be ripe, unlike the rest of
Europe, for revolutionary change and for a Marxist-inspired scenario of
anti-capitalist class struggle led by a newly united working class.[3]

In a curious alliance between extremes, Italy's uniqueness throughout
most of the 1970s stood as a guarantee for the preservation of the industrial modernization models of the liberal and social democratic planning intelligentsia (in America as well as Europe) and for the revolutionary hopes of the Left.

The presentation to an English-speaking public of some of the most
significant Italian sociological work of the last decade is intended to re-
fute the argument of Italy's 'specificity'. Although the texts presented
obviously provide a clearer understanding of Italy's particular social and
economic problems, this is not the primary purpose of the anthology. I
have chosen to present Italian sociology because the problems it ad-
dresses, the themes it analyses and the questions it raises are of great
importance internationally.

Italian sociological writing in the last decade can be characterized as
motivated by two key scientific and political concerns: first, a reappraisal
and understanding of the interpenetration of North and South in Italian
society beyond the traditional categories which saw the North as 'advanced' and the South as 'backward', and the former capable of pulling
the latter into the path of modernization; and, secondly, an analytical

search for a collective social actor capable of producing structural reforms which Italy needed, and capable therefore of uniting the necessary forces throughout the *entire* Italian peninsula.

In pursuing these two fundamental tasks, Italian sociologists in the 1970s may not have found any easy answers, but they were forced to confront some of the most significant problems of contemporary societies, while demystifying in the process the 'pet' theories of development (whether Marxist or non-Marxist) that have accompanied postwar social science in the Western world in general. In reappraising the links between North and South they have provided a major critique of modernization models, while delving deeper into the structural consequences of economic dualism and its side effects which have been surprisingly productive where least expected (in the traditional sectors and in the peripheral areas). In pursuing the search for a collective social actor, they have also criticized Marxist class analysis in respect of the role it accorded to the industrial working class and to the traditional and marginal sectors of society, while offering new insights into the role of politics and the welfare state in class formation, as well as the role and limits of collective movements and trade unions as social actors.

The result has been a sociology which, in explaining Italy's problems in the 1970s and in providing a critique of modernization, exhibits three tendencies. First, it is integrally intertwined with economic analyses of development and therefore markedly different from the French and American traditions where economics and sociology do not generally mix. Secondly, it is involved in a continuous dialogue with Marxist analyses while at the same time criticizing their structural positions and terminologies. Thirdly, it is directly implicated in the intellectual–political positions and choices of Italian society, and therefore composed of sociologists who are intellectual actors in their own right, *qua* sociologists.

The themes which we have just mentioned – the analysis of the labour market and its dysfunctions, the analysis of social classes, the limits of social actors in a political context and the analysis of the welfare state and the market economy – do not constitute abstract sociological topics pursued by an academic profession, but rather are historically defined and concrete responses to the very real problems besetting Italian society in the 1970s, and integral elements of the most important Italian intellectual and political debates of the decade.

Before analysing in detail the themes and texts presented in the anthology, it is important to provide the reader with two major background elements: a summary of the models of social and economic development which guided Italy's growth in the 1960s and against which contemporary sociology has rebelled; and a rapid overview of the multiple phases in postwar Italy's social and political development without which the references in the texts cannot be fully understood.

'Modernization' as a social and economic model

The texts presented here gather their full meaning when they are seen as reacting to the prevalent models of social and economic analysis which characterized postwar social science in the 1950s and 1960s in the Western world in general and in America in particular. They are opposed to a dream which failed to materialize, to the model of 'modernization', a social-science construct whose overwhelming power is drawing to a close. It is important to realize, however, that there were 'cracks' in the model well before the international economic crisis of the 1970s. Nowhere were these cracks more analytically visible than in Italy.

Firmly anchored to the star of economic growth, claiming the ability of this growth to foster both social harmony and political democracy, modernization theories found a fertile terrain in the 'reality' of the postwar world, especially in the years after reconstruction in America and Europe. With the advent of decolonialism in Africa and Asia, modernization theories above all conditioned Western analyses of the process of development in these 'underdeveloped' areas, where economic growth, national consolidation and social homogenization had to take place concurrently. They provided a global pattern of analysis with which to trace and chart change throughout the world.

This is not the place in which to enter into a profound analysis of the term 'modernization', whose archaeology (à la Foucault) and whose history would shed immense light on the essence of our postwar period. We would simply like to point out here the key tenets which accompanied this notion as it was translated practically in social-science writing of the 1950s and 1960s.

The first of these tenets was the placing of primary emphasis on economic growth as the motor of all social, political and cultural development, as the 'key' pole around which the rest of society would modernize. Perceived in a quasi-mechanistic manner, economic growth was believed to occur in stages of development, culminating in the creation of an industrial society after an agricultural revolution, marked migration to the cities and the establishment of industrial activity.[4]

Secondly, there was the creation of a structural–functionalist outlook which was directly linked to the belief in the centrality of economic growth, whereby all activities which fostered it were deemed to be functional and traditional or lagging sectors considered dysfunctional. This outlook, perhaps best demonstrated at a theoretical level in the work of

Talcott Parsons and Robert Merton, had a marked impact on perceptions of society, the state and politics, education, family and the role of
the intellectual.[5] We can examine these briefly in turn.

Society

Economic growth would lead to a profound transformation in
social structure, a transformation meant to favour the advent of the most
advanced industrial classes. Traditional sectors such as artisans, shopkeepers and peasants would decline, to be replaced by a consolidated
working class, a technically productive middle class and an advanced
industrial sector. Marxist and non-Marxist social thought concurred on
the primacy to be given to the economically advanced and productive
sectors of society. Disagreement arose over the relationship between the
advanced industrial working class and the capitalist sector, the Marxists
postulating the advent of a 'new' society through the class struggle,
whereas modernization theorists stressed that in an advanced industrial
society class conflict would be merely one conflict among many others,
not threatening the system as a whole but adding to its functional dynamism.[6] As the working class benefited from upward mobility, shared
increasingly in the benefits of society and above all performed highly
skilled work, society would become the rationally streamlined counterpart of an ever-expanding economy, where each individual would occupy a multitude of roles. The disappearance of the 'traditional' sectors
was assumed to take place automatically since their relationship to the
means of production (increasingly industrial and sophisticated) would
ultimately become dysfunctional.

The state and politics

Deprived of any normative transcendence, the state became a
vestige of a traditional historical epoch. By giving priority to 'civil society', its economic growth and social transformation, modernization theories assumed that the state could not shape social classes and economic
development. Its sphere diminished both in Marxist and non-Marxist
ideas. Its reincarnation as the 'welfare state' put it on a different plane
where it functionally redistributed the benefits of economic growth
throughout society, not unlike a broker.

In a parallel manner, politics was seen as the reflection of society's
economic and social interests, devoid of any independent mediating
function. With the increasing homogenization of society (one of the presuppositions of modernization theories), political life was expected to

5

lose most of its unbridgeable divisions, as parties became the conveyor belts for increasingly similar aggregate interests.[7]

Education

The functional conveyor belt of an industrial society, education was assumed to grow in proportion to the need for skills and culture generated by a growing economy and a modernized society. It was a motor for individual upward mobility, the breaking-point for traditional patterns of behaviour, perceptions and values, the melting pot for a modern mind.[8]

Family

Perceived as extended in traditional societies, the family performed an economic role for its members, each of whom participated in some productive manner to its internal organization. Through modernization the family was supposed to become 'nuclear', limited only to parents and children. Rather than performing an economic role (carried out by adults as individuals), the family was to become the locus of emotional and intellectual resources for its members. It would provide the non-functional affective core for a modern industrial society, transmitting 'values'.[9]

Intellectuals

No longer perceived as exalted anguished prophets, intellectuals were to become competent specialists with a functional role to perform on behalf of society both in the spreading of knowledge and in the pointing out of practical solutions for society's problems. As scientists of society, the new intellectuals were assumed to strive for a 'value-free' position.[10]

Eminently rational and positive eighteenth-century constructs, the intellectual foundations of modernization theories left little room either for the weight of history, culture and marginality or for clashing interests and passions. Harnessed to the motor of economic growth, they were supposed to bring even the most underdeveloped countries towards the goal of becoming harmonious advanced industrial societies. Readers of this anthology will readily recognize their own national version of these theories of the 1960s, fed by the presuppositions of an economic growth which was not susceptible to major crises, given the new regulatory failsafe mechanisms of Keynesian economics. This modernization dream was perhaps best epitomized in the ambitious social-science research programmes financed by the Ford Foundation in the 1950s and 1960s which influenced all Western social science.

The description of modernization offered here borders on caricature in its extreme simplification. We have only included it to provide a substratum against which the element of 'reaction' in the texts of Italian sociology could be understood. The texts included are all bent on reevaluating the fundamental assumption of modernization theories, i.e. the positive and functional consequences of economic growth and its derivatives. Paci, Pugliese and Ferrarotti point out the dysfunctional consequences of economic growth, industrialization and the creation of advanced economic sectors in Northern as well as Southern Italy. Barbagli counters the functional interpretation of education by stressing that it is not positively correlated to economic growth and can even be inversely correlated. Pizzorno and Donolo rethink the role of the state in the formation of class interactions as well as in the preservation of traditional declining sectors, while stressing that politics *can* determine the equilibrium of social classes far more than economics. Reyneri and Melucci reflect on the weight and limits of social actors with political responsibilities, such as trade unions and collective movements, both of which operate consciously outside and often in opposition to political parties. Balbo pursues an economic-structural analysis of the family in the context of the welfare state to show the degree to which it is still conditioned by economic imperatives. Paci stresses the degree to which Italy's economic vitality in the 1970s is the product of a new type of rationality based precisely on those traditional semi-agrarian classes and small industrial sectors whose end modernization theories had postulated. Capecchi's reflection on the role of the sociologist, which is included as an appendix to the anthology, counters the ideal of the social scientist as specialist operating in a 'value-free' setting with a vision of the intellectual/sociologist consciously involved in social engagement.

We will now examine in greater depth the Italian political and social setting in which these texts were written since they span in their references the entire postwar period.

The Italian context, 1945–1980

The brief summary which follows seeks primarily to present the main phases of Italy's postwar development insofar as they fit our sociological preoccupations. In a wider sense, however, this summary also tries to sketch the major turning points which Italy encountered in a far from atypical journey toward modernization. The key theme will be the interaction of Italy's North and South in the creation of a modern industrial society. It is precisely *vis à vis* this theme of North and South that the influence of modernization models mentioned earlier made itself most felt.

We can briefly distinguish four phases in Italy's postwar development with respect to the North–South theme, four phases which form a running commentary of Western perceptions of the solutions to underdevelopment: the years of reconstruction: 1945–1955; the years of the 'economic miracle': 1956–1962; the years of Centre–Left planning: 1963–1968; and the years of crisis: 1968–1980.

Reconstruction

This period, characterized by a climate of ideological tension and the effective existence of two Italies, spans the laborious process of rebuilding after the devastation of the Second World War. Northern industrial reconstruction took place in a climate of economic liberalism, with heavy unemployment at first, a certain amount of trade union repression, and with priority given to the export market, as Pizzorno stresses in his article on 'Middle Strata in the Mechanisms of Consensus'. The South was still seen as a vast traditional agrarian hinterland, a 'special' area the backwardness of which can only be understood in terms of a long-standing historical exceptionalism resulting from the uncompleted and distorted process of Italian unification.[11] It is this traditional emphasis on the 'Southern Question' that Donolo seeks to combat in his analysis of the South's problems and class structure, by stressing that the problems of the South in the 1970s are not at all the same as those it had traditionally confronted previously. The changes Donolo mentions in terms of the South began to take place precisely during the phase of Reconstruction and were embodied in two institutions: the Cassa del Mezzogiorno and the Svimez. The Cassa was created in 1950 to foster a 'special' public intervention on behalf of the South; it was designed to promote land reform by dismantling large landholdings in order to render Southern agriculture more productive. The Svimez was established to encourage the creation of industrial activity in the South.[12] As Pugliese stresses in his article, the Cassa in reality subsidized not only the lands but also the peasants living on them in an 'across the board' manner. The Svimez, on the other hand, sought to single out those structural areas with the greatest potential for industrialization. In both cases, however, during the years of Reconstruction, Southern development was seen as a 'special' case within the Italian setting, and was not yet struc-

8

turally integrated into the national economy. Both in the North and in the South the years of Reconstruction still carried the imprint of the weight of the past and its traditional agrarian predominance.

The 'economic miracle'

The 'miracle' in Italy's economic growth refers to the unleashing of unprecedented industrial and commercial energies in the wake of a very rapid reconstruction. From a static prewar society, Italy became an industrial nation with a yearly GNP growth of 7.9 per cent or more from 1956 to 1961.[13] This sudden and unexpected boom – due mainly to a non-recurring 'conjuncture' of a low-paid skilled work force, a vast reserve of unemployed, the opening of international and European markets and the inevitable consumer take-off after years of scarcity – altered the political and intellectual climate of the country. Emphasis was placed on technological innovation and growth in the industrial setting, on the dynamism of the economy and on the capacity of overcoming historical inertia and traditions. It was during these years of the 'economic miracle' that Northern industries, having fully employed the available Northern work force, began to attract Southern workers. The great migrations from the South to the North began to take place in 1957–58, contributing to Italy's growth in two ways: by providing needed workers for the North and by removing excess workers from a Southern countryside which required rationalization in terms of agricultural production. The movement from the countryside to the cities and from the South to the North was seen as an inevitable but positive dislocation in the passing from a traditional world to a modern industrial society. In the context of the 'economic miracle' the North was increasingly seen as the 'locomotive' capable of pulling the whole of Italy into modernization. This modernization was based less, however, on the actual interpenetration of Northern and Southern economies than on the moving north of Southern labour. This thus left intact a Southern hinterland which, it was assumed, would follow mechanically in the North's progress for the most advanced sectors, while the traditional sectors declined.

The North's booming consumer economy, the vista of constant economic growth and the crisis of Marxism after 1956, combined to give the impression that a new advanced working class, as well as a modern industrial bourgeoisie, were becoming the pillars of 'industrial society'. Pizzorno, however, shows that the 'economic miracle' was in effect spurred not only by exports but also by the traditional sectors of society, which in buying these new consumer goods with incomes largely derived from rent, in effect falsified the impression of a newly vibrant society in which those who produced were also those who consumed. Paci finds the key to the dysfunctional effects of the North's industrialization in the economic choices which called for massive immigration without a corresponding technological innovation during the boom years. Paci, Pugliese and Barbagli underline the negative consequences of the emigration of the South's best workers on that region's chances of 'catching up', or any rate of following, the Northern industrial model. The phase of the 'economic miracle' was more the product, as we have seen, of a fortuitous combination of social and economic factors. It was not 'planned' as such by the competent political authorities. One can truly speak of an economic surge which generated major changes in society and seemed to incarnate the tenets of modernization. However, the impact of modernization models in Italy did not take place during this phase of spontaneous growth, but rather in the years that followed which coincided with the planning hopes of the Centre–Left. It is for the developments of the 1960s that Italian sociologists in the 1970s would reserve their harshest critiques.

Centre–Left planning hopes

The formation of a Christian Democratic–Socialist political alliance in 1963 opened up vistas of a potential political harmony in a setting in which social and ideological tensions seemed to be minimized. Political planning of economic and social developments stressed Italy's modernization in the context of advanced industrial nations. Italy's reference points were no longer her internal history of the North–South divide but the European Economic Community and international markets. The North's 'economic miracle' was the first step in a national economic boom which would be furthered through judicious economic and social planning rather than the mechanisms of economic liberalism. The Centre–Left planning hopes of the early 1960s translated themselves into two visions: better social planning, community services and economic organization for the North (where the wave of Southern immigrants was significantly visible), and a new policy of development for the South which put the emphasis on its industrialization. With the renewal in 1965 of the Cassa del Mezzogiorno's 'special intervention' in the South, the notion of selective intervention gained ground among Italian planners. Rather than fostering global aid to the South's agriculture and peasantry as a whole, as the Cassa had done in the 1950s, selective intervention sought to concentrate its efforts in the areas of greatest economic potential. These areas then became 'poles of development' where high-level capital-intensive industrial activity should be fostered. Modernization of the South was conceived along the lines followed in the underdeveloped countries, i.e. through the establishment of key industrial sectors which were supposed to pull the area out of its backwardness by generating local demands and spreading goods and services, thus creating the economic prerequisites for an advanced self-sustained market. It was the consequences of this 'selective' intervention that sociologists in the 1970s, such as Pugliese and Donolo, criticized most severely.

In the context of modernization theories planners in the 1960s saw the 'Southern Question' as a technical problem which the economists could solve with the right social scientific instruments, and with the reorganization of the labour market already taking place through migration. Both in the North and in the South the years of the Centre–Left corresponded to a phase in which the social and political organizations linked to the ruling class significantly increased their power and effective influence in Italian society. A new class of entrepreneurs emerged, mediating between the state and contracting companies scheduled to carry out modernization projects. It is this new class of intermediaries and its *political* weight in the formation of economic change which Pizzorno and Donolo analyse.

The hopes generated by the Centre–Left alliance, the seemingly inevitable economic growth and the crisis of orthodox Marxism combined to make Italy adopt in the 1960s the social, cultural and political reference points of modernization theories whose content we have outlined in the preceding pages. These themes reflected in themselves the sociological concerns of the 1960s.

Italian sociology in the 1950s had largely developed on the margins of Italian cultural life, with a heavy Northern orientation and a major interest in the reality of working-class and factory life.[14] This interest in the most advanced industrial groups translated itself in the late 1950s into an interest in the major technological changes which the 'economic miracle' had made visible, along with an interest in the changing social composition of the working class and in the repercussions of economic growth on Italian society. The South was not a major subject of sociological research, except for those interested in analysing the traditional world of the peasantry in a quasi-anthropological perspective.[15] The Northern orientation of Italian sociological production was all the more intensified during the years of the 'economic miracle' and the Centre–Left, since the North's 'locomotive' was deemed responsible for Italy's development. When topics such as immigration were broached, they were typically perceived from the Northern end, and in terms of the social-psychological adjustment of the immigrants to a changed cultural setting.[16] The functional aspects of Southern immigration were unquestioned. The turning to a sociological analysis of the South in terms of its impact on national development was one of the key characteristics of the new sociological orientation of the 1970s which we are presenting in this volume.

In the 1960s Italian sociology spread out beyond an interest in industrial sociology and a concern for technological changes in society to encompass new themes directly linked to modernization models: analyses of mass society, consumerism, and the spreading of popular culture suggested that Italy had evolved away from a setting where working-class and 'highbrow' culture were the only poles of reference.[17] Politics, no longer perceived as the locus of insoluble ideological tensions became a field for sociological study, with patterns of analysis derived from the USA. Symbolic of these new concerns is Giorgio Galli's analysis of the Italian political system as a type of 'imperfect bipartism'.[18] Local-level studies of party militants in the Christian Democratic and Communist Parties encouraged the tendency to analyse political life in terms of interest groups and individual mobilization.[19] Sociologists evoked structural–functional ideas while studying social mobility and the tertiary sector, with the implicit assumption that as the economy expanded the qualitative result of Italy's full-fledged modernization would be the blurring of the old dividing lines between social classes.

Most importantly, in cities like Milan, at the Lombard Institute for Social and Economic analyses (ILSES), and in Turin and Rome, social and economic analyses of the transformations of Italian society began to be carried out in the context of modernization theories for planning desired social changes. Social scientists and modernizers seemed to share the same commitment to fostering a modern industrially advanced Italy. The theme of the 'labour market' was favoured among planners concerned with social needs as well as the manpower needs of Northern development.

One cannot understand Italian sociology in the 1970s without realizing that it constituted both a reaction to the failures of Centre–Left planning hopes, as well as a reaction to the modernization assumptions of its own sociological work in the 1960s.

The Centre–Left 'took off' precisely at the moment when the factors which had made the 'economic miracle' possible ceased to exist, and its hopes were quickly dashed. In 1963, Italy attained a level of nearly full employment, with the subsequent transformation of the bargaining positions of the working class, while at the same time the market for Italian goods was stabilized through the Common Market. Capital investment and technological innovation now took place in an extremely competitive international setting, where Italy's position was not strong. The social consequences of modernization (immigration, agricultural reconversion and newly available workers) began to take effect throughout Italy precisely at the time when the economic boom which underlay their presuppositions ceased, when the 'locomotive' of the North began to show its first weaknesses. The Centre–Left's inability to carry out reforms revealed the weight of the traditional sectors whose interests in modernization did not match those of the reformers. Not accidentally, the North–South division reappeared in this context, where the means provided for the 'selective' intervention in the South constituted new power bases and strengthened a new clientelary system linked to the state. The contradictions inherent in Italy's complex economic and social setting beneath the surface exploded in the late 1960s. The bulk of the articles in the anthology include the reactions of sociologists to the contradictions generated precisely by the modernization of the 1960s. The two main elements of modernization brought under examination were the mechanism of immigration to the North, with its dysfunctional repercussions on the imbalances of the labour market, and the 'selective intervention' in the South, with its dysfunctional social and economic perturbations in Southern lands and cities. These perturbations spilled into the Northern areas and thus brought *all* of Italy into a *common* social and structural crisis.

The 'crisis' years

The period which began in the late 1960s and continued in the late 1970s can best be understood as a series of four distinct phases, each comprising its own social struggles and political hopes. The sociological work included in this anthology is integrally linked to each of these phases, not only because it analyses their social consequences but also because the sociologists themselves were active participants in the elaboration of possible solutions to Italy's social and political problems throughout the decade. The four phases can be defined as follows:

1. *1967–1970:* the dashing of Centre–Left hopes and the rise of new social actors in the working class and the student movement.

2. *1970–1973:* the discovery of the 'Right' in power; the predominance of its social bases and economic structure, as well as the power of the traditional sectors of society.

3. *1973–1976:* the consolidation of a militant and diffuse Left in the trade unions, collective movements and the PCI, attempting to conquer power from the Christian Democrats and the traditional sectors they represented.

4. *1977–1980:* the confrontation, with two aspects in the Italian situa-

13

tion: (a) its major structural problems of a weak state, the lack of alternative political actors, the inability to provoke reform and the weight of terrorism; (b) Italy's 'defence mechanisms' against the weakness of any planning agent in terms of a parallel and peripheral or 'hidden' economy along with spontaneous adaptations to both the welfare state and the market economy.

1967–1970

Starting with the collapse of the barrier which separated Catholic working-class trade unions and student groups from their Communist or left-wing counterparts, which occurred with the explosion of the ACLI – the Associations of Italian Catholic Workers – in 1967, this period witnessed the spectacular rise of a united working-class militancy for new qualitative social demands (as opposed to simple wage increases), such as better pensions, job security and the abolition of outdated professional categories. Culminating in the massive strikes of the 'hot autumn' of 1969, the Northern working class (in whose ranks many new Southern workers could be found), led by the powerful Metal Workers' union, managed to obtain significant concessions from its industrial interlocutors while gaining official recognition in mediation by the state itself. Moreover, working-class protests also changed the trade unions' internal structure, making it more open to industrial democracy.[20] The working class had grown out of its traditional representative organizations just as the university students had grown out of theirs in the university in the student struggles of 1968.

Protesting against what were seen as the rationalizing values of a capitalist industrial society, its alienation, increasing work tempos, unfulfilled promises in terms of social services and the capitalist organization of work, workers and students seemed to form separately, as well as together, a new collective movement whose strength came precisely from the undermining of the political visions of modernization. These movements were not only separate from but also in opposition to the established political parties of the Right and the Left: they were 'extra-parliamentary'.

In the late 1960s a certain revolutionary 'euphoria' prevailed, provoked by the belief that since workers and students had obtained important concessions and changes in their respective milieus, the balance of power in Italy had swung away from the reformist modernizers and their 'misplanning' into the hands of socially innovative forces. One must stress, however, that these forces were 'Northern'. The great 'events' of the late 1960s took place mainly in Italy's industrial triangle. Anti-capitalist in their approach, generously borrowing from the Marxist tradi-

14

tion, both the working class and the student movement were merely trying to substitute a revolutionary 'head' to a modernization perspective which still continued to stress the most advanced sectors of society and the priority on the big industries of the North.

The 1970s in Italy are best characterized by the gradual moving away from this exclusively Northern perspective on the most advanced social classes. Italian sociology moved correspondingly toward a social vision which took into account the following factors: the presence, role and impact of the more traditional sectors of society, whether shopkeepers, artisans, or peasants; the distinction between a central and a peripheral working class and their often contrasting interests; and the awareness of Italy's territorial complexity and interpenetration beyond the North–South divide, specifically with reference to Italy's central regions. This gradual 'opening' to the other sectors of Italian society took place in the following years.

1970–1973

The hopes of the Left in the late 1960s were put to the test when it became apparent that the gains of the working class and of the students had not brought about significant changes in the political system. Indeed, frightened by the gains of the Left, Italy's 'Right' raised its head once more. In December 1969, neo-fascists dropped a bomb in a major Milanese bank, killing and wounding several people, in the hope of provoking a 'strategy of tension'. In 1970 there was an attempted coup d'état planned by right-wing generals, led by Borghese. More importantly, in 1971 and 1972 a series of massive uprisings occurred in the cities of the South, the most important of which was in Reggio Calabria, in which urban masses, unemployed and marginal workers issued contrasting demands: on the one hand, for jobs and social services, on the other, against the consequences of modernization and planning in the South. Theirs was a struggle against territorial as well as social marginalization. These social protests proved that the traditional sectors of society and even the 'lumpenproletariat' were not dying out, as modernization theories had presupposed, but were actually being reinforced by the immigration of former peasants thrown off the land by the modernization of the Southern countryside. Not readily integrated in the Northern trade union and collective movements, these social classes who were manifesting their frustration against the state and its social and economic planning, were in fact coopted by traditional right-wing groups of a Poujadist or neo-fascist persuasion. The importance of the South and its traditional classes for the *entire* Italian setting became rapidly visible, especially with the realization that working-class interests in the

North and in the South were often at odds. In the 1972 administrative elections, as the number of Fascist votes increased significantly in the South, the Christian Democrats formed their first Centre–Right government since the Centre–Left gains of the early 1960s, in an attempt not to lose to the Fascists their hold over the traditional classes and clientelary network of the South. Politics thus no longer reflected society's most advanced interests (which should have been those of the industrial, reformist, productive North), but rather cast light on the 'invisible' power (clientelary, landed, based on rent) close to the sphere of the state. The Southern case revealed the presence of marginal traditional classes. Elsewhere in Italy, even in the North, traditional classes began fully to show their weight in the same period, by using the slogans and techniques of the working class and student Left for their own often corporatist ends. Pizzorno mentions the tertiary sector employees whose revenue and status levels could not be compared with those of the working class but who chose to adopt class analyses in their own critique of capitalism. A Centre–Right government meant that the victories of the working class in the North were more than minimized when the moment came to translate them into effective national reforms. Italy's lagging sectors were in effect throwing their weight against the advance of the Left.

1973–1976

Starting in 1973 and with an ever-growing crescendo up to 1976, Italy witnessed the consolidation of the social conquests of the Left and their turning into an effective political alternative at the national level and no longer strictly in the North. One can speak of three different groupings for the Left: the trade unions, the collective movements and the PCI.

The trade unions, united in a common, coordinated strategy, in 1973 attempted to forge a plan for the renewal of Italy's economy, for a politics of employment and for a balanced distribution of resources between the North and the South. In this phase the unions strove to be the spokesmen not merely for the industrial working class of the North and their 'own' workers but for all workers and the unemployed, in a national strategy of economic and social renewal. They sought to take on in their national programmes the planning responsibilities which the political establishment had in effect abdicated. In the battle against the forces of 'rent' (i.e. the clientelary and traditional interests not only of the South but also of the North), which Pizzorno describes in his article, the trade unions were willing to collaborate in the drafting of an economic plan with the most flourishing enterprises in the country (FIAT, Pirelli, etc.). The front on behalf of reform was thus widened to include both sides of the industrial 'barrier', which had been opposed in the late 1960s. The key theoretical question in this context is: who were the natural allies of the working class?

Under the heading *collective movements* in this period one has to place the many issue-oriented movements which arose out of the student movement of the late 1960s: the feminist movement, hospital workers, teachers, tenants' unions, all gathered in 'collectives' and militant at the grass roots level. It is in these contexts, using petitions and focusing on clear, one-issue problems, that the collective movements formed the backbone for the reforms of civil society, their most spectacular results being the divorce referendum of 1974, the change in the family code of 1975 and the referendum on abortion of 1976. The advantage of such collective movements was that they could flourish throughout the country, in the Northern industrial cities as well as in the smallest Southern towns. They were not structurally wedded to an industrial setting nor to the presence of an organized working class as were the trade unions. Their significance as carriers of new social innovative demands is analysed in Melucci's article.

The spectacular rise in political significance of the Communist Party of Italy (PCI) was the third element in the Left's social and political consolidation along new national themes. The party's line, adopted after the lessons of Chile, of coming to power with the support of rather than against the Christian Democratic social base, marked an attempt to unite *all* reforming forces in society against the conservative poles. The party embodied in the mid-1970s the political complement to the social and economic struggle carried out by the trade unions and to the civil rights struggles carried out by the collective movements. As a political actor, it had the advantage of being able to mobilize forces throughout the country, which did not necessarily recognize themselves in the trade union movement, in a broad attempt to change the political equilibrium from below at the local level, against the conservative forces in power. The 1975 administrative elections marked the party's entrance into local government and the creation of 'red' city councils and mayors, beyond the classic example of Bologna. After its victories at the local level in 1975 and at the national level in 1976, the PCI sought to carry out the line of the 'historic compromise' with the Christian Democratic Party, in an attempt to come to power.

This phase was therefore marked by a great faith in the ability of collective social and political action to perform two essential tasks: to fight against the power of the traditional classes, 'rent' and the conservative forces of society; and to pursue a programme covering both the needs of the North *and* the South in a truly national policy of development, to redress the imbalances of a 'capitalist' interpenetration. In this programme the forces of the Left tried to win over other social groups whose protests might be added to the 'cause' (employees, functionaries, small businessmen, etc.). The political voluntarism of the late 1960s seemed to be giving way to organized political struggles.

1977–1980

After the successes of the Left's united collective action in 1973–76, this period was marked by a harsh confrontation with Italy's seemingly insoluble structural problems: a weak state, the lack of an alternative collective movement and a precarious economic situation. The PCI's entrance into the arena of government in 1977–78, in what was intended as a first step in the 'historic compromise' with the Christian Democrats, in fact provoked a series of divisive and even subversive reactions in the ranks of the Left, whose most extreme position was that of terrorism. This malaise translated itself in the trade unions, in the collective movements and in the creation of a disenchanted, politically and socially disaffected 'autonomous' area.

The trade union front whose strength in the late 1960s had come precisely from the avoidance of partisan politics inside a Left advocating structural reforms, threatened to break down, as Reyneri shows, on the issue of support or opposition to the PCI 'compromise'. Political divisions occurred precisely at the time when new social and economic conditions rendered the situation far more complex than the optimism of the late 1960s had warranted. The international economic crisis led the trade unions to abandon the global and ambitious reform programmes of 1973. Priority was given to their own traditional constituency of organized workers, facing potential lay-offs, economic reconversions and a constant battle against inflation.

Reyneri stresses how the power of the 'base' was being lost in the trade union organizations of the late 1970s. The same is true for the collective movements whose dynamism had been so vital in fostering society's reforms. Their grass roots' ardour was spent in a social setting in which reforms could not always take place by referendum and where political parties would espouse them. Melucci stresses the complexity of the relation to politics of these various movements. They needed to make contact with the political dimension but were also afraid of being coopted by it. While some of these forces were funnelled into political life through the Radical Party (a libertarian, issue-oriented, 'gadfly' party) in a newly revitalized Perliament, others strayed into private 'life-styles', social psychological pursuits, or into apathy and disenchantment. Their success in recruiting a mass-level base had little effect upon the power structure. A part of this frustration was seen in the 'events' of 1977 in Bologna where 'autonomous forces' marched in the streets protesting against the PCI's betrayal of its revolutionary mission and its entrance into the social and political 'establishment'. In his article Melucci criticizes the tendency of political parties (even on the Left) to see these protests as the product of marginal and deviant groups; he stresses instead their thorough and devastating critique of society, a critique which must be heeded. At a more extreme level, terrorism had sought to wipe out all tendencies to compromise within the PCI and to return it to its class positions in a revolutionary war, since the party seemed to be bogged down with all the responsibilities of power and none of its benefits. Moro's kidnapping and murder coincided precisely with the political accord which brought the PCI into the area of government.

It is perhaps significant that in this phase of political stalemate and social crisis national attention should focus on two 'old' elements, rendered once again relevant by the failure of the social and political voluntarism of the 1970s: the problem of the state and the presence of a peripheral, 'parallel' economy which keeps Italy running, despite the worst predictions of economic disarray, by adapting rapidly to the changing market situation. As was mentioned in the section on modernization theories, the state was supposed to lose its importance in an increasingly modernized society, giving way to a welfare state preoccupied with the maximal distribution of society's social and economic benefits. By the late 1970s, as Balbo's article shows, the welfare state had failed to materialize not only in Italy but also in even more advanced countries, where its premises no longer held. More importantly, in Italy references to the state took on an increasingly Hobbesian meaning as its weaknesses were analysed and its necessity in institutional political and defence terms was invoked against its numerous enemies.

A similar step backwards in terms of the assumptions of modernization theories was also made in the realm of Italy's economic development. Paci advances new interpretations of productivity that controvert Marxist and non-Marxist definitions which link economic growth to the most advanced social classes. Italy's productivity was not to be found in the big industries of the North but in the 'peripheral' economy in which agrarian activities complemented those in small industrial enterprises – precisely the two sectors which modernization theories had assumed would gradually die out. In this context, new definitions of privileged and non-privileged workers emerged, no longer along conventional Marxist lines but rather taking into account new criteria such as workers who are 'guaranteed' (with respect to job security, pensions, etc.) and those who are not (in precarious jobs, with no trade union support). The

19

very postulation of a productive 'peripheral' non-subsidized economy in Italy threw off the conventional conceptualizations of the country in terms of the North–South dichotomy, since it emerged that this new economy was located most often in Italy's central regions.[21]

One can say that by the late 1970s the decomposition of the modernization model had attained its peak. Some of its productivist tenets had been kept artificially alive in the 1970s by massive doses of political and social voluntarism. When social analyses referred to the spontaneous 'making-do' mechanisms of the Italian economy as the new leading sector of productivity, the very tenets of modernization came under fire, as, one may add, did the hopes of changing Italian society through social actors, whether in the trade unions or in the collective movements. The structural analyses which accompany Paci and Balbo's articles are not linked to any visible social collective actor which could enact change, as had been the case in the early 1970s. Their analyses offer social explanations of a market mechanism which continues to persist despite all efforts at social planning.

Italian sociology

Having provided a theoretical and political background to contemporary Italian sociological scholarship, we can finally turn to the texts included in this anthology. They can be most fruitfully divided along four main themes: the dysfunctional organization of the Italian labour market; the composition of social classes and their interrelation to each other and the state; the consequences of the integration of social and political action; and the interconnection between welfare state and the market economy in Italy.

We showed earlier how these texts embodied critiques of modernization theories and of Marxist analysis, as well as reflecting the limits of social and political movements in generating social change. We also stressed the direct links between these texts and the reformist ideals which dominated the Italian context in the last decade, and which the sociologists themselves shared. In this section we will turn to the theoretical implications and actual content of these texts.

Labour market

This economic term, long the preserve of socially oriented economists calculating the impact of emigration, 'human capital' and manpower needs for a modernizing society, was taken over by Italian sociologists in the late 1960s and used as a tool for detecting the dysfunctional mechanisms of modernization. It is, indeed, by comparing the original economic forecasts and assumptions for the late 1960s (drawn up around 1965) with their effective social consequences, that sociologists such as Massimo Paci in his 'Internal Migrations and Capitalist Labour Market' were able to show how Southern migration to the North was dysfunctional to the North itself. This migration did not in actuality fill new vacant jobs but instead generated a process of 'substitution' in the job market, where the weaker work forces of the North were no longer able to compete with the younger, less demanding forces of the South. The net result was a disruption of the regional labour market of the North and the importing of unemployment from the South, with a corresponding creation of pockets of underdevelopment in the North itself. Paci analyses this phenomenon by a careful collation of employment and immigration statistics, by interviews and by comparisons with projected objectives. His conclusions are a clear rebuttal of the tenets of modernization. Despite a massive upward shift in skill levels and an expansion of the most advanced sectors in Lombardy's economy, there has been no significant upward mobility either inside the working class itself or from the working class to the tertiary sector. Once again migrations account for the increase in qualified jobs and personnel in Lombardy. In analysing skill levels, Paci provides a useful explanation of the problems of working-class organization which led to the industrial struggles of the 'hot autumn' of 1969. He also anticipates the rise of severe unemployment in the North, even *before* such major developments as inflation or the international economic crisis had taken place. In searching for solutions to the imbalances of the labour market, Paci investigates a 'social policy of work' which would regulate the national labour market. This is an explicit reference to the hopes that the trade unions could become such a regulatory and policy-defining body.

Enrico Pugliese analyses the dysfunctional consequences of modernization on the labour market of the South in his 'The Mansholt Plan and the Mezzogiorno'. He shows how the creation of poles of development and the application of European standards of production in the South disrupted a delicate equilibrium. Traditional agrarian occupations were eliminated and new industries implanted, but the labour force could not be shifted from one sector to the other because the industries were capital-intensive and could not possibly replace the number of jobs lost in the traditional sector. Furthermore, these poles of development were really 'cathedrals in the desert', since they did not generate subsidiary activities which could lead to 'take off' in the South. The result was the creation of marginal workers, living at a peripheral and subsistence level, no longer able to rely on their traditional pursuits and without

21

access to the modern productive sector. It was the problems of this type of marginal worker forced to leave the countryside for non-productive cities which generated the uprisings of Reggio Calabria. Like Paci, Pugliese also looks to some national planning agent, such as the working class in its trade unions, to evaluate the entire Italian labour market situation before advocating given models of modernization for the South.

In his analysis of Rome's shantytowns, Ferrarotti shows their functional dualism in a capitalist city which was bypassed by the process of modernization, while Rome became Italy's bureaucratic and administrative centre. Rome's labour market is uniquely composed of 'men suspended between countryside and city and belonging to a world that is no longer peasant but not yet industrial'. The shantytowns are thus populated by those marginal groups which have been excluded from Marxist analysis, and whose real power in society cannot be underestimated. For Ferrarotti, the way out of Rome's problems is to be found in the strengthening of collective movements on behalf of basic human rights, such as housing and rudimentary social services. Working-class associations or trade unions have no place in this social universe, whose structural equivalents can be easily found in many of the cities of developing nations.

Barbagli takes the theme of the labour market into the realm of education, to counter the functionalist belief that education is a correlate of an expanding society and economy. He shows in historical perspective that education (especially higher education) grew as a function of economic backwardness and high youth unemployment. He gives as an example the high number of university students to be found in the South. Indeed, it is the more backward areas of the South which provided skilled labour for the most advanced areas of the North, thus perpetuating the peripheral condition of the South.

The category of the labour market is a useful tool in analysing the interpenetration of the North and South in the Italian setting, but it is a category which tends above all to emphasize the *economic* consequences of migration, in particular for the advanced working class in the North. It leaves untouched the problems of the traditional social classes and declining sectors particularly with respect to their importance in the realm of politics or the state. We mentioned earlier the political context of 'backlash' which led to the reflection on the nature of social classes in Italy. Let us now turn to its sociological implications.

Social classes

In Italy the debate on the composition of social classes was sparked off in 1972 by a short essay written by an economist, Paolo Sylos Labini, *Saggio sulle classi sociali*. This essay demystified the central notion held by the Left in Italy in the early 1970s that the strength of the working class in its trade unions was sufficient to carry out the structural reforms which Italy needed, especially if combined with the political need for change also exhibited by the 'productive' middle classes. The assumption underlying this analysis of the Left was that an increasing number of the middle classes were losing their social status and economic standing in a process of pauperization; this made them victims of 'Big Capital' and thus potentially allies of the working class. The formulation of this sociological category was particularly crucial for the political and social forces waging the battle against 'rent', i.e. for the trade unions and for the PCI which was already trying to widen its constituency.

Sylos Labini countered the assumptions of the Left by stressing two central points. First, rather than becoming 'proletarized', both the working and middle classes were instead occupying an increasingly strong position in Italy's economic life. If anything, their entente was possible because of their improved economic condition, not the reverse.[22] Secondly, and perhaps more important, Labini stressed that the interests of these so-called 'productive' middle classes were often not at all compatible with those of the working class, because they were in reality corporativist, traditional and even parasitic. Labini referred to the struggles of state employees or those in banks and insurance companies whose standing was far superior to that of the most advanced sectors of the working class. The conclusion for Labini was that the Left had first to rethink traditional Marxist analysis which saw society bifurcating, with an ever-growing gap between the haves and the havenots; and, secondly, to reconsider before incorporating in its ranks social strata whose corporativist interests were incompatible with those of the working class proper in what would otherwise be a paralysing dilution of its programmes.[23]

In the political context of the Centre–Right government and in the wake of the Reggio Calabria uprising, Labini's provocative essay led to a major sociological debate, on the one hand concerning the nature of social classes in Italy and their internal relations to each other, and towards the political apparatus on the other.[24] Spurred perhaps by the political desire of finding the 'correct' social allies for the working class in its quest for structural reforms, sociologists were led to analyze the complexity of the economic and political roles of the middle classes and the equally strong complexity of the working class.

The two articles dealing with this question in this anthology, Alessandro Pizzorno's 'Middle Strata in the Mechanisms of Consensus' and Carlo Donolo's 'Uneven Development and Social Disaggregation: Notes for an Analysis of Classes in the South', take into account the differences and similarities of the problem in the North and in the South. Both Pizzorno and Donolo refer to the impact of modernization and its negative consequences in their analyses of the interconnection between the middle strata and the marginal working class, a relation whose prime motor is not economic but political. Their emphasis on the political component in the formation of social classes contradicts the tenets both of modernization theories and Marxist analysis, but it explains the complex organization of a society at the crossroads between a welfare state and modern clientelary relations. For both Pizzorno and Donolo, the social composition of the South in the 1970s is the product of *new* social and political configurations created in the postwar period by 'special interventions', and thus does not bear a direct link to the South's traditional historical 'backwardness'. As Donolo says in his article, 'The Southern Question is dead.'

Pizzorno stresses the particular role which the middle strata performed in assuring mass consensus for the interest groups who were linked to Christian Democracy in the postwar period, i.e. groups which were the key mediators for that modernization whose structural effects Paci and Pugliese had already criticized. New 'parasitary' classes emerged as the by-product of modernization itself, but exercised a power which might be eroded by the very nature of the urban masses which the South's modernization had produced. For these masses, the product of migrations from the countryside, finding no jobs in the cities and having lost their traditional social structures, became free-floating, pursuing individual itineraries of economic survival, itineraries least susceptible to clientelary control. Pizzorno, however, is quick to point out that these Southern contradictions were not easily understood by a North whose reformist front was riddled by its own internal clashes between trade unions and industrialists.

Donolo, using Marxist-derived categories, analyses in depth the nature of the Southern working classes and their apparent inability to fuse into an organized whole on the issue of reform. Writing as a voluntarist in search of a political force capable of solving the South's problems, Donolo at times refers (perhaps too simplistically) to the role of the capitalist factory in the formation of a cohesive working class. Pizzorno, incidentally, sees this tendency to idolize the big factory as one of the great faults of the Italian Left. Despite his voluntarism, Donolo's analysis of the contradictions and incompatibilities inside the working class between central, peripheral and marginal workers is inexorable. It has obvious echoes in the underdeveloped world, where the central working class is a privileged force when compared to all those with marginal occupations. It is not a coincidence that Donolo often makes reference to work carried out in Latin America.

The fragmentation and internal incompatibility of the two principal reformist axes, the working class and the middle strata, when analysed in depth and with particular reference to their Southern aspects, helps to explain the failure of the collective actors to provoke change in Italy in the 1970s.

Social actors and politics

How can social action be translated into effective political action, and how can large-scale national change arise from specific, often regionally circumscribed, groups? These are the dilemmas which Italian trade unions and collective movements (whose strength lay particularly in the North) had to confront in their attempt to embrace Italy's global social problems.

Reyneri deals at length with the dilemmas of the trade unions confronted by political forces (in this case the PCI) pursuing the same goals of reform. Taking on a global strategy without compromising one's sectorial responsibilities is the central problem of the trade unions caught in the tension between the central working class, which is their primary constituency, and the marginal and peripheral working classes which they have not organized but whose economic status and social role cannot be overlooked when charting a national reform policy. Reyneri also places the power of the trade union base in perspective by looking at a longer time period of trade union activity and its cycles of centralization and decentralization.

Melucci examines the political role and social actions carried out by different collective movements. He examines how their 'essence' is often lost in political translation, while at the same time their key goals cannot be fulfilled at a local or grass roots level. Without a coherent political vision collective movements which deny or criticize society run the risk of anomie, marginality, violence or even terrorism. Melucci stresses, however, the degree to which 'marginality' itself becomes an ideological category of those political forces (on the Right and on the Left) which are bent on disarming the subversive impact of collective movements whose vision of change is far more dramatic than that allowed for by political mediators. The tensions between collective movements and political organizations are also those which exist between a social activism based on issue-oriented problems, in which all interested social groups or individuals can participate, and a social activism perceived in terms of class interests and therefore open only to a restricted constituency.

Of the texts presented in the anthology, Melucci and Reyneri's are the least economic-oriented, but they are integrally linked to the other texts by the political and social questions addressed by Italian sociology in the 1970s.

Dualism, the welfare state and the market economy

In the texts presented so far the negative consequences of modernization have been underlined: its dysfunctions and its creation of peripheral and marginal social classes and areas of development, both in the advanced industrial North and in the less developed South. The failure of modernization could only be matched by the apparent failure to find a collective force capable of carrying out Italy's structural reforms. The relative weakness of the working class on a national scale, and its internal divisions, seemed to undermine the bases for organized change and for an alternative vision of society, postulated in the euphoria of the late 1960s. Italian sociology seemed to be an exercise in analytical frustration.

The last two texts presented in the anthology are cast in a somewhat different light and underline some of the functional or at least newly productive consequences of Italy's dualism. They are in a way 'explanations' of why Italy, despite her major political, economic and social flaws, still manages not only to survive but to keep steadily afloat. Laura Balbo's analysis of the family in the Italian welfare state and Massimo Paci's study of the Italian class structure interpret what could be called functional adaptations to a dysfunctional setting, whereby families as well as entire social classes learn to 'make do' with what is available, given the clear absence of political and economic planning. In a sense both Balbo and Paci's texts underscore Italian ingenuity, albeit analysed in structural economic and social terms. They are also reflections on the coexistence and interdependence of the services of the welfare state and those of a market economy.

Balbo analyses the organization of family life in Italy as a function of the resources available to it from paid employment, social services and domestic work, in what is a realistic appreciation of the peripheral economy which offers the greatest potential for alternative solutions when compared to the enormous difficulties of life in the industrial factory setting.

Paci performs a thorough analysis of the social and economic structures of the peripheral economy as it exists in Central Italy. Here small industries and enterprises hire a semi-urbanized peripheral working class that has still kept one foot in traditional occupations of domestic work and even agriculture. Given the diversification of its tasks, this working class is thus able to absorb the shocks of the international market and economic cycles more easily.

Paci stresses that this peripheral working class has nothing in common with traditional or parasitary classes but is a fully productive social group which does not even rely on the services of the welfare state to carry out its activities. The analysis of Italy's peripheral economy thus makes it imperative to redefine the notion of 'productive' beyond the standard references either of modernization theories or conventional Marxist analyses. This productive dualism is perfectly adapted to the international division of labour and is far less rigid than the major industrial concentrations of Italy's Northern regions.

Italy's central regions and peripheral economy constitute at present the frontier of most active sociological work in Italy. This new emphasis, ironically, marks a return to that type of small-scale productivity which modernization theories had regarded as obsolete and dysfunctional, both for the advanced countries and those on the road to development. It could well be that a more harmonious small-scale interpenetration of industry and agriculture, which this peripheral economy represents, is more in keeping with the effective structural reality of the world's economy, since it respects more well-established traditional equilibriums.

Italian sociologists as political intellectuals

The texts included in this anthology have all been written by authors who were directly involved in the social and political life of Italy in the 1970s. Sociologists have participated in the work of trade union study centres in trying to map a plan of common economic and social action; they have analysed the sociological composition of the industrial working class to assess its strength and bargaining power more effectively. They have set up and animated collective groups by seeking to gather data on marginal economic and social conditions, particularly in the South but also in the North, with respect to interest groups ranging from students to teachers and hospital workers. In brief, they have shared the hopes and disappointments of Italy in the 1970s. The line between professional research and personal political and social engagement has been deliberately blurred in a vision of how to pursue sociology, best illustrated (even if in an extremist manner) in the pages written by Capecchi which we have included in the appendix.

The sociological treatment of terrorism in Italy has been a significant exception to this situation. The relative newness of the phenomenon, its clandestinity and its seeming marginality during the days of social and political voluntarism have not made terrorism a popular topic with the sociologists we have included here. Their structural socio-economic analyses have not proved adequate to apprise events which cut across political and even social-psychological lines. So far terrorism has been examined in essays which were more the product of concerned citizens, whether journalists or social-psychologist-oriented sociologists than the product of full-fledged sociological *research*.[25] Analyses of terrorism are absent from this anthology because none meriting the label 'sociological' has yet appeared, although work is at present being carried out on the topic.

Italian sociology's political engagement can easily be accounted for. The discipline attained academic legitimation very late and its full institutionalization really dates from the 1970s.[26] Until then, Italian sociology had lived the ups and downs of reformist, modernization-oriented intellectuals in postwar Italy. Sociological work was principally carried out in social and economic research centres generally linked to regional planning agencies, deeply influenced by the model of modernization. The best example of such a planning institute was the Lombard Institute for Social and Economic Studies (ILSES) where most of the sociologists included in the anthology have worked at one time or another (Pizzorno, Paci, Capecchi, Balbo, Reyneri). Others such as Melucci and Pugliese, along with most members of the younger generation of sociologists, attended as students the parallel school for sociological training, the Istituto Superiore di Sociologia, in Milan in the late 1960s.

The critique of modernization theories was for Italian sociologists a critique of the assumptions and climate in which they had carried out most of their work in the 1960s. The rise of political and social voluntarism in the late 1960s was bound to generate new definitions of the role of the sociologists and the search for collective social forces to carry out major changes. In the 1970s most sociologists rallied to the trade unions as the principal collective force, as well as to collective movements, but retained a clear preference for the former and its organizational 'clout'. The Italian sociological work presented here cannot therefore be separated from a certain political activism of the Left. Significantly, its privileged forums for publishing initial phrases of research have not been the professional periodicals created in the 1950s and 1960s, such as the *Rassegna di Sociologia* or the *Quaderni di Sociologia*, but alternative periodicals of counter-sociology such as *Inchiesta*, which sought to promote the new sociology that Capecchi, *Inchiesta*'s editor, had advocated in his article. Other cultural journals of the Left include the *Quaderni Piacentini*, *Problemi del Socialismo*, and the less politically defined progressive journal, *Il Mulino*. Many of the articles included in the anthrology were published in these non-professional journals. Another privileged vehicle for sociological research has been the periodicals linked to the trade unions, such as the *Quaderni di Rassegna Sindacale*.

This phase of dispersed sociological research is now coming to an end. As the younger sociologists have been integrated in the university structure the professional exigencies of career patterns are slowly giving new life to the older professional periodicals mentioned above. One must also underline the pivotal role played by the publishing house Il Mulino in reprinting collections of these combative articles into integrated volumes, thus 'professionalizing' work done in a para-political and *engagé* intellectual context by the generation of sociologists formed in the 1960s. This has been the case for Paci's first volume, *Mercato del lavoro e classi sociali in Italia*, and for Pugliese's book, in collaboration with G. Mottura, *Agricoltora mezzogiorno e mercato del lavoro*.

The sociological research published in this anthology constitutes in most cases a portion of ongoing projects. Each of the authors in the anthology has full-scale sociological works in progress, some of which have recently appeared, and all of which, we hope, will be translated into English. One can already cite among the most recent volumes Emilio Reyneri's *La catena migratoria*, a study of emigration and its impact on the labour market both in the point of origin and of arrival; Massimo Paci's *Famiglie e mercato del lavoro in un'economia periferica*, a study of social and economic life in the peripheral economy of Italy's central regions; and Laura Balbo's *Interferenze: lo stato, la vita familiare la vita privata*, co-edited with R. Zahar, a study of the social and economic function of the family *vis à vis* the 'failed' welfare state.[27]

We hope that this anthology of Italian sociology will have contributed to a better knowledge and understanding of an important current of social science research which is of equal interest to all types of national experiences of development and underdevelopment.

Notes

[1] Cf. Vera Lutz, *Italy, a Study in Economic Development* (London 1962); Maurice F. Neufeld, *Italy: School for Awakening Countries* (Ithaca, N.Y. 1961); George H.

Diana Pinto

Hildebrand, *Growth and Structure in the Economy of Modern Italy*, (Cambridge, Mass. 1965).

[2] The volume edited by Cavazza and Graubard, *Il caso italiano*, 2 vols (Milan 1974), carries contributions by the following English-speaking scholars: Charles P. Kindleberger, Andrew Shonfield, Suzanne Berger, Stanley Hoffmann, Robert N. Bellah, Gerald Holton and Graubard himself. One can also add to the list the 'Europeans' such as Juan J. Linz, Karl Kaiser and Jacques Le Goff. The volume edited by Luigi Graziano and Sidney Tarrow, *La crisi italiana* (Turin 1979), contains articles by Tarrow and Peter Lange, and was the product of initiatives by the Einaudi Foundation, the Council for European Studies and the International Studies Center of Cornell University. Percy Allum and Joseph La Palombara participated in the discussion sessions.

[3] This current of the *operaisti*, who saw working-class struggles as the spearhead of revolutionary action is best represented by Mario Tronti. His 'Sindacato, partiti et sistema politico' in A. Accornero, A. Pizzorno, B. Trentin & M. Tronti (eds.), *Movimento sindacale e società italiana* (Milan 1977), argues for Italy's exceptionalism among other countries confronted with trade union struggles.

[4] As indicative of this interpretation one can cite Walter Rostow, *The Stages of Economic Growth: a non-Communist Manifesto* (Cambridge, 1960); and at a more 'refined' level, Raymond Aron, *Dix-huit leçons sur la société industrielle* (Paris 1962).

[5] Typical of this outlook are Talcott Parsons, *Politics and Social Structure* (New York 1969), and *Structure and Process in Modern Societies* (Glencoe, Ill. 1960); Robert Merton, *Social Theory and Social Structure* (Glencoe, Ill. 1951 and 1968).

[6] One of the best arguments for this interpretation is Ralph Dahrendorf's *Class and Class Conflict in Industrial Society* (Stanford, Calif. 1959).

[7] Cf. Gabriel Almond, *The Civic Culture: Political Attitudes and Democracy in Five Nations* (Princeton 1963); or S. M. Lipset, *Political Man: the Social Bases of Politics* (New York 1960); Gabriel Almond & James S. Coleman (eds.), *The Politics of the Developing Areas* (Princeton 1960).

[8] Cf. R. Clark, 'The Study of Educational Systems', *International Encyclopaedia of the Social Sciences* (New York 1968), vol. 4.

[9] Cf. Neil J. Smelser, *Social Change in the Industrial Revolution* (London 1959), and *The Sociology of Economic Life* (Englewood Cliffs, N.J., 1963).

[10] See Talcott Parsons, 'The "Intellectual": a Social Role Category' and Edward Shils, 'The Intellectuals and the Powers: Some Perspectives for Comparative Analysis' in Philip Rieff (ed.), *On Intellectuals* (Garden City, N.J. 1969).

[11] Among the most important *meridionalisti* works are: Sidney Sonnino, *La Questione meridionale* (Rome 1902); Giustino Fortunato, *Il Mezzogiorno e lo Stato italiano*, 2 vols (Bari 1911); Gaetano Salvemini, *Scritti sulla questione meridionale (1896–1955)* (Turin 1955); Guido Dorso, *La Rivoluzione meridionale* (Turin 1925); and Antonio Gramsci, 'Alcuni temi della questione meridionale', written in 1926 and now regrouped with other writings in A. Gramsci, *La questione meridionale* (Rome 1951). For an overview of the Southern question in Italian political life, see Massimo L. Salvadori, *Il mito del buongoverno* (Turin 1960).

[12] Giuseppe Galasso, *Passato e Presente del meridionalismo*, 2 vols (Naples 1978), I, 56–61.

[13] Hildebrand, *Growth and Structure in Modern Italy*, p. 12.

[14] F. Ferrarotti, *Sindacalismo autonomo* (Milan 1958); L. Gallino, *Progresso technol-*

ogico ed evoluzione organizzativa negli stabilimenti Olivetti (Milan 1960); A. Pizzorno, *Comunità e razionalizzazione* (Turin 1960).

[15] Edward Banfield, *The Moral Bases of a Backward Society* (New York 1958).

[16] F. Alberoni, *Contributo allo studio dell'integrazione sociale dell'immigrato* (Milan 1960).

[17] F. Alberoni, *Consumi e società* (Bologna 1961).

[18] Giorgio Galli, *Il Bipartitismo imperfetto* (Bologna 1967).

[19] F. Alberoni, *L'attivista del partito: una indagine sui militanti di base nel PC e nella DC* (Bologna 1967).

[20] A. Pizzorno (ed.), *Lotte operaie e sindacato in Italia (1968–1972)*, 6 vols (Bologna 1975–8).

[21] Arnaldo Bagnasco, *Tre Italie: la problematica territoriale dello sviluppo italiano* (Bologna 1977).

[22] Paolo Sylos Labini, *Saggio sulle classi sociali* (Bari 1975), p. xii.

[23] *Ibid.*, pp. 135–7.

[24] Massimo Paci (ed.), *Capitalismo e classi sociali in Italia* (Bologna, 1978); Paolo Calza Bini, *Economia periferica e classi sociali* (Naples 1976).

[25] Recent works on terrorism include Sabino Acquaviva, *Guerriglia e guerra rivoluzionaria in Italia* (Milan 1979), and Franco Ferrarotti, *Alle radici della violenza* (Milan 1979).

[26] Cf. Diana Pinto, 'La sociologie dans l'Italie de l'après-guerre: 1950–1980, *Revue Française de Sociologie*, xxi, 2 (April–June 1980), 233–50.

[27] Emilio Reyneri, *La catena migratoria* (Bologna 1979); Massimo Paci, *Famiglie e mercato del lavoro in un'economia periferica* (Bologna 1980); Laura Balbo & R. Zahar (eds.), *Interferenze: lo stato, la vita familiare, la vita privata* (Milan 1979).

I: The Labour Market

1. Internal Migrations and the Capitalist Labour Market *

Massimo Paci

It is a well-known fact that in the last ten to twelve years the phenomenon of internal migration in Italy has touched a significant portion of the mass population. In the Lombard region alone, to which we will refer in particular in these pages, the net migratory total from other Italian regions (not counting therefore migration abroad or migration within the region itself between Lombard provinces) between 1959 and 1968 amounted to 630,000 units.[1] Obviously this major movement of population has significantly altered the nature of the work force in the different regions and the functioning of the labour market. We possess very little knowledge about the social aspect of the migratory phenomenon. Even in the official documents dealing with national and regional economic planning these problems are treated more in terms of hypotheses and deductions than on the basis of objectively reliable data.

In the following pages we will try to fill this gap by replying to a specific question: are the internal migrations of labour forces towards the Northern regions necessary to fill an excess of job vacanies in such regions – an excess which would otherwise remain unsatisfied – or do these internal migrations constitute a threat to the local work force because of greater competitive advantages (possession of specific skills in demand on the local market such as youth, resistance to the new work tempos, low cost, willingness to move, etc.)? Simply by asking this question we are casting doubt on the prevalent view that migrations to the North take place because of its excess of job opportunities. Even the most fervent advocates of the Italian Mezzogiorno have not seriously questioned this view. Yet this interpretation is crucially important for the very battle which the Mezzogiorno is waging. As long as internal migrations appear

* First published in *Problemi del Socialismo*, no. 48 (September–October 1970), pp. 671–87.

vital to the job market of the Northern regions they are open to criticism for their human and social costs or for their indirect economic consequences (on the community structures financed by the Northern administrations). They cannot, however, be criticized in terms of purely economic advantages.

Once these migrations are shown to produce a *process of substitution* of the local work force by immigrant work forces, in effect 'importing unemployment' from the South to the North, any argument based on the necessity of balancing in the short term job opportunities and demand loses its validity.

We must determine first of all, therefore, the identity of those labour forces which have migrated to the North in order to evaluate their contribution to the demands of the job market in these regions in recent years. With respect to Lombardy, for example, it is important to establish what percentage of the 630,000 immigrants in the last ten years were actually members of the work force. As a first estimate, one can say that if 40 per cent of the Lombard population is engaged in work activities the percentage among the immigrant population will certainly be higher, given the greater concentration of such a population in the central brackets of the age pyramid, and also given the fact that they migrated in the first place precisely in search of a job. The Project for the Regional Economic Development for Lombardy, produced by the Committee for Economic Planning for Lombardy in 1966, for instance, predicted that *two-thirds* of the net migration in the years 1966–71 would be composed of members of the employable population.[2] In this case the percentage of work activity for the immigrant population was estimated at 65–66 per cent, markedly higher than the percentage of the resident population. A more cautious and perhaps reliable evaluation was formulated by Adina Ciorli and Franco Momigliano. Using a series of hypotheses linked to age composition and the relationship between males and females in terms of age and schooling in the immigrant population, these authors estimated that in the period 1966–71, out of the net migration of 276,000 persons, 136,000 were employable, i.e. 49.2 per cent.[3] On the basis of a sampling carried out in the autumn of 1968,[4] we found that nearly 10 per cent of all workers in Lombardy were immigrants who had arrived in the previous ten years. When translated in absolute terms, this percentage corresponds to nearly 320,000 persons and therefore to a rate of employment slightly higher than 50 per cent for the population which had immigrated in the decade. We therefore feel we are very close to the truth in stating that nearly half of the net number of immigrants to Lombardy from other regions was composed of an active work force. This means that out of 630,000 immigrants to

Lombardy between 1959 and 1968 315,000 were active members of the working population.

We can now compare this figure with the number of new job openings in the region during the same ten-year period, a figure amounting only to 88,000 jobs. *The number of immigrant workers thus appears to be three to four times higher than the number of new jobs available during the period under study.* Confronted by such a disparity between these two figures, we cannot refrain from thinking that internal migrations did not simply fill new and additional jobs in the North otherwise destined to remain vacant but that they also replaced in work activities certain members of the local population of working age who were either currently working or potentially employable. It is in fact true that for the years 1959–68 unemployment did not increase in Lombardy; the number of unemployed and of those looking for a first job had actually fallen by 50,000. But it is also true that during this same period the percentage of the employed population in the region dropped significantly: for men from 65.3 per cent in 1959 to 59.9 per cent in 1968, and for women from 29.3 per cent to 23.7 per cent. This fall is not compatible with the claim that there was an excess of job supply over job demand in the region.[5] From the data, one has the impression that the immigrant work forces had a much more profound impact on the job market than has hitherto been thought. They not only filled the extra jobs available but also compressed to such an extent the job market that they persuaded certain sectors of the local population to leave it or even not to enter it. One can assume that the immigrant workers, because they were younger, more amenable to change, more adaptable to new work tempos, and above all less well paid, competed with certain local work forces (women, older workers, workers in declining sectors or possessing outdated skills). These workers became progressively marginal to the regional work force and slowly entered the ranks of the non-active population.

The female work force in the region, for example, declined by 67,000 jobs in the years 1959–68, falling from 32.3 per cent of the total work force to 29.3 per cent.[6] In the decade under study, in other words, there was a progressive 'masculinization' of the work force, especially visible in the industrial and service sectors. This decrease in female employment expressed itself by a decline in female work activity from 29 per cent to 23 per cent rather than in an explicit situation of unemployment. During the first years in which it was observed this decrease in female work was assumed to reflect the improvement of the average family's life-style, as well as the increase in female schooling. More careful observers nowadays are becoming worried, since they see the decline in work activity as a sign of hidden or 'discouraged' unemployment.[7]

Massimo Paci

A similar analysis could probably be made for the older workers, who also disappeared from the work force in the period under study. Unfortunately, however, there are no official statistics on regional work forces broken down by age. A certain indication can be had, however, by looking at the levels of activity of the male population over fifty from 1961 to 1967. Within the limits of any comparison between different data sources and age ranges one can still note a marked diminution in the level of work activity of older males (over fifty). This falling-off of work activity is too massive to be attributed to a bettering of living conditions inside the family.[8] More probably the transformations of the productive structure inside the region, in agriculture as well as in industry, led to the expulsion from active working life of vast numbers of older workers, either in possession of obsolete skills or no longer capable of adjusting to the new work rhythms. Faced by the competition of the new younger immigrant workers, these older workers seemed to have preferred to withdraw from active life ahead of time.

In more general terms one can assume that the profound modifications which took place in the last ten years in the sectoral division and structural function of the job market in the region occurred through a process of 'indirect' substitution of the work force. Immigrant workers flocked toward the expanding sectors and professions while local workers fell out of those sectors and professions in decline. This mechanism of substitution in the work force seems to be confirmed by the fact that there has been practically no professional or sectoral mobility of the work forces resident in Lombardy in the last ten years, as has been shown in recent research.[9] Given the profound transformations of the job market, such a scarce mobility in effect does not seem surprising.

The sectoral modifications of the job market appear fully in the following statistics: in ten years the agricultural sector lost 230,000 workers and the textile industries 120,000, while the metallurgical industries gained 200,000 workers and the chemical industries almost 70,000. Faced with such massive structural changes one could have expected to see a vast process of job mobility from one sector to the other inside the local work force. In our research we discovered instead that in the ten-year-period only 10 per cent of those working in the service sector in Lombardy had been working in industry in the region; only 3 per cent of those working in the industrial sector had been in the service sector; and only 1.4 per cent of those working in the non-agrarian sectors (industries and services combined) had worked in the agricultural sector.[10] This last figure appears to be surprisingly low (in absolute numbers, only 30 out of 2,800 persons interviewed had been working in Lombard agriculture ten years previously). The number of workers who came from the other declining sector of the region, the textile industry, was equally low. It seems evident that the great majority of those who abandoned these sectors did not look for work in other areas of activity and swelled the ranks of the non-active population. If one compares these data with those collected in the same research on the sectoral distribution of the immigrant workers in the previous ten years, *which shows the degree to which they entered the most active sectors,* one can clearly see the mechanism of substitution at work and its repercussions on the sectoral composition of the job market.[11]

Beyond the sectoral changes, one can make similar observations with respect to the qualitative changes in the job market which have been equally important in the last ten to fifteen years. Between 1958 and 1967, for instance, the number of managers and employees increased by 150,000 persons, while the number of independent workers and their helpers decreased by more than 80,000. The number of industrial workers, on the other hand, increased by 170,000 workers in the first five years of the period, only to decrease markedly in the following five years, so that the net total of increases only amounted to 90,000, a figure which was clearly inferior to the increase in the number of managers and employees. If one considers only the dependent workers in the industrial sector, which constitute the principal occupational nucleus in this region, one could observe a marked modification in their composition according to their varied skills. Statistics are only available up to 1966 for the province of Milan which, however, contains by itself 40 per cent of the regional work force. Two different tendencies emerge clearly from these data. On the one hand one sees a general increase in the average level of job qualifications, due to the increase in numbers of employees, managers and highly skilled workers.[12] On the other hand one can observe, at the working-class level, a strong diminution of those two categories which constituted the steps to a career as skilled worker, i.e. the category of apprenticed and qualified worker, while the mass of the unskilled workers and labourers remained unchanged.[13] One can therefore speak of two parallel processes in the qualitative structure of the regional work force: a process of qualification which touched above all employees, managers and to a lesser extent highly skilled workers, and a process of dequalification which touched the central area of the working-class hierarchy (skilled workers, apprentices and unskilled workers). Inside the working class itself one can see an important process which entailed on one hand the emergence of new specializations to replace more traditional skills, especially with respect to the problems of machine maintenance, assemblage, control and repairs. On the other hand this process further entailed the formation of a large mass of semi-skilled workers, which form the central nucleus of the working class. Inside this core one can find not only the current unskilled workers but even a great proportion of the current skilled workers, especially those who have become qualified in recent years. In other words, these skilled workers now constitute a 'hybrid' category, composed less of workers trained for a specialized career and increasingly more of workers who are not differentiated in their tasks from the unskilled worker linked to an assembly line. One should note in passing that for these workers directly linked to the productive process the label of 'skilled' loses all professional connotation and has meaning only in economic and salary terms. For them classification as skilled and unskilled depends increasingly on the contractual bargaining of the trade unions rather than on the effective professional content of the work performed. One can stress that at the core of many of the industrial struggles of 1969 lay the demand on the part of the unskilled workers to be reclassified as 'skilled'.

Confronted with these qualitative changes in the restructuring of the work force, one would expect once again to see an important 'vertical mobility' of the work force itself through the different categories of qualification. The data gathered in our research seem to deny this hypothesis. They refer to the simple shift in skill categories in the decade 1958–68, and show that for all skill levels the percentage of upward mobility from the next lower level never surpasses 20 per cent.[14] In particular the upward shift from worker to employee status was only 5 per cent, which means that only an infinitesimal minority of the employees who formed the category growing at the highest rate came from the working class. The ten-year period studied is sufficiently long to warrant an expectation of higher mobility. Another significant finding which emerges from our research was the two-way mobility of the working class, between skilled and unskilled workers. The rate of upward mobility between these two categories was 18 per cent, whereas the rate of downward mobility was 13 per cent.[15] The circularity between these two categories seems to confirm the thesis of the homogenization of tasks in skilled and unskilled workers alike, and the formation of a new semi-skilled category in the industry of the region.

At this point we shall turn to the impact of immigration on these qualitative transformations of the job structure of the region. The data at our disposal indicate that, contrary to the prevalent stereotype, which sees the internal migrations of our country as a phenomenon of the most unskilled work forces of rural origin, Lombardy attracted a strong current, mainly of urban origin, with a high level of instruction and professional qualifications. Nearly 20 per cent of I and II category employees and of highly skilled and skilled workers was composed of workers who had immigrated to the region in the previous ten years. The percentage is 17 per cent for civil servants and managers, and 15 per cent for employees of the III category.[16] It seems, therefore, that the role of internal migrations has been equal to if not superior to that of 'vertical' mobility of the local work forces, in the study period even with respect to the filling of specialized jobs. This means that one can also discern a mechanism of 'indirect' substitution with respect to the qualified work force similar to that described in the sectoral transformations of the job market. Indeed, it is possible to believe that while we are witnessing a flux of immigrants whose level of qualification is expanding (employees, managers, skilled and semi-skilled workers on the production line), we are also witnessing a parallel movement towards non-productive life of local workers whose category and qualifications are on the decline (independent workers and helpers and workers in traditional jobs). Those portions of the local work force most affected by departure from the job market, even in this case, should be the 'weakest' – those least capable of surviving the competition waged by workers from other areas, i.e. women and workers in the older age brackets. The possibility of verifying these hypotheses is slim given the absence of data, particularly with respect to the older work force. In terms of women one can compare the industrial censuses of 1951 and 1961. From these censuses it is clear that skilled female workers were eliminated by the restructuring processes undertaken in the industrial sector. Their number declined from 49.2 per cent to 34.1 per cent of the total number of women working in industry.[17]

At this stage one should perhaps clarify briefly the time factor inherent in the substitution mechanism of local work forces by immigrant ones. The process of substitution seems to have taken place in two phases, profiting from, so to speak, the economic 'conjoncture'. The first phase, that of the migration of workers from other regions, corresponded to the years of economic expansion. The second phase, that of expulsion of local workers (women and older workers) from declining work sectors and job skills, was completed in the phase of economic recession.[18] The absorption of so many immigrant workers from other regions was made possible by the phase of economic expansion. Almost all sectors displayed during those years a rise in job levels, or at least a certain stability. Even the textile sector, in constant decline since 1951, seems to have 'held its own' during the five years of economic 'boom'.[19] The bulk of immigration therefore took place without provoking at the *same time* the removal of the local workers from the work force. This removal from active life of the local workers began to take place in 1963.

To resume, the labour market of the region during those years seems to have worked through an 'accordion' mechanism of job expansion and contraction. This mechanism, however, contained elements of severe imbalance since it provoked the substitution of local work forces which were still employable (women over 25–30 years' old, and men over 50–55) with work forces coming from other regions of the country. It is true that the numbers of local workers cut out of active life did not swell the ranks of the unemployed in the region, but simply entered non-active life. But in many cases behind this difference lies the same fact: an under-use of the potential work force of the region and an increase in the 'family burden'. It should be clear that if we are drawing attention to this phenomenon it is not out of some absurd kind of provincial 'jingoism', or 'regional Malthusianism'. Rather it is because we think that the worst possible way of solving the problem of Southern occupation is by 'exporting' unemployment from the South to the North of the country. In reality these internal migrations appear to us to be doubly harmful. First to the South, because they deprive it of its best work forces (we have identified them as technicians, managers and qualified personnel), and secondly to the North because they provoke a dualistic or unbalanced mechanism in the local labour market, which produces the falling-out of the weaker work forces. There are also territorial repercussions to our analysis carried out so far on the level of the regional labour market. One can indeed claim that the substitution mechanism we have been describing leads to the creation of unemployment areas inside the Northern regions. It is possible that the loss of jobs in the agricultural and textile sectors takes place in different areas from those where the influx of new work forces and the expansion of the most dynamic sectors occur. One thus runs the risk that inside an industrial region such as Lombardy veritable pockets of hidden unemployment and 'invisible misery' will emerge, similar to those known in other industrialized countries.

The dangers we have underlined appear, however, to be intrinsic to the spontaneous functioning of the labour market in a capitalist economy. In such conditions the internal migrations of the labour force and the processes of substitution which we have described seem inevitable. It is difficult to think that the productive system of the North and especially single firms would prefer to bear the costs of a sectoral reconversion and a professional retraining of the local labour forces when they could instead substitute them with work forces from other regions of the country which already possess the required training. In the absence of a labour policy with planned employment, the productive system will spontaneously choose the solution which in the short run will prove to be least costly to employers. Confronted with the increase of sales during the 'boom' years, local firms had before them two possible alternatives of development, besides that of creating new plants in the South. The first required investment in new machinery, in new technical and organizational methods, and therefore a reallocation and requalification of the local work force. The second alternative entailed a simple 'across the board' increase in occupation through the insertion of additional workers in the productive process linked to the increase in numbers of machines, and thus led to the internal migrations. The first alternative was without doubt the more costly at first, but it would have certainly paid off later, by raising the levels of productivity and by permitting a more stable insertion of the work force in local firms. The second alternative was instead less costly (at least at first) and was chosen with the consequences which we all know: once the need for greater productivity manifested itself when our economy entered the European market it led to the expulsion of the 'weak' components of our labour force, dumping on them in effect the costs of the necessary productive reconversions.

Today we are probably at the beginning of a new massive wave of migrations; there are some who speak of 70,000 new immigrants in Lombardy in 1969. Everyone knows that FIAT alone has hired in its Turin plants 15,000 immigrant workers. If this process were to continue in succeeding years the imbalances which we have described for the labour market of the North can only worsen. One would very rapidly pass from the problem of the falling-out of the weaker work forces into a hidden non-employment to the problem of true unemployment 'tout court'. It is true that some analyses (e.g. Project '80 of the ISVET) forecast for 1981 an excess of job opportunities over job demands in Northwest Italy, but it is also true that such projections probably underestimate the potential number of job demands in these regions. There is ample margin for uncertainty since different authors cite widely varying figures. Livi-Bacci evaluates the number of job demands for Northwestern Italy in 1981 at 6,850,000 units,[20] one million more than the ISVET figure.[21] One should also add that these estimates, based on the 1961 census, do not take into account the continued rise in birth rate in the years after 1961, especially prevalent in the Northwestern parts of Italy and whose consequences will be felt around 1981, when those born after 1961 will enter the job market. But the principal argument against such projections of job demands refers to the definition given to the rate of activity of the population at the end of the period. Such forecasts assume in general a constant rate of activity (for instance that of 1961). But the rate of activity of a population is not a natural fact before which one can take a neutral stance; it is a factor which can and should be the object of a precise political choice, striving to attain those levels of participation in

41

productive life, equally distributed among all categories and segments of the population and held to be compatible with a certain 'model' of civic life. What is the meaning of projecting on 1981 the rate of activity of 1961 or of assuming that the falling tendency of the rate itself and its unequal distribution in the various categories of the population (especially between men and women) will remain unchanged? In the same study of the ISVET cited earlier (which evaluates job demands in terms of the level of activity of 1967) there is an observation that 'one needs to proceed with "political" evaluations of the rate of activity deemed necessary for a balanced socio-economic situation. In our opinion this level should be significantly higher than that of 1967.'[22]

With respect to Lombardy in particular, we can recall certain significant data gathered by recent studies in the field. Based on an ILSES research carried out in 1967, for instance, one can predict that the aggregate of new job demands in the region in 1971 will be between 296,000 and 322,000 units.[23] The interest in such an estimate lies for us in the fact that it is based on the assumption that the number of women in the work force in terms of job supply and demand will grow between 1966 and 1971 in a similar proportion to the known growth rate in the same period of the job offers in the non-agrarian sectors. In these conditions, and by adopting hypotheses which are not unrealistic for the probable dynamic of job opportunities in the different economic sectors, one comes up with an unemployment total for 1971 of between 119,000 and 145,000 units (corresponding to 3.57 per cent or 4.20 per cent of the work force). The fact that unemployment in the region is not increasing for the time being in terms of these predictions appears to be largely due to the fall in the rate of activity of women, which was greater than anticipated. The expulsion of women from employment, which we mentioned earlier, has by and large prevented the open manifestation of an explicit unemployment which would have emerged had the original hypothesis of the number of female job demands been borne out.

In a longer perspective, the future of employment possibilities in Lombardy is worrisome. According to recent research by Luigi Frey on the employment perspectives in the region for 1981, it seems that if one assumes a 'neutral' or 'semi-neutral' trend in the development of job opportunities in Lombardy, a high level of unemployment would ensue, equal to nearly half of the projected increase in the work force in the period.[24] This result is based upon the following assumptions: (1) a maximum ratio of 6 per cent between the agrarian work force and the resident population of the whole Lombard region in 1981 (a ratio judged to be very optimistic in terms of agrarian employment); (2) an increase in revenue from the industrial sector at an average rate of at least 6.5 per cent per year and an average increase in productivity in the sector of at least 5 per cent per year, judged by the author to be 'reasonably low in the light of any observable industrialized experience'; (3) an increase in employment in the tertiary sector at the rate of 1.2 or 1.5 per cent per year (in the absence of any radically new interventions at the political and economic level); (4) an increase in job demands of the work force in the region at the average annual rate of 0.88 per cent, versus the 0.75 per cent level in Northwestern Italy and the 0.70 per cent level for Italy as a whole according to Svimez hypotheses.[25] At least half of this increase would be due to the net immigration of work forces, estimated at an average of 17,500 persons per year in the period considered (1966–81); (5) a distribution of the new jobs in the industrial sector in the different Lombard regions as a correlate of the number of available workers liberated from the agrarian sector and the distribution of new jobs in the tertiary sector as a correlate of the resident population density in the different Lombard regions. Even assuming all of the above one is still faced with an excess of job demand (703,000) over job offers (477,000) in the non-agrarian sector: of the 703,000 job demands 203,000 are due to the migration away from agriculture. Therefore there is an added unemployment level of 226,000 units, which means that there will be *an explicit unemployment rate of over 8 per cent of the work force in the region by 1981.*[26]

Perhaps what should be underlined most in Frey's analyses are his observations on the qualitative composition of the future work force seeking jobs in the region, i.e. its composition in terms of sex, age and professional qualifications. These observations, the product of interviews with experts in all sectors of economic life, lead the author to predict major imbalances and difficulties of adaptation between job offers and demands in the years ahead. These imbalances, in the absence of necessary interventions in the politics of the labour sector, will further aggravate the dangers of unemployment for the region. In this context, Frey observes:

the survey on youth employment has revealed a situation which is profoundly different from the expected tendencies of job offers and demands in the region by age bracket. On the one hand the explicit added unemployment, i.e. the difference between added job offers and job demands, should concern particularly the older workers; on the other hand for the young under 30 the opposite situation should arise, i.e. there should be an excess of job offers over job demands, which carries with it the danger of provoking an even greater net immigration of young workers than originally predicted. One would therefore have increasing unemployment among older workers, eliminated from the productive process for structural reasons linked to the sectoral dynamic, to the level of instruction of the workers, to the capacity of adapting to change, and to their attitude in face of phenomena of dequalification, etc., next to a dearth of youthful workers.[27]

Similar considerations can be seen with respect to the sex and professional qualification structure of future job offers in Lombardy: the difficulties of adaptation which the local work force experiences for available jobs would cause, according to Frey, a further immigration of work forces from other regions, stronger than the one envisaged with 'neutral' or 'semi-neutral' trends of development. This would effectively provoke a further increase of unemployment in the region.[28] The conclusions which Frey reaches by looking at the area of job opportunities thus appears to be strictly complementary to those which we reached in the preceding pages by looking at the problem of adaptation to job demand. In both cases the results show that in the Northern regions there is a mechanism of substitution which is presently in its initial stages but which is destined to increase, between local and immigrant work forces, with a corresponding increase in such regions of unemployment or underemployment.

The question which we must address at the end of this analysis is whether it is possible to eliminate this spontaneous mechanism of the labour market without profoundly modifying the very nature of the national economic system as it is at present. The answer to such a question, in our opinion, can only be negative. Even if not entirely eliminated, this mechanism can be corrected through an efficient work policy and the effective planning of employment, especially if it were to take place through and under the control of the trade unions and working-class organizations. The working-class struggles of last year (1969), beyond the demands for higher wages, called for a major participation and recognition of the workers in the economic and productive system. This need translated itself in a series of precise demands: greater rights of trade union representation, new organizational frameworks, reevaluation of skill categories, greater possibilities for promotion, greater job security and reduction of working hours. All these demands acquire a specific meaning if we place them in the framework of the labour-market mechanism as we have described it: functioning essentially through disequilibria and contradictions, through massive expansions and contractions in the immigration process and through expulsions from work which are equally massive, through the compression of workers at the lowest skill levels and through a sudden lack of skilled manpower, through geographic and professional mobility which is imposed on the workers rather than chosen and whose costs are entirely borne by the workers themselves.

The fundamental problem remains one of political nature. The eventual 'rationalization' of the labour market, or better of certain aspects of its currently imbalanced functioning, even if it is operated through the initiative and control of the trade union organizations of the working class, can never be complete. It is our conviction, indeed, that the principle of 'disequilibrium' (or better 'contradiction') is inherent in the very functioning of the capitalist labour market. Any rationalization performed in certain areas (whether regional or sectoral) of employment is possible only through the introduction of new elements of irrationality (under-use of resources, costs linked to immigration, chronic instability of employment, 'redundant' phenomena, superfluous costs of assistance and of instruction, etc.) in other areas or sectors. This is a principle which brings us back to the well-known problem of the 'dualist' nature of capitalist development. If there is any novelty in our analysis, it lies in the attempt to use this principle of contradictory and imbalanced development no longer to describe the relationships between metropolis–colony and city–countryside, as others have done, but to use it in describing the relationships *inside* the areas which are economically developed, between the population which is involved in productive life and that portion which is left out.

The implications of such an analysis for the political and trade union struggles in our country are not to be neglected. It is obvious that this analysis reevokes in new terms the problem of the 'alliances' of the working class, perceived as the central nucleus of the population linked to the productive system, with those sectors of society which have been marginalized by the system. It also raises the problem of the fusion of objectives and demands inside the productive working class (issues of salary and working conditions) with those demands linked to problems outside the productive sector *per se* (migration, economic insecurity, problems of housing and schooling and so on).

Notes

The majority of the notes which accompany this article refer to other portions of Paci's research undertaken for the Institute of Lombard Social and Economic Development (ILSES). These analyses, not readily available in their original research form, can now be found in Paci's book *Mercato del lavoro e classi sociali in Italia* (Bologna 1973), where a shorter version of this article also appears. The reader wishing to refer to the tables and statistics which underline this analysis can turn to this book or more recently to an article written in English by Paci: 'Class Structure in Italian Society', *Archives Européennes de Sociologie*, xx, (1979), 40–55 (and pp. 206–21 below). [*Editor's note*]

[1] See Table 7 (based on ISTAT, *Annuario di statistiche demografiche*), in M. Paci, *L'Evoluzione dell'occupazione in Lombardia e gli squilibri del mercato del lavoro*, December 1969, in Atti del Convegno Regionale sulla Occupazione, organized by

the Regional Committee for Economic Programming in Lombardy, Milan, 7–8 February 1970.

[2] Regional Committee for Economic Programming in Lombardy, *Progretto di Piano di Sviluppo economico e regionale,* April 1967, section IV, p. 17.

[3] A. Ciorli, *Popolazione e forza di lavoro in Lombardia al 1971,* ILSES, Milan, April 1969, p. 86.

[4] M. Paci, *L'Evoluzione dell'occupazione in Lombardia e la mobilità delle forze di lavoro,* ILSES, December 1968.

[5] See Table 8 (based on ISTAT, *Rilevazione trimestrale delle forze di lavoro*) in Paci, *L'Evoluzione dell'occupazione . . . ,* February 1970.

M. Paci, E. Rasi & G. Ziliani, *L'occupazione femminile in Lombardia,* ILSES, June 1969, Table 17, p. 39. One should note among the results which emerged from this research the absence of any reference to the recovery of the rate of activity in the female work force older than 30–35 years. According to what was observed in nearly all the Western industrialized countries, one should expect such a recovery in Lombardy. *Ibid.,* pp. 41–7.

[7] 'L'evoluzione del mercato del lavoro' in *Congiuntura Economica Lombarda* (monthly review of the Cassa di Risparmio delle Provincie Lombarde), 9 September 1969, p. 18.

[8] Cf. Tables 9 (source: ISTAT, *Census of the Population, 1961*) and 10 (source: ISTAT, *Rilevazione trimestriale delle forze di lavoro*) in Paci, *L'Evoluzione dell'occupazione.*

[9] Paci, *L'Evoluzione . . . mobilità delle forze di lavoor,* pp. 30ff.

[10] *Ibid.,* Table 13, p. 46.

[11] *Ibid.*

[12] G. Barile & M. Paci, *La qualificazione del lavoro nell'industria lombarda,* ILSES, December 1969, Table 5, p. 25 and Table 9, p. 30.

[13] *Ibid.*

[14] *Ibid.,* pp. 122ff., Graph 2. The percentages relative to the unit of mobility are calculated on the total of those having the skill 'at arrival'.

[15] *Ibid.*

[16] *Ibid.,* Table 49, p. 131.

[17] Paci *et al., l'occupazione femminile in Lombardia,* pp. 15ff.

[18] Paci, *L'Evoluzione . . . mobilità forze di lavoro,* pp. 13–20.

[19] The variation in working-class occupation in the textile sector between 1958 and 1963 was only 0.86 per cent. See *Ibid.,* Table 6 (source: Ministry of Labour).

[20] M. Livi Bacci & E. Pilloton, *Popolazione e forze di lavoro delle regioni italiane al 1981* (Rome 1968), pp. 24ff.

[21] ISVET, *Idee per una nuova politica del lavoro in Italia,* documenti ISVET, n. 20 (Milan 1969).

[22] *Ibid.,* p. 19.

[23] Ciorli, *Popolazione . . . in Lombardia al 1971,* p. 101.

[24] L. Frey, *Politica degli investimenti e politica dell'occupazione in Lombardia,* December 1969, in Atti del Convegno Regionale sulla Occupazione, Milan, 7–8 February 1970.

[25] Livi Bacci & Pilloton, *Popolazione . . . delle regioni italiane al 1981,* pp. 24 ff.

[26] Frey, *Politica . . . in Lombardia,* Table 5, p. 14.

[27] *Ibid.,* p. 9.

[28] *Ibid.,* pp. 11–13.

2. The Mansholt Plan and the Mezzogiorno *

Enrico Pugliese

European capitalist integration and the 'underdevelopment' of the Mezzogiorno

The process of European capitalist integration tends to widen on the one hand the gap between developed and underdeveloped areas of capitalist development, and on the other hand to modify the relationship of development–underdevelopment inside the economic system of the European Community, while also altering the corresponding system of class relations.

The class alliances which the bourgeoisie carries out vary according to the various phases of capitalist integration, as do also the class relations inside the 'underdeveloped' areas.

With respect to the Mezzogiorno, the current process of integration aims at the progressive extension in the Southern hinterland of the capitalist productive system which has as its consequence the crisis and falling out of traditional sectors and productive activities. The global result is the worsening of the labour market and a relative deterioration (at times even absolute) of the living conditions of those social strata (above all large sections of the proletariat) which are not integrated in the modern capitalist sector, and which constitute the majority.

The internal differentiation of the 'underdeveloped' regions also tends to increase in conjunction with the process of capitalist integration. In the Mezzogiorno those areas which are in a disadvantaged position from the start tend to find themselves progressively emarginated since the modern productive sectors tend to bypass them while the traditional activities which they contain enter into a state of crisis similar to that experienced by the developed areas.

The 'underdevelopment' of the Mezzogiorno is not therefore the product of the absence of capitalist development, but the result of specific choices made by the capitalists and of the presence of capitalism

* First published in *Inchiesta* (Winter 1972), pp. 11–20.

inside the Mezzogiorno itself. This underdevelopment tends to increase with the progress of capitalist integration.[1]

The historical class roots of underdevelopment in the Mezzogiorno were correctly identified by Gramsci in his analysis of the fusion of interests and political alliance between the backward landed-agrarian 'grand' bourgeoisie of the Mezzogiorno and the industrial bourgeoisie of the North (the historic bloc). But the terms of this analysis have been radically altered by the choices which the Italian bourgeoisie – and in particular the strongest capitalist groups – have made in the last quarter of a century. The carrying out of the Land Reform and the creation of the Cassa del Mezzogiorno at the beginning of the 1950s have marked the definitive crisis of the historic bloc, the subsequent crisis of the landed bourgeoisie (as a class of power) and the beginning of profound changes in the social and economic configuration of the Mezzogiorno.

These interventions in the Southern economy have led to two results: the loss of primacy of landed rent and the creation of structures, especially in the agrarian sector, that could foster the growth of its productive capacities. In this manner, the bases were laid for the acceleration of the process of capitalist integration. This process began in the early 1960s in conjunction with the implementation of the politics of development 'by poles'; and with the differentiation of the intervention in the Mezzogiorno itself.[2]

In the Southern hinterland this policy of intervention has increasingly acquired the explicit connotation of 'assistance' and has been primarily used in regulating the process of departure and emigration. In those areas marked for capitalist development (the areas of irrigated plains where the most important interventions in agriculture as well as in the industrial sector are concentrated), the policy has instead had the purpose of creating modern capitalist structures capable of realizing a more efficient use of resources (not least of which those of manpower easily available in considerable quantity and at low cost), and integrated in the national and international market.

The interventions bent on eliminating external uneconomical processes, the incentives given to agricultural and industrial enterprises, the setting-up of public industries in the Mezzogiorno – all of these policies could not bring about an effective 'self-propelled mechanism of development', capable of transcending the fundamental aspects of Southern underdevelopment, much less of eliminating its very existence. The reasons for this failure will appear more clearly if we consider the essential characteristics of the Italian economic system and the role which it has in the international economic system. As is well known, the Italian economy is increasingly based on a modern industrial sector geared to the production of consumer goods for the internal market as well as for export. This sector is characterized by high levels of productivity, moderate use of manpower, high work loads and tempos, relatively low wages (with respect to other advanced capitalist countries), and a concentration of the work force.[3]

The characteristics of this modern industrial sector are in contrast with the other sectors from which the work force comes, and, after having been the object of intense exploitation, to which it returns (agriculture and the tertiary sector). The increase in production of this advanced sector does not yield a comparable increase in the use of the labour force. This is because the type of technology and the organization of production this sector utilizes derives from countries where there is (in contrast to Italy) a labour shortage. For these industries to remain competitive at the international level the use of increasingly advanced technologies is crucial.

As the process of supranational capitalist integration progresses, the dualism between this advanced sector (which produced the greatest portion of revenue) and the rest of the economy increases. In the agricultural sector, the fact that it contains a relevant portion of the 'industrial reserve army', produces necessarily a lowering of its levels of productivity, taking the sector as a whole. In the tertiary sector, the levels of productivity can only be very low since it is filled by an underemployed work force, or at any rate one integrated in activities of low economic productivity. With the increase in dualism there is also a corresponding worsening in the living conditions and future prospects of those portions of the proletariat in the poorest sectors.

If one accepts this analysis and if one considers its territorial implications, the fundamantal aspects of the 'underdevelopment' of the Mezzogiorno appear more clearly. It is in the Mezzogiorno that all the poorer sectors are ultimately localized. The slow diffusion of industrial activities of the modern sector in the South does not make up for (either in terms of occupation or in terms of revenue of the workers) the progressive crisis of the traditional economic activities, on whose destruction this modern sector is based.

The change in policy in Brussels and the 'Mansholt Plan'

The flow of workers towards industry, functional in terms of the development described above, has been effectively regulated in the past through an agrarian policy which permitted on the one hand the capitalist development of agriculture, while maintaining a peasant sector from which the efficient and productive forces were removed.

Enrico Pugliese

A profound dualism was thus created in agriculture between a capitalist sector capable of achieving high levels of productivity (especially through the use of technologies minimizing the use of labour) and the peasant sector which was relatively less productive but played a significant role in terms of the high labour forces it employed. In the Mezzogiorno, as in the rest of Italy, it makes no sense to talk of agriculture as a traditionally homogeneous sector. One should talk rather of the coexistence between a dynamic and productive agriculture and a subsistence agriculture kept alive by policies for 'advantages to the peasant enterprise'.

The keeping of such an 'industrial reserve army' and the regulation of its entrance into the advanced sector of the economy remained possible while structural policies were still formulated at the national level. But in 1968 a change took place in the agrarian politics of the European Community. Aware of the glaring contradictions in the previous agrarian politics of the Community – bent essentially on favouring the integration of agrarian markets and on defending the price levels of the products – and moved by the need to restructure European agriculture along lines that were efficient in capitalist terms, the Community decided to initiate a new course. The goal was to carry out rapidly the transformation and homogenization of the agricultural structures of the six countries in the Community. The first step in this new policy was the presentation of the 'Memorandum on the Agricultural Reform of the Community', better known as the "Mansholt Plan'. The Memorandum was the subject of very heated political debate, which necessitated the reexamination of the position of the Commission on a series of specific issues. Even at the time when the Commission had judged conditions to be sufficiently ripe for the new proposals and guidelines to be implemented (April 1970) new amendments and changes had been made to the original 'Plan'; further changes also appeared in succeeding documents.[4]

Nevertheless, both in terms of the fundamental objectives of the 'Plan' and the general considerations which inspired it, as well as in terms of the principal means considered to implement it, the 'proposals and directives' and the succeeding documents reflected the orientation of the original Memorandum. An evaluation of these implications will not suffice if it is only made with reference to the agrarian sector. It is therefore necessary to keep in mind the choices made in terms of general economic policy, since it is from this policy that the situation of the labour market and the social organization which would be consolidated in the Mezzogiorno depended. We will refer to these aspects in our concluding paragraphs. It is nonetheless important to concentrate on the agricultural sector and its choices because of its relevance for the Mezzogiorno, all the more so because the sudden change in the agrarian policy which the Mansholt Plan entailed, threw into crisis the complex mechanism of capitalist development and control of the labour market which had been implemented by national agricultural policy. Before entering into a detailed analysis of this problem, it is necessary to dwell on the effects up to now of the agrarian policy of the Community as well as that of Italy on the evolution of agriculture in the Mezzogiorno, for the following reasons: first, to provide a clearer picture of the situation into which the proposals of the Mansholt Plan would be introduced; secondly, to indicate the types of change entailed and the structures which would be needed to carry out the Mansholt model; and thirdly, to show that the class interests which the new structural policy favoured remained essentially the same as those privileged by the old 'market policy'.

The Mezzogiorno and the agrarian politics of the Community

As is well known, article 36 of the Treaty of Rome, which defines the objectives of a common agricultural policy, refers both to the need to improve the productive structures of agriculture and to that of stabilizing the markets as well as guaranteeing supplies and distribution. The tool with which these objectives were to be realized in the Community was the FEAOG (The European Fund for Agrarian Orientation and Guarantees), a common fund from which to cover the expenses of the progressive integration of the agricultural sector of the Community.[5]

The FEAOG was to have intervened through its two sections by regulating the situation of the agrarian markets (the Orientation section) and by favouring the improvement of the agrarian structures (the Guarantees section). In the phase before 1968, i.e. the phase of the 'market policy', the FEAOG budget had markedly increased, and an ever-increasing percentage of Community expenses went towards the price support of agrarian products. In the period between 1965–66 and 1968–69 alone, the Guarantees section of the FEAOG saw its expenses grow tenfold from $240 million to $2,600 million, while the expenses of the Orientation section rose only from $80 million to $285 million.

The reasons for which the politics of price supports were given priority in this first phase must be sought in the decision-making mechanisms of the agrarian politics of the EEC and in the class interests which they reflected. The policy described above consolidated the interests of the advanced capitalist agrarian sectors, of the backward agrarian sectors and of the monopolies linked to the agricultural sector (Federconsorzi, etc.).[6] The only group to have suffered were the small peasants. In reality, the 'market policy' was always proclaimed as acting in defence of the incomes of the poorer peasants in greatest difficulty, but it was clear to all from the start that the only beneficiaries could be the large agrarian landholders.[7]

The policy of 'market policy' entered in crisis only when a contradiction developed between the interests of agrarian capitalism and those of the general European capitalist system, for which the growing public cost on behalf of agriculture became increasingly dysfunctional. The different national destinations of this local cost have been unequally distributed, and Italy was certainly not among the favoured nations. After Germany it is the country with the highest passive total (the differences between amounts deposited and amounts received) while at the same time the country with the highest number of dependants in the agrarian sector. Furthermore, Italy *pays* the FEAOG each year 58 billion lire (the difference between the amounts deposited and those received) while France *receives* 230 billion lire.

The Mezzogiorno in this context appears as a particularly underprivileged region both in the type of enterprises which have benefited from price support and in the type of products which have been privileged. It has the largest number of small peasant holdings (those which have suffered most severely from the price support policy carried out by the Community) and contributes the greatest portion of the Community's Mediterranean agricultural products. These products have always ranked second in terms of preference to the clearly privileged continental production.

The super-privileged products,[8] such as cereals, sugar and dairy–cheese goods have practically no significance in the Southern agrarian economy, where fruits, vegetables, wine and olive oil are most relevant. Besides oil, which up to now has benefited from price support, no other Southern agrarian product has been privileged.

Fruit and vegetable production, which entails an important use of manpower and which thus offers the possibility of improving the level of employment, benefits from partial support, while other Southern products, such as wine, do not benefit from any support whatsoever. Cereal production, which is super-privileged, needs a minimal input of manpower and its subsidy presents no benefit at all to the Mezzogiorno. The support which this cereal production has received has proven to be a form of finance for the big agrarian enterprises at the expense of small peasant holdings, whose grain output is modest and often destined for domestic consumption. Furthermore, the increase in the cost of cereal production has had an indirect negative consequence for small peasant enterprises. By increasing the production cost of the livestock which use cereals as fodder, this increase has prevented the growth of animal breeding which could have constituted another source of income. This added income could have guaranteed work opportunities for a family labour force which is chronically in excess of work demand.[9]

The previous agrarian policy of the Community has therefore produced an accumulation of consistently negative decisions for the Mezzogiorno. These decisions have not been accidental, nor are they to be explained – as Italian technocrats often claim – by the incapacity of our representatives at the EEC to defend Italian interests. These decisions are simply the result of the different political forces and pressure groups which operate at the Community level. From this fact we can note that the decisions which are unfavourable to the agrarian economy of the Mezzogiorno do not affect all classes alike.

It is true that Italy's role in the EEC economy, and the necessary expansion into European markets of its national industrial consumer products presuppose certain sacrifices (in terms of lost protection) for Southern agriculture. It is also true that the interest of the Northern agrarian producers, especially of the Po valley (who are those best organized), coincide more often with those of the European agrarian capitalists than with those of the South, in relation to the products which should benefit from price supports. More importantly, when there is a practice of 'discrimination' or of 'privileging' of a given agricultural sector, the effects are profoundly different depending on the economic dimensions of the enterprises concerned (and therefore of the class positions of the landholders). The example of grain policy is the most obvious, but others can also be made.

'Discrimination in relation to Southern agriculture' is a term which in reality translates itself essentially in the relative worsening of the small peasantry. It is the advanced capitalist sector of the Southern producers which has profited most from the margins of expansion produced by the integration of the markets of the Community as well as from the margins of expansion inside the national market. Neither the backward capitalist nor the peasant sectors could profit from these conditions. The former sector could not benefit because it was tied down by archaic work contracts and was therefore not inclined to carry out profound transformations in the structures of the enterprise. The peasant sector could not take advantage because it was incapable of entering profitably into the existing commercial channels and because it lacked the necessary capital with which to enact appropriate changes in culture to match the new type of demand. Furthermore, the advanced capitalist sector has benefited from measures with which to combat a 'crisis' from which it never really suffered.[10]

Enrico Pugliese

The effects of this support policy for the markets of the South have been worsened by the agrarian policy and structural interventions carried out in Italy. This policy has not only been in contrast with that practised in the other European countries but it has also helped create productive structures which gave the advantages of a price support mechanism to an ever-diminishing number of Southern enterprises. While other countries have had for years a policy of favouring land sales by holders of enterprises deemed too small, in Italy as late as 1960–65 the creation of small enterprises for cultivation was still being encouraged.

The rationale of the Mansholt Plan is to foster the demise of all agricultural enterprises below a certain level of efficiency or a certain economic size. Italy's past structural agrarian policy, bent on maintaining a relevant portion of the industrial reserve army in the agricultural sector, has not only encouraged the continued existence of these small and backward enterprises, but it has even favoured their creation. The enterprises created by the Land Reform are all smaller than the minimum size judged viable for economic survival by the Mansholt Plan. The interventions of the first and part of the second Green Plans, and in the South the activity of the Cassa del Mezzogiorno, have stimulated a series of productive and unproductive investments which have brought these enterprises into great difficulties, while tying a significant number of Southern peasants to their enterprises.

In the capitalist sector of Italian agriculture, even in the South, the policy of structural intervention has effectively led to a modern and efficient restructuring. Conversely, however, the policy of structural intervention in the peasant sector seemed to be motivated largely by a desire to keep this excess work force tied to the land (by freezing them in small peasant enterprises) for fear that it would push dangerously on the job market.[11] Of the two principal functions of agriculture (the productive one and that of deposit of the industrial reserve army) it is the latter which has clearly prevailed in Southern agriculture. As a result these productive structures and social organization are completely different from those of the EEC and far more backward. This is why the number of enterprises judged too small for development by the Mansholt Plan has more severe repercussions in the Mezzogiorno than in any other region of the EEC, and why a very high proportion of the agricultural work force deemed to be superfluous by the EEC is concentrated in the Mezzogiorno.

The Mansholtian ideology and the neo-rural utopias of the Memorandum

The proposals of the Memorandum will be applied in the situation characterized in the preceding pages, and it is in such a context that they should be evaluated. One should perhaps stress the wide-ranging considerations and the interpretations of facts from which these proposals have arisen.

The Memorandum denounces clearly the preceding 'market policy' for not having confronted the following problems: that 'the immense majority of rural families has lagged significantly behind in relation to income and living standards'[12]; that neither governments nor agricultural organizations have been able to 'formulate a clear response to or an improvement in the situation of those concerned';[13] and that because of 'a general evolution an increasing number of agricultural enterprises are relegated to the category of marginal enterprises'.[14] Not only has the 'market policy' not solved these problems but it has also favoured the increases in food surpluses and in the super-profits of the larger enterprises.

According to the Memorandum, the problems of European agriculture have their origin in its scarce contractual capabilities, the inadequacy of its peasant productive structures and the excessive use of manpower in the enterprises. Given this analysis, the alternative solution proposes the widespread realization of industrial-capitalist type productive structures, characterized by larger enterprise sizes, smaller levels of manpower, greater capital intensity, a bigger concentration in the territorial and managerial unit and above all, in the marketing of agrarian products. Only these measures, according to the Memorandum, can bring about that equality of revenue between those working in the agrarian sector and those working in other production sectors, while also solving at the same time the problem of surpluses. These measures should restructure the Community's allocations for price support, which have reached astronomical figures.

The ultimate goal toward which all these measures suggested in the Memorandum should strive is an ideal situation in which every agricultural worker would enjoy an adequate income, in which all risks of surplus production are eliminated, in which there is an equitable relation between the prices of agrarian and industrial products, and in which the agricultural workers would have the same social and economic opportunities as the workers in the other sectors. In reality, however, this vision expressed in the Memorandum is a neo-rural utopia. Indeed, in formulating his project, Mansholt assumed the existence of common interests between the 'agricultural workers' beyond class conflicts. He left aside completely all considerations linked to the general economic situation of the Community and the link between agriculture and other productive sectors. Above all, he underestimated the constrictions of the system itself in the realization of the project as it was conceived and in the carrying out of its declared objectives.

The realization of these objectives implies the expulsion from agriculture of five million workers and a containment of the global agricultural production of the Community through a significant reduction in the cultivated surface area. The massive expulsion of the work force should come about through the curtailment of all forms of incentives to those enterprises smaller than a given economic size, and through incentives to abandon agricultural activity to the owners, associates and dependants of these enterprises. There are three types of incentives: a lump sum payment for those who accept to turn over the agricultural areas which they abandon to enterprises which are modernizing; annual payments in the form of early pensions to those workers who are over 55; or premiums for professional requalification for the heads of families who are younger and who personally run their enterprises.

One should underline that these measures concern only those workers who are heads of enterprises; only in certain cases are their collaborators and dependants included. No similar advantages are planned for those agricultural labourers who do not work in a permanent manner for a given person and whose jobs are clearly at stake in the restructuring process envisaged by the Mansholt Plan. This mass of agrarian workers (which in Italy comprises over 80 per cent of the dependant agrarian work force, in absolute numbers more than a million workers) is mentioned neither in the Memorandum nor in the succeeding documents.

The problem of agricultural work and employment is perceived in the Memorandum uniquely in terms of a surplus of work forces for the agrarian sector. The Commission does not seem concerned by the problem of alternative job prospects in other productive sectors of the economy. Generic references are made to the need to create new jobs (paragraph 88 of the Memorandum) and to the fact that in prevalently agrarian regions 'one should envisage the possibility of keeping the agrarian work force on the land for a few more years'. No mention, however, is made of the criteria with which jobs will be guaranteed for those who lose theirs because of the restructuring process. In reality there is no plan for solving the problem.

The worsening of perspectives for the poor areas: from the Memorandum to the directives

There are two fundamental points to the Memorandum: the need to concentrate all agricultural production in enterprises of a given size and to expel all surplus labour. These points are expressed in categorical terms in the 'proposals for directives' which have followed the Memorandum. In all the directives there are three fundamental types of provisions for carrying out the Mansholt Plan:

(*a*) Measures favouring the modernizing of enterprises;

(*b*) measures encouraging the cessation of agricultural activity and the ceding of lands;

(*c*) measures directed toward the professional qualification of the agricultural workers.

There are some variations in the different proposals for determining which enterprises are chosen for survival or the cost to the Community of the measures to encourage the abandoning of agricultural activity. The choice of capitalist concentration of agrarian production and the definitive undermining of backward structures, however, remains constant. The need for a 'regional policy of the EEC' is underlined on every occasion, along with the desire that a renewed Social Fund could contribute to the creation of new productive structures in the least privileged areas. For the time being, however, all agricultural policy decisions are taken without reference to the implications they will have on the general productive structures as well as on the labour market. This is a particularly serious problem in the poorer areas where the number of peasants forced off the land is highest and where the possibility of non-agrarian work is smallest.

One should not harbour illusions on the regionalization of the community's agricultural policy. Even if one were to set aside the fact that the capitalist restructuring of agriculture by expelling workers will still aggravate the labour market, other problems are raised in the hinterland with respect to the issue of productive development and the global increase in revenue of agriculture. The EEC does not appear willing to make a supplementary financial contribution for the major expenses which such a restructuring would entail, nor is any particular aid envisaged in terms of the programmes of development in these areas. The regional articulation of the Community's agrarian policy appears to be firmly tied to the principle of 'carving equal parts out of inequality', and no significant changes have been made in this principle since the Memorandum was presented.

The only expression of greater flexibility in the latest EEC documents has been over the definition of 'agricultural enterprises marked for development'. In the original 'proposals for directives' of May 1970, these agencies (meant to enjoy the benefits of the agrarian policy) were defined as those capable of realizing a production of at least 10,000 units (dollars) per worker. In the latest directives, this minimum threshold is no longer fixed and the member states have the possibility of keeping alive those enterprises capable of 'attaining a work revenue comparable to that produced by the non-agrarian sector in the same region as well as an adequate recompense for invested capital'.[15]

Despite the references to 'work revenues' and 'regional parameters' in defining the minimum sizes of enterprises, the improvement is only one of appearance. The agricultural enterprises capable of meeting the above standards can be counted – if they exist – on the fingers of two hands. Suffice is to show that in the Mezzogiorno the average income for an agricultural worker amounts to 540,000 lire, while non-agrarian salaries are beyond 1 million lire.[16] Furthermore, the concession of a different size parameter for defining those 'enterprises fit to survive' means very little if the EEC refuses to provide a higher percentage contribution of the amounts destined for the development of these enterprises in the least privileged areas.

The Community has shown itself willing to provide a higher contribution to the cost of early retirement and for the 'premiums for restructuring' means for those excluded from the agricultural sector. But these provisions are least advantageous in the poorer regions. The exodus from these regions has only negative consequences if there are no guarantees of work elsewhere. As G. G. Dell'Angelo observes, in these areas 'the exodus does not produce increases in the rate of productivity, but simply shifts the unemployment somewhere else. The incentive to leave agricultural activity produces in these cases a drop in agricultural production which is not compensated by any other benefit'.[17]

The choices of the Mansholt Plan translate themselves for the poor regions into a shifting of unemployment and precarious employment from the agricultural sector to the other sectors (especially the tertiary). Technically efficient enterprises which will be rational in capitalist terms will emerge even in the poorer areas. But this will take place at the expense of the overriding majority of peasants, who will be left out of the EEC intervention. It will be small consolation for those expelled from the agricultural sector or transformed into a pauperized rural mass, and at any rate excluded from all contributions and policy on behalf of agriculture, to know that others (those who remained in competitive enterprises) will finally be able as the Mansholt Plan says, to 'participate in the general well-being'.

The development of a few capitalist enterprises and the acceleration of the proletarization and pauperization process of all others will therefore be the most significant result of the Mansholt Plan for the poorer regions. The consequences of this process will be felt far beyond the agricultural sector. The mechanisms generated by this unisectorial plan must therefore be considered in the light of the general process of capitalist development and of its regional articulations.

The acceleration of the process of underdevelopment in the Mezzogiorno

The relative underdevelopment of the Mezzogiorno has increased through the processes described above. In comparison with other regions of the EEC, the Mezzogiorno stands out as a 'particularly depressed area'. Revenue levels are the lowest of all regions in the Community. They range in the Mezzogiorno from 200 to 300 thousand lire per inhabitant, while the average per capita revenue in the community is 625,000 lire.[18] Despite the very high levels of emigration (capable of accounting in the years 1958–69 alone for a net migration of 2,639,351 persons), the rate of unemployment is still very high, amounting to 5 per cent of the active population. The rate of activity (relation between the work force and the total population) is also very low, given the selective character of the exodus and the emigration, composed mainly of the youngest and most competent forces.

The industrial sector is undeveloped in relation to the other regions of the Community, and the agricultural sector still occupies a high percentage of the work force (29 per cent versus 20 per cent for Italy as a whole and 13 per cent for the EEC in 1968). It still contributes in a relevant measure to the creation of revenue in the region (18.1 per cent as against 9.8 per cent for Italy and 5.7 per cent for the EEC). Furthermore, the level of development attained by Southern agriculture is the lowest in Europe. The net amount of gross added value for Southern agriculture in 1968 was of $1,420 units compared to 1,729 for Italy and 2,129 for the EEC. The setting described so far for analysing the context in which these measures will take effect is inadequate if one does not analyse the internal configuration of this context, i.e. the different existing situations within Southern agriculture. The figures cited above refer to the Mezzogiorno taken as a whole and do not convey the levels of development reached in the most advanced areas and the levels of underdevelopment in the others. The implications of the new agrarian policy will be different depending on the existing level and character of development of the different areas. Since they will be conditioned by the

59

different departure levels, it is important to examine these in detail.

Natural and historical conditions on the one hand and the type of territorial configuration of the most recent public intervention on the other have created in the Mezzogiorno two fundamental social and economic realities: one of areas destined towards progressive marginalization; and the other of areas tending towards economic development.[19] The former covered in 1961 73.2 per cent of the agricultural and forest area, and employed 53 per cent of the total of agrarian workers, contributing only 45 per cent of the net agricultural and forest total. This area is composed of the traditional extended regions of the Southern Appennines as well as of the traditional regions of mixed agriculture. The latter areas were originally characterized by a less poor type of agriculture. The persistence of archaic relations between the agrarian enterprise and the work force, and the traditional use of a soil which was not adapted to the new methods of cultivation, have rendered any increase in their potential quite problematic and warrant their being included in the group of areas due for progressive marginalization. The term 'progressive marginalization' has been chosen to underline the fact that this process is already going on and that the new course of agrarian policy will only hasten it.

Already in the late 1950s, when the special intervention on behalf of Southern agriculture (through the Cassa of the Mezzogiorno) became more selective at the territorial level, these areas were removed from the principal productive interventions. Their exclusion, however, became definitive in 1967 with the law of renewal of the Cassa, which limited drastically its areas of intervention (currently operating on only two million hectares [one hectare = 2.471 acres] of irrigated land which include those areas with the greatest potential for capitalist development), thus removing from special assistance the greatest portion of the territory of the Mezzogiorno and the near totality of its poor areas. The result of this choice has been the consolidation on these lands of a subsistence type of agriculture which will probably not disappear through the application of the Mansholt Plan but in which the living conditions of the workers will worsen. Inside these areas the only enterprises which will be able to benefit from the 'premiums of modernization' will be the big capitalist enterprises willing to enact further processes of expansion (enlargement, massive expulsion of the labour force, and forest–pastoral use).

Despite the probable development of a few extended capitalist enterprises, the effect of the Mansholt Plan in these areas of progressive marginalization, which comprise in area three-quarters of the Italian Mezzogiorno, will be to increase their economic 'backwardness' and to produce the definitive loss of any relevant productive function (except that of producing labour forces for migration).

The problem is entirely different for the other type of areas, given their greater wealth and potential for economic development. In these areas, comprising the traditional areas of intensive culture of the Mezzogiorno, and especially those sectors of recent irrigation, the concentration of productive investment has yielded a consolidation of highly productive capitalist enterprises, and has favoured a general increase in global production and productivity. In these areas the number of enterprises which will meet the standards of the Mansholt Plan are numerous, but here too the number of small and medium owners or lessees (who had survived thanks to the preceding policy of non-selective contributions and subsidies) who will be expelled from the productive process is very high, even though as G. Mottura writes, 'it is not clear if this will also entail expulsion from the countryside'.[20]

Given the insignificant number of agrarian holders of 'enterprises destined for development', it has been noted that the calculations of the Mansholt Plan in relation to the number of persons interested by the contributions for those who abandon agricultural activity (700,000 units for the EEC) are wrong. At first glance this number of workers interested in the contributions seems impressive. But leaving aside all reference to the possibility of surviving or supporting a family on the premiums paid for abandoning agricultural work, one must realize that not all workers will be interested in ceding a piece of land which in the past represented, even if minimally, a guarantee at a time when the job market is so highly unfavourable to the workers.

The proletarization of the small peasant enterprises and their exclusion from the benefits of the agrarian policy does not automatically mean that they will cease their activity. Suffice it to say that while for Italy as a whole the predictions of decline for the agricultural work force have been largely surpassed (one and a half times as much as expected by the First Plan of economic development of 1966–70), in the Mezzogiorno, where agricultural development was weaker, the work force diminished less than had been expected. This fact implies that the 'push' factor cannot determine by itself the high level of exodus; it is the general situation of the job market which will determine the final destination of those rendered marginal in the agricultural productive process. Only by analysing the labour market can one determine whether these agrarian labourers will become workers in other productive sectors, remain frozen in the primary sector with an essentially non-productive role, or simply become a 'marginal mass' (rural and urban poor for whom no productive integration is envisaged, regardless of their availability).

61

Enrico Pugliese

Some conclusions

Having ascertained that the Mansholt Plan entails for the Mezzogiorno an expulsion and marginalization of the work forces from the productive agricultural process, it is necessary to evaluate the employment perspectives in other sectors of this region.

The industrial sector is undergoing a process of capitalistic concentration which does not necessitate any improvement in the employment levels. This process has not been slowed down but has instead been accelerated by the public intervention on behalf of the industrialization of the Mezzogiorno.

Any significant industrial investment in the Mezzogiorno is not integrated in a 'desert' but concurs in strengthening the process of capitalist restructuring already under way, thus accelerating – without being able to immediately provide a needed alternative in terms of job openings – the crisis of the traditional productive structures.[21]

The policy of intervention has proven incapable of confronting the problem of the labour market in this phase of capitalist development; to this problem must be added the strong possibility that this type of intervention will itself diminish. Such a diminution is the result of the supernational process of capitalist integration, exemplified by the type of integration currently taking place in the agricultural sector and by the criteria for regionalization of the Mansholt Plan itself. In this light, the analysis of S. Vinci appears very convincing when he speaks of the 'rosy' perspectives for the Mezzogiorno of the EEC integration:

as the process of European integration advances, the Italian economy will come into contact with far more developed economies . . . this will necessitate even in the more advanced regions of Italy a greater public intervention, both in terms of infrastructures and in terms of direct production . . . in order to match successfully the competition of the other countries in the EEC. A similar situation will produce a shift in the order of priority of the various problems . . . and this shift cannot possibly take place in favour of the Mezzogiorno.[22]

In his quoted report on the employment policy of the EEC Donat-Cattin [Italian Minister of Labour] is now denouncing 'the prevailing attitude inside the Community which will inevitably lead to a strengthening of pre-existing disequilibria', and demystifies 'the adoption of the correctives [articles 54 and 56 of the CECA Treaty, the Social Fund and the European Investment Bank] which modify only marginally and to a minimal extent the effects of the principal policies adopted by the Community'.[23]

It is accepted even in official circles that the process of European capitalist integration has worsened the conditions of underdevelopment of the Mezzogiorno, both in terms of the marginalization of its traditional productive structures and of the increase in unemployment as a structural phenomenon. The general results of this process can be summarized in the following terms: first, a proggresive restructuring of industry which leads in turn to: (*a*) the crisis and closing down of small enterprises and a drop in employment levels; (*b*) the creation of very advanced productive structures in contrast with the rest of the local economy. These new structures will only be able to absorb a modest portion of the available work force, because of their high technological level or their relatively modest consistency. Secondly, there is a process of capitalist restructuring in agriculture similar to that going on in the industrial sector, and which will manifest itself: (*a*) in the hinterland, in terms of abandonment of vast areas and the progressive deterioration of the subsistence agriculture rooted there; (*b*) in the richer plains, where the process of capitalist development has been concentrated in recent years, in terms of a marked restructuring of agriculture which will produce on the one hand the demise of the backward capitalist sector and of the peasant sector (through the policy of structures), and on the other hand the consolidation of the advanced capitalist enterprises.

The effect of these changes on the labour market will be an expulsion from the productive process of quantities of the work force far greater than can be absorbed by the system. Consequently, the processes generated can be seen as processes of proletarization as well as of marginalization and pauperization. Given the internal differentiation of the Mezzogiorno, one or the other process will prevail depending on the different situations locally, just as the internal composition of the proletarian or semi-proletarian strata will vary. The political implications will also vary according to the situation. In the hinterland, where the pauperization process will prevail, precisely because of the demographic degradation which characterizes these areas (due to the emigration of the most competent and spirited militants), one cannot exclude the possibility that these processes will take place, as they have always up to now, without profound social tensions. In these areas of capitalist development, however, such calm will not be possible – as has been shown by the social revolts which the Mezzogiorno has already experienced. The rapid process of proletarization of ever-growing sectors of the peasantry, the worsening of living conditions of the proletariat (by loss of work places and by the increase in exploitation of those who remain inside the productive process), and finally the frustration of expectations aroused by the politics of intervention in the Mezzogiorno (which is

Enrico Pugliese

strongest in the more advanced areas), tend to determine the growth of conflicts which are increasingly less capable of being controlled by the existing power structure.

Notes

This article, with others by Enrico Pugliese and Giovanni Mottura, has now been republished in a volume published by Il Mulino: G. Mottura & E. Pugliese, *Agricoltura, Mezzogiorno e Mercato del Lavoro* (Bologna 1975). (*Editor's note*)

[1] One can therefore see that it is meaningless to set up an interclass contrast between 'underdeveloped South' and the rest of the country. A correct analysis of the processes of acceleration of 'Southern underdevelopment' implies an analysis of the evolution of class relations which correspond to these processes.

[2] For a more detailed analysis of the nature of capitalist development in the South, see Centro di Coordinamento Campano, 'Sulle recenti tendenze dello sviluppo capitalistico in Campania', *Vento dell'Est*, no. 22, 1971.

[3] For an analysis of the implications derived from the international position of the Italian economic system for the labour market and for the composition of the work force in different productive sectors, see M. de Cecco, 'Sviluppo del sistema economico italiano e sua collocazione internazionale', *Rivista di Scienze economiche e commerciali*, 1971.

[4] See 'La riforma delle strutture agricole nella Comunità Economica Europea', *Rivista di Economia Agraria*, ii–iii, 1971, and in particular G. G. Dell'Angelo's commentary.

[5] The fund was already anticipated in article 40 of the Treaty of Rome but its actual creation goes back to 1962.

[6] See A. Zeller, *L'imbroglio Agricolo del Mercato Comune* (with preface by M. Rossi-Doria) (Milan 1970), p. 28.

[7] For the mechanisms whereby the policy of price supports favours the big enterprises and accelerates the processes of proletarization in the small enterprises, see G. Mottura & E. Pugliese, 'Agricoltura capitalistica e funzione dell'Inchiesta', *Inchiesta*, no. 3 (1971), pp. 12–13.

[8] The agricultural products of the Community are divided into three categories: those which benefit from a nearly total guarantee of prices and markets, which represent about 70 per cent; those which benefit from a partial guarantee (20 per cent); and those which are practically not guaranteed. See Zeller, *L'imbroglio Agricolo*, pp. 28–9.

[9] See D. Tabet, 'Cerealicoltura e zootecnia nel MEC Agricolo', *Critica Marxista*, no. 1–2 (1970), p. 199.

[10] One can think for example of the generous compensations given to the fruit producers of the South to favour exports inside the EEC, incentives which were pocketed by those who were already exporting successfully.

[11] See G. Mottura, 'Piano Mansholt e mercato capitalistico del lavoro', *Quaderni Piacentini*, no. 42, 1970; and Mottura & Pugliese, 'Agricoltura capitalistica e funzione dell'Inchiesta'.

[12] European Community Commission, 'Memorandum for the Reform of the Community's Agricultural Structures', para. 33.

[13] *Ibid.*, para. 30.

[14] *Ibid.*, para. 37.

[15] European Community Commission, 'Modified Proposals for the Directives of Agricultural Reform', 7 June 1971, no. 1 article 4.

[16] Not of the *peasant sector* but of agriculture as a whole.

[17] Dell'Angelo, 'Lariforma delle strutture agricole', pp. 42–3.

[18] 'CEE Employment Policy', Memorandum of the Italian Minister of Labour to the Council of Ministers of Social Affairs of the EEC, *Mondo Economico*, no. 39, xxvi, 1971.

[19] The singling-out of these two fundamental socio-economic realities is based on M. Rossi-Doria's 'L'analisi zonale dell'agricoltura italiana' (Ministry of the Budget 1969), as well as on Rossi-Doria's classic 'Strutture e problemi dell'agricoltura meridionale', reprinted in *Riforma agraria e azione meridionalistica* (Edagricole 1976).

[20] Mottura 'Piano Mansholt', p. 50.

[21] G. Mottura, 'Verso una riduzione dell'intervento', *Economia Pubblica*, no. 1 (1971), p. 20. One can find useful notes on how the setting-up of big industrial enterprises leads to the crisis of the existing small enterprises in A. Graziani, 'Grandi imprese e intervento pubblico', *Economia Pubblica*, no. 1, 1971.

[22] S. Vinci, 'Il ruolo del MEC', *Economia Pubblica*, no. 1 (1971), p. 26.

[23] See 'CEE Employment Policy', p. III.

3. From Capital to Periphery[*]

Franco Ferrarotti

The myth of the naturally harmonious city

The study of the *borgate* [peripheral poor suburbs] and *baracche* [shanty-towns] of Rome is important because it destroys the myth of the city as the expression of a naturally harmonious integrated and balanced community. As though it were an extraordinary social laboratory, through an analysis of its various phases of development and in particular the violently asymmetrical character of its growth, Rome allows one to isolate and deepen certain fundamental problems of Italian society taken globally. Such a study, in other words, does not represent a concession to the current populistic fashion or to the neo-decadent or pseudo-revolutionary taste for situations of human marginality. The Roman *borgate* are currently a fashionable topic. The centennial of the opening of Porta Pia and of Rome as capital is imminent [it took place in 1971], and the rhetorical celebrations do not wish to stumble on such a bitter and visible reality. Responsible authorities appear to be sensitive to the topic because they are planning to eliminate as quickly as possible this 'ugly mark, memorial of sad times'. But is it really a matter of ugly marks, of a few remnants of urban terrain that must be rehabilitated, or, as has been said, of a few thousand 'troglodytes' who must be reeducated? Or are the slums and shantytowns of Rome the symptom instead of deep structural cleavages and contradictions, the changing and even picturesque surface symptom of an asymmetrical social relation of submission–domination or exploitation–profit which has remained fundamentally unchanged in its essence and which is rooted and justified in the logic of an entire life pattern?

It is from the silences more than from the words that one can intuit here what is important. There is no ability and no will to establish the essential connections. The myth of the shantytowns as pure marginality, as less than true humanity to be listened to and saved, containing immigrants that must be educated to urban living, perpetuates itself. In this

[*] First published in *Roma da capitale a periferia* (Bari 1974), ch. 1, pp. 6–13, 27–38.

66

human interest, one can always find present a taste for close observation which is more sadistic than paternalistic, because it takes place at another (superior) plane, as an entomologist who observes minutely his insects under the lens or as a biologist who analyses his germ culture. One is blind in face of the fundamental nexus whereby the shantytowns are a necessary function, the inevitable and uneliminable product of the capitalistic city as it is structured in its active forces and in its real social relations and in its harsh objective demands. The shantytowns are the city's reserve force. The current image of the shack dweller is wrong and needs to be redressed. One always thinks of the shacks as the product of an emergency situation linked first to the war and later to immigration. But the shack dweller is not simply a refugee, even if he continues to live in such a precarious state. Our researches have proven that the number of illegal squatters and shack dwellers is increasing; they come from elsewhere but also from within the city, pushed out because of its competitive tensions, of the lifting of rent controls, etc. In a city based on the principle of the maximization of profit, shacks are the norm: luxury neighbourhoods and ghettos of misery are equally necessary. This is true for the capitalist city in general since it is by definition a divided city, but it is even more true for Rome which has remained a 'parasitic' bureaucratic city, one that is only indirectly productive, and one which for many important aspects remains a pre-capitalistic city. We have already mentioned that a productive, technological dimension lies behind the modern city's genesis and development. No such technologically productive factor is to be found at the basis of modern Rome's life. What can be found is a need to present an imposing facade: there is a bureaucracy, there are the imperial eagles, there is the centre of Christianity. What is missing, however, is the reality of production and distribution, which is replaced instead by a need for conspicuous consumption and the demands of status representation. The tradition of the ancient clientelary crowds transforms itself here into the precarious existence of a lumpenproletariat, better defined really as a 'semi-proletariat', i.e. an intermittent proletariat, occasionally working in a building trade which is fragmented into myriads of small enterprises run archaically and suspended between an agricultural world which is disappearing and an industrial culture which is slow to grow.

If no truly innovative changes are made, the alternative is tragic. Rome will incarnate the case of a pre-modern city which has become decrepit without ever having come industrially of age. Let there be no misunderstanding, however, for what is said above does not stem from the illusion that industrial maturity, measured according to current indices which are 'neutral' and therefore 'meaningless', such as median per capita income and productivity per man-hour, can constitute an ultimate solution for the problems of human coexistence. Industrially mature societies are not more functional or less problematic: they are simply closer to the point of rupture of the internal contradictions inherent in the logic of capitalist growth. The importance of the analysis of Rome's semi-urban proletariat stems from the following paradox: those social groups which are at present the last on the scale of industrial development – the marginals, the excluded, the masses from the underdeveloped countries – which have up to now been the passive providers of human and mineral resources, have a great historical privilege in the possibility of a development which does not reproduce the model either of private industrial capitalism or the system of state capitalism.

A new role for the urban semi-proletariat

The city therefore is a contradictory, dialectical reality in constant motion. The development of a new political and social conscience within the ring of *borgate* which surrounds Rome, constitutes from a sociological point of view, the most interesting result of the recent very violent struggles over housing. The housing problem epitomizes at the end of 1969, even if in a deformed manner, the most strident contradictions of Italian capitalist development. This is particularly true in Rome, the capital and the dividing line between North and South, where over one thousand families coming from the shantytowns occupied empty buildings, both private and public. Hundreds of other families have begun collective struggles in opposition to evictions and self-proclaimed rent cuts, thus reproducing forms of civil resistance and insubordination which had emerged elsewhere. The use of catch phrases and the formation of local control mechanisms, are reminiscent, even in their differences, of the councils of the student movement and those of the working class inside the factory. After years of being passive participants in a political struggle that was always above their head, and whose decisions were taken by others given their own total lack of social organization, the shantytown dwellers are slowly and painfully beginning to acquire a collective consciousness of themselves in society.

Two facts, essential for a global understanding of Italy's political and social development, emerge from this new consciousness and from the new rallying cries of 'occupy empty houses' and 'rent strikes', with the subsequent radicalization they entail. On the one hand, there is the definitive unveiling of the class character of the city's organization, which emerges in the events themselves and in people's consciousness. On the other hand, the deficiencies and faults of the Left's urban renewal housing policy carried out in the 1950s and 1960s come to light. This policy was based on the notion of a public intervention coming from above, designed to create a more 'photogenic' urban renewal to modify the chaos brought about by profit-based development.

The notion that Rome was the centre of the structural backwardness of a system, a centre which would be gradually and naturally absorbed by its own further development, is a legend which has failed. Furthermore, it becomes clear that the present situation (16,000 families in the small peripheral towns; 69,000 in cohabitation; and 900,000 in the shantytowns, and 32,000 empty houses) – whose original and 'understandable' *raison d'être* dates back to the Fascist urban renewal and to the choice of the housing industry as the lynchpin of development during the years of reconstruction – is not a dysfunctional situation with respect to the rest of the 'miracle economy'. This housing crisis is integrally linked to the logic of development–underdevelopment which in Rome finds ample justification even in terms of social policy, given the type of migratory flux which the city attracts.

We will examine schematically some of the forms which this housing process has taken. In the last few years there has been an effective integration of private capital, urban rent and public capital. This fusion has in effect transformed the area of public intervention (through laws or the action of public organisms) into a support for the private sector, whose big private concentrations often owned the land which they were also developing. The private sector in effect asked the state and the town municipalities to underwrite those infrastructural and 'social' costs which were not profitable, whereas the overall development of the area continued to follow the logic of the profit motive. Thanks to this mechanism one has reached the actual extreme divergence between the type of housing offered, generally very expensive, and the type of demand. In social terms this discrepancy between supply and demand translates itself into a housing insecurity, and in Rome in the plague of the shantytowns and squatting, which has a clear function of social control of the immigrant force.

Thus a city which is split in two is born. It is composed of an immense peripheral ghetto with new homes at a high rent (in Rome it is estimated that nearly 60 per cent of the inhabitants do not own the house in which they live), with shacks, and with 'model neighbourhoods', all of which are ten kilometres away from the centre, and deprived of services. The centre of the city is fast becoming an archaeological island for wealthy tenants. From 1955 to 1964, while Rome's population increased by one-third, the centre of the city experienced a significant loss of inhabitants: Campo Marzio 19,937 to 12,598; Campitelli 1,761 to 1,027; Colonna

8,488 to 4,583; Trevi 10,154 to 5,574. This depopulation of the centre is the most macroscopic fruit of a politics of eviction of the old inhabitants and of transformation of the houses to be rented to new social groups or to wealthy tourists.

The response of the Left to these developments was neither fast enough nor adequate, and assumed that Rome was merely a wart in the system. Gradualistic reform proposals were made which accepted the logic of the social division of housing and spoke in terms of ownership of one's house through very long-term loans. What is worse, the only speculation which was identified and attacked was that linked to the 'black' aristocracy [close to the Church, translator's note] and to the more backward sectors of the capital. Coupled with an emphasis on the public sector, these elements reduced the clash to a purely 'political' level, one that could be resolved only through the mediation of representative institutions. In this context, and given the total lack of organization of the most desperate sectors of the city, the political line which the parties followed, even when they were close to the needs of the masses of the citizens, still remained essentially 'paternalistic'. In reality, the anger of the poor has remained undiminished and did not even affect the proposals for reform. It is not a coincidence that public investment in housing has dropped in the last few years from 25 per cent to 6 per cent, while the budget for building highways has greatly increased.

The housing struggles of 1969, which followed by one year those of the students, mark an important change in direction. Once people have understood that the struggle for housing is not only a struggle for a different organization of the territory or for a new redistribution of the social product, but also represents an action against some of the essential mechanisms of the Italian capitalist system, the merely 'political' dimension of the struggle disappears and its 'social', class character reemerges. The shack dweller has his landlord once again as interlocutor. Economic and social power, as a structure, are contested and not merely the political power which acts as facade. The housing clash puts the landlord directly into question by occupying the houses which he leaves empty or by pushing towards self-determination those rents which are speculatively high. The empty image of the 'citizen' fighting for his housing disappears to be replaced by that of the worker, whether he be a construction worker, a metallurgist, an agrarian worker, an employee, or technician, who uses in this struggle his entire experience and social definition.

Among the shack dwellers, who in Rome are for the greater part immigrant construction workers, new forms of political organization and consciousness are formed. This is the first painful response, even if often poorly organized, against that social disaggregation which is favoured by those in power. The daily press is thus beginning to speak of new types of unitary committees composed of social forces which are not based on representation but apply direct democracy. These committees on the one hand manage the housing conflict, and on the other are also giving life at the territorial level to new centres of alternative power.

Such struggles are naturally still at the embryonic stage, and one can find emotional and adventurist extremist positions coexisting with fear and real inexperience. The phenomenon of collective action is still not widespread. Often the assembly of those who are occupying a building splits into four or five different meetings composed of students or of the more politicized shack dwellers while the others applaud. But in certain sectors and areas new openings for action are developing and the old state of submissive subjection is fast disappearing.

Having overcome the ghetto of the shack, increasing numbers of construction workers carry their working-class identity even outside the work place. It is in this context that the new line on housing becomes relevant by negating the notion of housing as a property right and proposing housing as a 'social service'. This interpretation has come down to the masses from the desks of the urban planner and constitutes their first experience with real democracy. 'Housing is a social good and should belong to all' is the slogan in the assemblies. The usual sceptical attitude towards all criticism of the management of public agencies or of the behaviour of those in power is now being replaced by a positive movement towards politics linked to real experience and not divorced from daily life. The housing struggle thus has managed to fuse, both objectively and in subjective consciousness, with the struggle for wages and for new power conditions inside the factory. It has become an important phase in the struggle for democracy as real participation and self-determination rather than as theoretical periodical control through representation.

The economic paradox of Rome*

One must examine Rome's economy as a whole in order to understand why the city cannot cope with the demographic pressure it faces today and will increasingly face in the future, and also to understand the role which the peripheral semi-proletariat, whether of recent or old immigration, plays (marginal and occasional jobs, hourly domestic service, work done at home, etc.). Rome's economic framework is paradoxical.

Ibid., pp. 27–38.

Franco Ferrarotti

In 1967 the net income of Rome and its province amounted to nearly 2,456,900,000,000 lire. In the list of Italy's seven richest provinces, Rome ranks second, with a provincial income of 7.42 per cent of the Italian total, where Milan had 11.10 per cent. But these figures are misleading. If one breaks them, down for 1967, in percentages for different national sectors of activity, ascribing the figure 100 for overall Italian production, for Rome the greatest productive sector is that of the public administration (12.90 per cent). This sector is immediately followed by that of tertiary activities (10.55 per cent), and far behind are the industrial (4.38 per cent) and agrarian sectors (2.48 per cent). This subdivision is directly linked to the very structure of Rome's earnings as well as those of its province, and is substantially homogeneous with respect to the figures registered since 1963. Agricultural, forestry and fishing activities in 1963 comprised 2.30 per cent of net revenue; 2.22 per cent in 1964; 2.24 per cent in 1965, and 2.30 per cent in 1966. This uniformity was confirmed by the trends in the industrial sector, whose variations from 1963 to 1966 were only of the order of 0.2 per cent, and by the commercial sector. The transport and service sector, on the other hand, registered an increase of 0.5 per cent compared with 1963, the highest rise of all.

The largest chunk of Rome's income, and therefore of its economy, comes from the public administration and from the service sector. Rome's only big industry is that of the bureaucracy. Truly productive industrial structures have a difficult time emerging or are lagging behind. If we analyse in percentage terms the composition of revenue produced by the different sectors even for 1967 we are confirmed in our views: first place in the whole net revenue of Rome is held by tertiary activities (50.30 per cent). All of this is widely known but needs to be repeated so as not to fall into abstract ideological schemas, and so as not to lose sight of the specific character of Rome's proletariat, lumpenproletariat and semi-proletariat. Here the clientelary and employee tradition of a mass of people waiting at the door of the powerful is not an historical relic but an essential daily experience.

An analysis of working-class occupations in the province of Rome provides direct proof of the contradictory character of a substantially unbalanced development. The data furnished by the INAIL are instructive, even though they do not provide a definitive total. They are elaborated on the basis of employers' declarations of the workers they hire. Many of the figures concerning workers in small enterprises are probably missing, since these enterprises tend not to declare their workers, given their high mobility and frequent replacement. They can thus avoid the social costs which accompany any properly registered worker, and therefore lower the median cost of work. The small and very small industries prefer to transfer a part of this work cost to the undeclared wages of the worker, as a way of encouraging overtime or work done beyond the hours accepted by the trade unions. One must add also that the INAIL's figures do not include artisanal enterprises which are governed by their own special laws.

Despite the above reservations, a clear tendency appears from the available data and one which militates against any potentially optimistic interpretation. Working-class employment in all sectors has declined since 1964. The drop is impressive especially when one considers that the years after 1965 were a time of recovery after the slump of 1963–4. The crisis furthermore touched the heart of working-class activity in Rome: the construction industry. With respect to the total industrial occupation in Rome, this industry accounted for 25.30 per cent in 1964; 1964; 23.93 per cent in 1965, 22.75 per cent in 1966 and 20.74 per cent in 1967. Rather than a decline these figures represent a true collapse. The processes of capitalist restructuring after 1965 have been paid by the workers in terms of loss of jobs, dequalification, slowing down of work tempos and cuts in working hours. This was the real price for the rationalization of productive cycles and for the increase in capital input imposed by new production needs once the recession was overcome. The expulsion of construction workers from employment not only confirms the seasonal character of the construction industry but took on for the affected workers the characteristics of a life sentence, since in practice it implied the definitive expulsion from the labour market of the greater number of workers with a low job qualification. Their reintegration in the productive cycle depended on a readaptation that they could not easily perform while unemployed even if enjoying social benefits.

The Roman working class is therefore easily pruned without serious consequences either because it is employed in tertiary activities which are not strictly necessary (concierge activities, middlemen offices: miscellaneous activities which could be cut down in hard times without harm), or because it is tied to a construction industry which is still largely para-industrial, and whose workers commute from agricultural areas or from the shantytowns – men suspended between countryside and city and belonging to a world that is no longer peasant but not yet industrial. A third characteristic of the Roman working force, and one which is important in our research, is the role exerted by the phenomenon of apprenticeship. Ninety per cent of the apprentices in the Roman region (Lazio) are concentrated in Rome. The official ratio of apprentices in the enterprises hiring them is 2.4 per cent, but this figure is not credible given the high number of very small enterprises extant which mainly hire apprentices. The large industries, for instance Fatme, Rome's biggest metal industry, do not take on apprentices. When the labour market offers qualified workers the bigger industries tend to avoid the costs of a professional training, especially since it is easy for them to attract from the smaller industries, generally run along family lines, those former apprentices they would need. In the Roman situation, the apprenticeships constitute a visible type of sub-salary and a clear form of exploitation. It is out of the question for the apprentices to sue their employers. Besides the problem of the slowness of the judicial system, such an act would mean that they might leave their jobs, only to find themselves a few months later in the same circumstances elsewhere. For the smaller enterprises, the exploitation of apprentices is simply a question of economic survival. Thanks to it they can survive in a competitive market which would otherwise tend to eliminate them. These small enterprises, however, play a crucial role in the continuation of archaic and underdeveloped work relations.

The economic paradox of Rome hinges on the link between the increase in net revenues and the yearly production of capital and the absolute diminution, percentage-wise, of working-class employment. While revenues hold up in terms of national standards, the average of working-class employment has, with the exception of isolated cases, undergone a noticeable decline. Following the recession of 1963–4, Rome's productive network has reconstituted itself with respect to national standards along two characteristic lines: first, by performing drastic cuts in the average levels of employment and in comprehensive salary levels; and, secondly, at the same time by cutting on production time, thus augmenting the productivity of each worker while letting the subsequent reduction of jobs fall as 'social costs' on the workers themselves. It is in this respect that the backwardness and contradictions in the Roman productive network become apparent. This network is characterized by those sectors which are slightly more backward than the national average (construction, small and very small industry, and agriculture). It is the working class which pays the cost, because it functions as a shock absorber with respect to the fluctuations of the market, both in terms of employment and wages. When there is a period of recovery, it finds itself in a position of weakness *vis á vis* the attacks of the industrialists. But one should also immediately consider the other aspect of the Roman economic structure, the public administration. There is no point in entering the polemic against the parasitic bureaucracy which has its strongest advocates in cities like Milan and Turin. Italy's public administration is perfectly functional in the context of the capitalist division of labour seen as the manifestation of a wider political and administrative management. This functionality should not, however, hide the fact that the public administration is never called upon to pay directly for unemployment, for wage cuts, for underpayment, for chronic underemployment, or for the massive loss of job qualifications which characterize the present economic order.

The reasons for this research: power seen from below

An analysis of the integration and life conditions of the growing peripheral Roman population acquires great significance in the light of Rome's particular development. The problems of this population composed, properly speaking, of second-class citizens, are not generally studied analytically by Marxists. These problems are assumed to be sufficiently clear inside a simple macrosociological profile of the development of the economic system; they are either made to fuse with the problems of the productive working class perceived in rational and specific terms, or they are discarded as the problems of a politically irrelevant historical fringe. This manner of perceiving reality reflects a tendency to underevaluate marginal and excluded human groups which is characteristic of the Marxist tradition. Because it does not participate in a regular and systematic manner in the productive process, the lumpenproletariat is considered by Marx and by the Marxists not as a 'class' but as a stratum which 'forms a mass neatly distinguished from the industrial proletariat', according to the formula used by Marx in *The Class Struggles in France.* Already in the *Communist Manifesto,* the passive characteristics of this mass are underlined. The indistinct mass comprising the lumpenproletariat does not even constitute the backdrop of society. For the proletariat is considered as the lowest strata of society; its uprising cannot take place without the shattering of all the superstructures composing official society. The lumpenproletariat as such disappears from the framework of society and its extremely marginal position makes it a residue which need not be taken into account. If Marxist analysis on the one hand focuses on the most visible aspects of the lumpenproletarian condition (passivity, great fragmentation, precarious living conditions which determine and are determined in turn by an inconstant link with the world of work, i.e. the absence of that element which makes a class fully class conscious), on the other hand, such an analysis seems arbitrarily to exclude from the game of politics a relevant portion of the population. One must take into account the human beings which the disparaging term 'lumpenproletariat' tries to describe. In reality, one of the major

75

factors which accounts for the 'depoliticization' of the lumpenproletariat can be found precisely in the theory which calls this population 'lumpenproletariat'.

The fact that such a social group remains confined to the margins of history is determined to a certain degree – and the nature of this degree must be examined – by revolutionary Marxist theory itself. By having accorded privileged status to the urban proletariat in the revolutionary process, Marxism closed off the potential revolutionary role of the lumpenproletariat. The limitations in Marx's analysis can be explained either as the conditioning of his time, or by the fact that in the whole of his work Marx focuses on the capitalist process in the most advanced industrial nations of Europe. Given this approach, certain social categories were inevitably underestimated in what was in reality a very intellectual exercise. It would be an important and interesting task to perform an 'archaeology' of Marx's work looking for all the elements which formed the notion of the 'lumpenproletariat'. The purpose of such an exercise would not be to search for a formal coherence but to evaluate how given judgements at the theoretical level influenced practical actions. Marxist analysis never defined itself as an instrument of mere knowledge but as a method with which to change and revolutionize a given social reality. So what was its influence on this reality in relation to the lumpenproletariat? What role did it play in making the lumpenproletariat *be* in effect lumpen' and *remain* so?

Beyond these theoretical considerations, the fact remains that the phenomenon of the lumpenproletariat, once its irrelevance has been deliberated, acquires the ineluctable character of a natural phenomenon to which one adapts because it is held to be both normal and unchanging. In reality the world of chronic poverty and that of marginal human populations is extremely complex. Its institutions and forms of behaviour defy commonly held categories. We have systematically studied the Roman shantytowns for years to find out who lives there, when, for what reasons, from where they have come, and since when. Many assumptions of sociological literature and many accepted beliefs have fallen. People do not go directly from the countryside to the city, from agrarian to industrial labour, from tradition to reason. There is an infinite series of intermediary positions which can only be clarified through research. Shantytowns are a waiting room. People wait: it can last twenty years or an entire lifetime. People come there from the villages, from the Roman Agro, from the Puglie, from Lucania and Calabria; but they also come from Rome's central neighbourhoods, pushed out by some misfortune (sickness of the head of the family, especially if it entails an operation, with the subsequent loss of a job, excessive rents, falling into debt, and so on), pushed or downtrodden by the process of proletarization. Rome has become our social laboratory. We have the Third World at home.

A community of shack dwellers is essentially a community of the excluded. Even if it is entrenched and at times surrounded and besieged by the structures of the modern city which expand like an oil slick, such a community still remains cut off. Shantytowns often grow on makeshift ground, on pieces of flatland, outside culture and history. Deprived of what makes existence civilized, the shantytown dwellers remain and wait in silence and despair. We have noted above the beginning of a new social role for these dwellers through the recent housing struggles. But these struggles constitute merely timid opening gambits, and in the hierarchy of misery the shantytown dwellers are on the lowest rung of the ladder. Having fled depressed areas, mortified by a millenarian misery, they have reached the capital. But their initial hopes have little by little given way to waiting and to their customary resignation. A stable job, a decent house, an education and hence the possibility of participating directly in political and social life are all distant objectives. In a situation which tends to crystallize, these objectives are now perceived to be unreachable if not by some fortuitous event. All terms of comparison here lose their meaning. Current standards of judgement become inadequate. Applied to an ahistorical and asocial community, any historical and social orientation becomes meaningless.

In the following pages we will try to begin an analysis of these problems. We will examine life in the peripheral suburbs and in the shantytowns in relation to social structure and to the struggle of interests, to job possibilities, to source of income (amount and frequency), to family size, to the raising and socializing of children, to the school and to cultural opportunities, to health and social services, to local political activity and to the links between individuals, families and established authorities. The purpose of this research is the following: to study the top of society and the centres of political and administrative decision-making. From the perspective of the shantytowns these summits of society can be studied from the bottom up, at the terminal point of all decision-making, or rather most often at the end point of the lack of decisions. One of the powers of power is precisely that of not exercising power, of letting things go, in the name of spontaneous evolution, the nature of things, nature *tout court,* or even providence.

4. Some Hypotheses on Education in Italy*

Marzio Barbagli

It is not an easy task to reconstruct and explain educational characteristics and trends in Italy in the last hundred years. To the difficulties normally entailed in such a project one must add the more serious consequences of the last few years: when education spreads, when it encompasses all, when it appears to be a concrete, solid reality, it becomes all the more elusive and unapprehendable, impossible to penetrate and to understand. Our conceptual castles, built with years of effort and work, have revealed themselves to be structures of shifting sand, our interpretative schemes and hypotheses old rusty tools. But above all, it is our fundamental attitude toward education and the unlimited trust we have placed in it which has come under critical scrutiny.

Faith in the powers of education was probably never so strong as at the end of the 1950s. Modern priests praised its virtues. Supported and financed by governments and foundations, sociologists and economists invested their best energies in this fascinating enterprise. They dusted off old concepts or presented new ones; they gathered, elaborated and pored over data; they filled the pages of their books and articles with austere mathematical equations intended to guarantee the scientific validity of their discourses. They also tried, however, to be understood and so they bustled about, giving lectures and writing short works of popularization. From these works the many finally grasped the virtues of education. They understood that it was enough for it to be planted, to take root, to grow healthy and strong for all the evils which besieged man to end, for tyrannies to crumble, for misery, unemployment and underdevelopment to disappear. The rapid diffusion of this modern myth was sharply interrupted by the student struggles. It is unnecessary to recall here the accusations which were levelled by the 'men of '68' against school and society alike. Suffice it to say that the crisis which they provoked was so widespread and profound that it promptly caused even the priests of the new religion to vacillate. Those who at the beginning of

---

*First published in *Disoccupazione intellettuale e sistema scolastico in Italia* (Bologna 1974), pp. 11–27.

the 1960s looked with confidence at the perspective of educational growth and considered the notion of intellectual unemployment as a 'vague expression',[1] would announce later the 'warning signs of a storm', noting that 'a portion of the credits allocated for the educational system serve instead to produce groups of protesters and unemployed.'[2] Those who in 1961 in Italy thought they were facing a lack of qualified personnel,[3] write today that 'the serious danger confronting all countries, and ours in particular, is that of an excess of persons with degrees compared to the job opportunities available at such a high cultural level.[4]

Nevertheless, the old conceptual edifices having fallen new ones have yet to appear. Some have been hastily constructed and already show their first structural faults. The affirmation made in 1969, that 'we are all little more than blind kittens in confronting the major problems of education' remains valid even today.[5] What hypothesis, then, can guide us in interpreting the development of Italian education in the last one hundred years?

As a society undergoes industrialization and modernization, its instruction of the young becomes extensively differentiated, internally complex, and elaborately connected with other features of society. Education becomes more necessary for the economy and linked closely to it as a major mediator between manpower demand and labor supply. Occupational competence, general and specific, is increasingly certified by schooling and achievement is thereby prefigured, as labor shifts from manual to mental and from low to high degree of skill. In the aggregate, those who leave school early, are designated for unskilled work, and those who remain on the educational escalator are carried to the jobs for which general education and specialized vocational training have earmarked them. Higher education is also deeply involved in technological advance, as a location for scientific work and as the enterprise that trains the modern researcher and technologist. Thus, education becomes a way of investing in human capital across many levels of skill.[6]

This passage, written by an authoritative scholar for an authoritative work in the social sciences, offers a good example of the approach used most often to explain the relationship between the development of education, the job market and the system of social stratification. It is defined as the 'functional theory' approach or 'functional differentiation' model by its advocates and the 'technocratic concept of education' by its detractors.[7] According to this explicative model, the expansion of education would be the consequence of modernization and of growing institutional differentiation. Such an expansion in effect would be the consequence of society becoming more complex, of its articulation in a multiplicity of institutions and roles, some of which would necessitate 'strategic human capital.'[8]

In more analytical terms, this interpretative model, which is nothing more than the application to education of the more general functional theory of social stratification,[9] can be broken down into the following propositions:

(1) The level of occupational qualification necessitated by industrial society grows through two different processes: (a) there is first of all a tendency towards growth in the number of jobs which require a high level of qualification and a parallel tendency towards the diminution of low-skill jobs; (b) there is also a second tendency for the *same* jobs to require an increasing level of qualification, in order to be filled.

(2) It is the instruction offered by the school system which should provide the necessary levels of qualification needed. This implies that: (a) education creates a more productive work force; (b) this education is provided not by many sources but only by one: the school.

(3) Consequently, as the levels of qualifications needed by industrial society increase, the percentage of the population which must go through the school system also grows, as do the number of years in school.[10]

Can this model be useful in explaining the evolution of Italian education in the last hundred years? Only partially. One cannot deny of course that the increased domination over nature, the changes carried out in the organization of work, the growing application of science to the economic process, with the subsequent increase in the level of qualification of a number of tasks, have influenced the development of education. Nevertheless, studies carried out in a number of different countries and covering different historical time periods show that the functionalist model cannot by itself explain the phenomena which interest us. Several contrary points have been made, for example. Especially in those countries which have passed a certain threshold of industrialization only a portion of the increase in education levels can be attributed to the increase in the percentage of highly qualified jobs. Often it was not the supply of qualified jobs which produced an increase in the number of qualified job demands, but on the contrary the former grew in size only to fulfill the pressure of the latter. In many capitalist countries there is a tendency to underutilize the level of general and specialized knowledge of vast numbers of the population. Education does not always increase the productivity of the work force but can also produce opposite effects. In certain cases the only type of valid instruction is not that produced by schooling but by other institutions which were not designed for that purpose (for example on the job training).[11] In the Italian case, without wanting to anticipate here the results of our analysis, presented throughout the volume, one can say that it would be impossible to give an adequate interpretation of the evolution of education in the last hundred years by relying uniquely on the functionalist model.

Let us move away for a moment from the functionalist model and consider the school in capitalist society as an institution which confers status and privileges. It then becomes legitimate to think that the development and stagnation of instruction are due not only and not so much to the rise and fall in the demand of technical qualification – as functionalist theory sustains – but rather to the power relationships among different social groups and to the attempts they make to maintain or improve their own position in the system of social stratification. Two specifications must be introduced, however, in examining more analytically this interpretative hypothesis, which lies at the basis of our study. First, the internal structure of the schooling system is a fundamental intervening variable to keep in mind in explaining the evolution of education. Secondly, when speaking of 'social groups' we do not refer here only to social classes, i.e. the bourgeoisie or the proletariat. If it remains true that these two social classes have been the protagonists in the Italian national setting, that they have been the collective subjects whose actions formed and transformed the educational system, it is equally true that other actors have performed important roles in the script: those social groups, and in particular the intellectuals, who received life and legitimacy from the educational system.

Among the many mechanisms through which the school system filters and sifts the population, selects and contains its demands for education, certainly the most important is to be found in the system's internal structure. In the course of this study I will examine this structure at two different levels: the junior level of the secondary system and the senior level.

The internal structure of the junior level of the Italian school system varies in terms of its greater or lesser openness according to the historical period studied.* I use the terms 'openness' and 'closedness' to refer to the degree of specialization and internal differentiation. More specifically, I consider a school system 'closed' when it has, parallel to the school which prepares for secondary and university studies, one or more self-contained schools which constitute ends in themselves and which do not permit entry into the senior levels. Conversely, I consider a system to be 'open' when it has none of these cul-de-sac schools. To give some examples, the most open type of school system in Italy was that enacted

---

*Each of these school systems is explained in the pages which follow. They are all characterized by different degrees of 'openness' in relation to one central factor: access to higher education and the university. Certain schools only allowed students to enter specific technical faculties, while only the elite lycees provided an opening to all higher education; still others gave no access at all to the universities. *Editor's note.*

at the end of 1962; but the one created by the Casati law was also fairly open. The system created by the Gentile reforms by contrast was closed, and even more closed, if possible, was the one which Bottai, with his *Carta della Scuola,* and Gonella proposed in 1951.[12]

The internal structure of the senior secondary level of the school system varies with respect to the historical period considered and in terms of its major or minor emphasis on 'professionalization'. I consider a system to be professionalized when it has, parallel to the school preparing for the university, other schools which do not allow access to the university but which train the middle levels of society (for instance technical specialists or teaching staff). I consider instead a system to be deprofessionalized when its secondary schools give access to the university system and lose most of their original function of training middle-level professionals. To cite some examples: the most deprofessionalized system Italy has had is that formed at the end of 1969. But, as we shall see, there were other phases of deprofessionalization in the periods 1870–75 and 1930–35. The most professionalized system was created by the Gentile reform.

Class and strata struggles have played differing roles in the degree of openness and professionalization of the Italian school system. Above all it is clear that as the school becomes progressively more institutionalized, as its function of distributing degrees is socially recognized, the demand for instruction on the part of families will rise, provoking aspirations and counter-aspirations in the various social classes in order to preserve or to improve through these degrees their position in the stratification system. The social classes excluded from the higher levels of instruction struggle, often organized by a party, but at times even spontaneously, in order to break down those barriers which exist in the school system so as to render it more open. Or, if the system is already sufficiently open, they rally in its defence against the threats emanating from the dominant classes or other strata. This is how the most profound transformation of the school system of the postwar period – the creation of a single junior high school in 1962 – came about. The proletariat wanted access to instruction and change, and the working-class parties, after years of uncertainties, vacillations and errors, seized on this demand and articulated it. Similarly, if, after realizing at the turn of the century that the school system enacted by the Casati law was no longer adapted to the new situation, it took the bourgeoisie over two decades to render it more closed and restrictive, this was due partly to the presence and resistance of the working-class movement. The partial failure of the Gentile reform, which compelled this Fascist philosopher and his successors to review a law which had been so carefully constructed, was provoked by a type of passive and spontaneous resistance of those social classes which the law mean to keep out (the lower middle classes and the higher levels of the proletariat).

All these struggles, whether defensive or offensive, organized or spontaneous, have had one characteristic in common. They never questioned the fundamental principle upon which the functioning of the school in capitalist society is based. They carried in themselves 'the rarely conscious and from the start unresolved ambiguity between an "egalitarian" push for the right of all to knowledge and the acceptance of the concept of "promotion" which takes for granted the notion of the technical as well as the social division of labour'.[13] This fundamental ambiguity did not prevent the struggles from being harsh and bitter. Nor did it prevent them from producing with time (because it is an obvious, if often forgotten fact, that the consequences of changes in school systems are only felt after many years) profound effects on the functioning of the labour market, major revisions in the models of social stratification, and cracks in the entire social edifice.

One should not think, on the basis of what has been said so far, that the dominant classes have always and only opposed themselves to the development of education or that they have done everything possible to keep the school system closed or to render it so. If this has been the prevalent tendency on the whole, cases are not lacking, even in Italy, in which these classes have behaved differently. In effect, even the bourgeoisie has required at certain moments an expanding educational system, and for two sets of reasons which can be defined as economic and political. For economic reasons, because it is through the education furnished by the school for better or worse, that they were able to dispose of the personnel of high- and middle-level qualification needed for industrialization and economic development. For political reasons, because schooling, from elementary classes through to university, has always had the characteristic of transmitting not only knowledge but also values, of providing not only a technical qualification but also an ideological preparation, of shaping not only the cognitive aspects but also the affective elements of personality.[14] In our country, the dominant classes have shown on several occasions in varied situations that they were aware of the role performed by schooling in the political socialization of the young. This was certainly the case in 1959–60 when they looked, with less hostility than previously, at the possibility of opening and democratizing the school system for two reasons: in anticipation of the rapid increase in demand for technicians and graduates, and also because they were convinced of the need to furnish through education the necessary ideological basis for those work forces which were in the process of shifting from the primary to the secondary sector of the economy.

The awareness of the importance of education as an ideological apparatus of the state, however, goes back much further in time, to the very formation of the nation state. Inside the dominant classes of the time, two different conceptions clashed: the first saw the most effective form of social control as keeping the majority of the population both ignorant and illiterate (according to an old eighteenth-century proverb: 'if a horse knew as much as a man, I would not like to be its rider'[15]); the other current saw the enactment of such a control rather in the diffusion of education. The school system which was born in Italy – that of Casati – had a relatively open structure because, for a time, inside the dominant classes the second notion prevailed: i.e. the persuasion that the only way for the new state to set roots and reinforce its own authority was by enlarging primary instruction and above all by developing secondary and more advanced schools, the only ones able to furnish a core of ideologically trustworthy and competent functionaries. The dominant classes have found themselves at times confronted by what we would call the dilemma of selection–socialization. In order to function efficiently as an instrument of social control, a school system must be structured in such a way that it will perform both functions in a balanced manner. If the system gives too much weight to the selective factor, and therefore has a closed internal structure, it runs the risk of not having a sufficiently diverse number of youths stay in its ranks for a sufficiently long period of time to socialize them properly in political terms. If, on the other hand, it gives too great an importance to the socialization function and therefore has an open internal structure, it runs the risk of not properly carrying out a selective process and of therefore producing a surplus of qualified personnel. This explains at least in part why, when the Italian bourgeoisie tried to confront the phenomenon of intellectual unemployment (both during the Fascist period and after the Second World War) by emphasizing the selective function of schooling, it nonetheless never lost sight of its socializing function. This is why it did not limit itself to the simple expulsion of 'excess' students from the secondary level, but tried instead to channel them into dead-end schools, capable of holding them for a given number of years, of giving them an adequate ideological training, without however permitting them to continue their studies.

Finally, the role of the intellectual strata has been doubtless very important in terms of the influence which they had in the internal structure of the Italian school system. The excess of supply of university and school graduates over demand which – as we shall see – has been an endemic characteristic of Italian society from the 1880s to the present, has often placed the intellectuals in a situation of status disequilibrium,[16] of incongruence between the degree obtained and subsequent occupation, revenue level and prestige which the *social norms of the time* considered to be correspondingly appropriate. Like all other groups in such a situation, the intellectuals also tried to escape from it, to redress their own status, to occupy equivalent positions in all hierarchies. This need led them to act collectively through their professional organizations, to modify the market conditions, and therefore to put pressure in two different directions: in the sense of an increase in job offers and a diminution of qualified workers. In reality the various categories and organizations of intellectuals were not always in agreement on the line to be followed. The efforts of secondary school teachers to increase the number of job offers (and so expand the school population) at times clashed with the efforts of doctors and engineers to restrict the number of job demands (and so contract the school population). The pressures of university students and graduates to reduce the flux of job demands by introducing rigid mechanisms of admission to the universities (fixed numbers) often clashed with counter-pressures of those with high school degrees wanting access to higher education. These counter-pressures, naturally when in conjunction with other conditions, have often been at the origin of deprofessionalization processes at the secondary level. One can say, however, that on the whole among the intellectual strata the prevailing line on school politics has been Malthusian.

In more general terms, the situation of status disequilibrium among intellectuals has led to a strong political radicalization. It is hard to say whether this political radicalization in our country has been left- or right-oriented, if it has turned the intellectuals – as Wilhelm Riehl said in the last century – into 'the true *ecclesia militans* of the fourth estate',[17] or whether it has instead made them adhere to Fascist movements.[18] The outcome depended on a multiplicity of historically variable factors and conditions and also on whether the intellectuals were in a situation of partially blocked upward mobility or of partial downward mobility.[19] The first situation occurred in a phase of stagnation or of moderate economic growth when the number of qualified job offers increased more slowly than the number of job demands, and led the intellectuals (especially those who had just obtained their degrees) towards left-wing positions. The second situation occurred in phases of economic crisis, characterized by the collapse of job offers for qualified personnel, and pushed the intellectuals (especially those already with a position) towards right-wing positions. Regardless of the outcome, it is certain that the political radicalization of the intellectuals has always caused concern

85

among the dominant classes and has led them to espouse a politically Malthusian line in terms of schooling.

The hypothesis outlined in the preceding paragraph, however, is not sufficient. It should be integrated and elaborated. Besides examining the struggles carried out by different social groups to modify or preserve the educational system, to increase or reduce the level of instruction of the population, it is necessary also to examine the economic context in which these different actors performed. Once the school asserts itself as an institution both authorized and capable of conferring status and privileges, it automatically produces demands and counter-demands between the excluded social classes bent on obtaining an education and the privileged strata bent on preventing such access or at least bent on ensuring that such an exclusion should take place at a higher level. It is also true, however, that the intensity of these different pressures varies according to the economic situation and its trend.

If we try, however, to go beyond such a generalization, things become much more complicated. There is no doubt that economic trends play a part in private demands for education (i.e. on the demands made by the young and their families). But in which direction? What is the link between the two variables? Unfortunately, the great majority of studies carried out on the links between economics and education have considered the latter and not the former as the independent variable. When education has been considered as the dependent variable, the conclusion has always been that there was a positive correlation between the two variables. In reality the situation is significantly different. Despite the evident character of the above correlations at first sight, the argument is unable to give an account, without introducing important specifications, of the evolution of education in Italy in the period under study.

During the last century in Italy, the links between economics and education have varied according to the level of the school system. If we examine the compulsory school (compromising for a long period only the primary level), we note that between economics and education there is always a positive correlation. Such a relationship can be at times disturbed by the interference of other variables, can be reduced, and even weakened. But it always persists. The situation is completely different if we move to the secondary level or to the high school level. Here any analysis of the links between the two variables becomes very difficult. For certain periods there is an absolute lack of data with respect to those economic indicators without which one cannot construct any larger argument; furthermore the data on education are also very scarce. It is additionally very difficult to keep other variables under control, to be able to say, for instance, whether the development or stagnation of education were due to trends in the economy or to changes in the internal structure of the schooling system. But even with all due caution there are many elements which, as we shall see, lead us to state that for the period under study there is either no link or an actual reverse link between economics and education (at the secondary and superior levels).

How are we to interpret this fact? In an important study, Joseph Ben David tried to explain why in the twentieth century in certain European countries such as Germany or France there were many more students than in Great Britain, Belgium or Switzerland (to the point of producing in certain periods an excess number of university graduates), when one took as an independent variable the 'presence or absence of other channels of mobility beyond that offered by higher education'. According to Ben David, in England and Switzerland

there existed a strong and well articulated middle class, formed before the rise of the modern universities, during the nineteenth century. . . . The professionals did not constitute a separate class, were not hostile to and formed instead an integral part of a rich and educated middle class. Higher education was never the only or the privileged channel for mobility, through which it was possible to elevate itself from the 'masses'.[20]

This interpretation is also valid for our country. The lack in Italy, for the period studied, of any relation between trends in the economy and trends in higher education, or even the presence of an inverse relationship, indicates that there were no other channels of mobility in our country beyond those offered by the school, or that they were far weaker than in other countries. Therefore the demand for education, the impetuous expansion of students registered in secondary schools and in the university, the unemployment of university and high school graduates, which have characterized long periods of post-Risorgimento Italy, and which had moralistically been attributed to an obscure psychological tendency for 'diploma hunting' can be explained, beyond the variables used above, by referring to the peculiar characteristics of Italy's economic development: the lateness of its beginning, its dualistic nature, its sudden halts. These peculiar characteristics of the Italian economic system, and the subsequent lack of any alternative channels for social mobility have made the demand for promotion through education – a demand which the school itself by its regulatory principles as well as the nature of the stratification system in which it operates, provoked in all capitalist societies – much more strong, persistent and even desperate in Italy.

Marzio Barbagli

Notes

[1] Cf. P. H. Coombs, in E. A. G. Robinson & J. E. Vaizey (eds.), *The Economics of Education* (London 1966), p. 684. This volume reproduces the proceedings of the colloquium organized in 1963 by the International Economic Association.

[2] P. H. Coombs, *La crisi dell'educazione nel mondo* (Rome 1968), collana 'Formazione e Lavoro', p. 52.

[3] G. Martinoli, *L'università nello sviluppo economico italiano* (Milan 1962).

[4] G. Martinoli, 'La conferenza sulle strutture future dell'insegnamento postsecondario', *Quindicinale di note e commenti*, 15 September 1973.

[5] F. Ciafanoni & C. Donolo, 'Contro la falsa coscienza del movimento studentesco', *Quaderni Piacentini* (July 1969), p. 40.

[6] R. Clark, 'The Study of Educational Systems', *International Encyclopaedia of the Social Sciences* (New York 1968), vol. 4, pp. 510–11.

[7] S. Bowles & H. Gintis, 'I.Q. and the U.S. Class Structure', *Social Policy* (Nov.–Dec. 1972/ Jan.–Feb. 1973), pp. 65–96.

[8] In using the term 'strategic human capital' we refer to those highly qualified personnel who should carry out 'the strategic occupations in modern society': entrepreneurs, managers, scientists, engineers, doctors, architects, teachers, etc. F. H. Harbison & C. Myers, *Education, Manpower and Economic Growth* (New York 1964).

[9] For the functionalist theory of social stratification see the collection of essays edited by R. Bendix and S. M. Lipset, *Class Power and Status: Theories on the Class Structure* (New York 1953).

[10] I have taken these propositions from R. Collins, 'Functional and Conflict Theories of Educational Stratification', *American Sociological Review*, xxxvi (1971), 1002–19.

[11] For the results of these studies and for a profound critique of functionalist theory in education see Collins, *ibid*. Among recent studies on the links between education and the labour market in the United States the most important is certainly that of I. Berg, *Education and Jobs: The Great Training Robbery* (New York, 1970); see also Bowles & Gintis, 'I.Q.'; M. Vaughan & M. Scotford Archer, *Social Conflict and Educational Change in England and France, 1789–1848* (Cambridge 1971).

[12] It is important to clarify that the expression 'open system' does not refer to the problem of access to schooling of youths coming from the lower scoial classes, but rather to the dimension of the quantitative flux of students which the system allows to go on to the higher levels. Owing to the presence of other factors (for example examinations along meritocratic lines) the two issues do not always coincide. This is supported by the fact that England has always had a number of university students (as a proportion of the actual population) inferior to that of Italy, but at the same time a higher percentage of students coming from the lower social classes.

[13] R. Rossanda, M. Cini & L. Berlinguer, 'Tesi sulla scuola', *Il Manifesto* (February 1970), p. 22.

[14] On the role of the school in ideological formation and of the importance of the latter on the productivity of the work force in capitalist societies, American economists of the New Left have done a lot of work. See for example, Cf. S. Bowles & Gintis, 'I.Q.', p. 79; H. Gintis, 'Istruzione, tecnologia, e caratteristiche della produttività del lavoro', *Rassegna Italiana di Sociologia* (July–Sept.

1972), pp. 535–58; S. Bowles, 'Contradictions de l'enseignement supérieur', *Les Temps modernes* (Aug.–Sept. 1971), pp. 198–240.

[15] Quoted by L. Stone, 'Literacy and Education in England: 1640–1900', *Past and Present* (February 1969), p. 85.

[16] By the term 'status disequilibrium' we mean the situation in which certain persons find themselves when they occupy a high position in one social hierarchy and a low one in another: the 'new rich' who have high revenue levels but low levels of education or prestige; black professionals in American society who occupy a high position through education but a low one through ethnic group. For an overview of the most important researches carried out an status disequilibrium see A. Pizzorno, 'Squilibri (o incongruenze) status e participazione politica, *Quaderni di Sociologia* (July–Dec. 1966), pp. 372–86.

[17] W. H. Riehl, *Die bürgerliche Gesellschaft* (Stuttgart 1851), cited by L. O'Boyle, 'The Democratic Left in Germany, 1848', *Journal of Modern History* (Dec. 1961), p. 377.

[18] For the other countries it is important to note that according to O'Boyle intellectual unemployment 'had an important role in 1830 and 1848 in France and in Germany. Where it did not constitute a serious problem such as in England, the danger of a revolution was minimized.' L. O'Boyle, 'The Problem of an Excess of Educated Men in Western Europe, 1800–1850', *Journal of Modern History* (April 1970), p. 498. Kotschnig has held that unemployment pushed many intellectuals towards the Nazi movement: see his *Unemployment in the Learned Professions: An International Study of Occupational and Educational Planning* (London 1937). On the importance of unemployment in the diffusion of communism in Asia see M. Watnick's article in Bendix & Lipset, *Class, Power, and Status*. For other bibliographical indications see W. Kornhauser, *The Politics of Mass Society* (Glencoe, Ill. 1959), x, pp. 183–94.

[19] For this distinction see G. Germani, *Sociologia della modernizzazione: L'esperienza dell'America Latina* (Bari 1971), especially pp. 130–5.

[20] J. Ben David, article in Bendix & Lipset, *Class*. Ben David's second hypothesis is not as valid: he holds that intellectual unemployment is due to the rigidity of the higher educational system, to its incapacity to adapt to the changes which take place in the economic system. According to Ben David, in the interwar period intellectual unemployment occurred in countries with a rigid system such as those in Europe, which continued to produce the same numbers of qualified personnel as in the preceding century (especially of lawyers and doctors), whereas this phenomenon of unemployment was unknown in countries with a more flexible system such as the United States and the Soviet Union, which rapidly adapted to the transformations of the economy and gave greater importance to the training of teachers and engineers. Ben David's hypothesis does not hold when faced with the facts for the simple reason that in the European countries in the 1920s and 1930s unemployment not only hit doctors and lawyers but also teachers, engineers and scientists.

5. Education and Internal Migrations[*]

Marzio Barbagli

It is only after having treated the tendencies of intellectual unemployment and education in the postwar period that I can broach a topic left untouched so far: the internal migrations of intellectual work forces. The results of my analysis on the relation between the uneven development of Italy's economy and the evolution of secondary and higher education can lead to several questions. We have seen that from the beginning of the century, and not just in the postwar period, the economically underdeveloped areas of our country have always produced a higher number of high school leavers and university graduates than the more developed areas (with reference naturally to the present population). Is there not a contradiction between these data and our image of Italy as a country split in two even in terms of the distribution of education, with the Northern population possessing a higher level of education than the Southern? Is it not with such an image, together with an economic theory which attributes extraordinary importance to education for initiating or accelerating economic development, that for years the notion was held whereby to fight underdevelopment in the Mezzogiorno one had only to increase the numbers of high school and university graduates in the technical and scientific disciplines?[1]

I think I have shown sufficiently in this study that illiteracy and surplus production of intellectual work forces are not in logical contrast but represent, in the underdeveloped areas, two sides of the same coin. How then can one explain the fact that after having produced for decades a significantly higher quantity of intellectual forces than the North, in 1951 the South should have (in relation to the population over six years old) only 0.9 per cent of university graduates and 2.6 per cent of high school leavers compared to the North's 1.1 per cent and 3.6 per cent respectively? On the basis of data compiled in 1968 on a sampling of work forces in Lombardy, Massimo Paci observed,

contrary to the prevalent stereotype which sees the internal migrations of our country as a phenomenon of the most unskilled work forces of rural origin,

[*] First published in *Disoccupazione intellettuale e sistema scolastico in Italia* (Bologna 1974), pp. 465–78.

Lombardy attracts a strong current, mainly of urban origin, with a high level of instruction and professional qualifications.[2]

The results of this research showed that indeed in the decade 1959–68, while immigrants constituted 10 per cent of the total work force, the figure was of 17 per cent for managers and civil servants and 20 per cent for the employees of the first and second categories, and 15 per cent for the third.[3]

Given these data, the apparent incongruity between the cultural backwardness of the underdeveloped areas and their overproduction of intellectual forces is easily explicable on the basis of a constant and heavy migratory flux of university graduates and high school leavers towards the developed areas of attraction. If we try to extend the analysis made for Lombardy to the whole of Italy and beyond the decade 1959–68 studied by Paci, we encounter severe difficulties due to the lack of data at our disposal.

What took place after the Second World War? For the decade 1951–61 one can try to give an answer by taking into consideration the data of the two censuses on the one hand and the data on the number of high school leavers and university graduates produced in the different areas of the country on the other.[4] This comparison does not permit us to evaluate the number of leavers and graduates who transferred themselves from the South to the North or vice versa during the decade. We can only gather approximately the net result of these movements in the intellectual labour force (which is what we were most interested in). Table 1, which contains the significant data for such a confrontation, needs some commentary. Lines A and B contain the numbers (in thousands) of those with high school diplomas and university degrees in the censuses of 1951 and 1961. Line C represents the increment produced during the decade. The data of the three successive lines, which indicate the percentages of high school leavers and university graduates in the population over six years old, allow us to see that in this last decade the distance between North and South has not only not diminished but has actually increased. The data of line G represent an estimate of the increase in leavers and graduates, once the effect of internal migrations has been factored out, which occurred in the decade, i.e. evaluating the different contributions effectively given to the North and the South by the production of high school leavers and university graduates.[5] By subtracting the value of G from the value of C one obtains the approximate value of the migratory current from South to North and vice versa. From such a comparison the following results emerge: in the decade 1951–61 the South had a net gain of 211,000 high school leavers and

Marzio Barbagli

Table 1. *High school leavers and university graduates, 1951–1961, and estimate of the migratory totals North–South for the decade* *

	High school			University		
	North	South	Italy	North	South	Italy
A 1951 Census (absolute numbers)	980	392	1,372	293	136	429
B 1961 Census (absolute numbers)	1,361	570	1,931	405	186	591
C Census increases 1951–61 (B − A) (absolute numbers)	+381	+178	+559	+112	+50	+162
D 1951 Census % of population over 6 years old	3.62	2.57	3.24	1.08	0.89	1.01
E 1961 Census % of population over 6 years old	4.64	3.50	4.24	1.38	1.14	1.30
F Increase 1951–61 (E − D)	+1.02	+0.93	+1.00	+0.30	+0.25	+0.29
G Estimate of net increase 1951–61	+348	+211	+559	+99	+63	+162
H Migratory total (C − G)	+33	−33	—	+13	−13	—

Note: North also includes the Central regions.

63,000 university graduates. 33,000 high school leavers (15.6 per cent) and 13,000 university graduates (20.6 per cent) emigrated to the North or to the Centre of Italy. These figures explain why even during this decade the gap between the level of instruction of the population of the North and that of the South increased further despite the greater production of leavers and graduates inside the South itself.

Only the results of the 1971 census, when published, will permit us to confront the internal migrations of the intellectual work force in the decade 1951–61 with that of the following decade. But we can already see what occurred in this last decade. The problem has been treated by CENSIS in its survey of the university graduates in the academic year 1965–6, which I have already cited. By comparing the place where the degree was obtained with the work place of those questioned, the CENSIS study points out that while Northwestern Italy presents a 'markedly larger number of work places than the number of degrees conferred', the other two areas offer a negative balance with, however, a fundamental difference: that it is 'high' for Northeastern and Central Italy while it is 'modest' for Southern Italy and the Islands.

According to CENSIS, these data show first of all that there is 'the existence of a "brain drain" inside the country to the benefit of those areas of greatest economic development' and, secondly, that this phenomenon has negative consequences not so much for the less developed areas *where the development of education has* not yet reached the necessary thresholds to satisfy fundamental internal local needs, but for those areas which are already developed in terms of education but which are technically, scientifically and economically subordinate to those areas where there is a concentration of 'software' phenomena.[6]

It is hard to understand how CENSIS can refer to the intellectual work force, holding that 'in the underdeveloped areas, the development of education has not yet reached the necessary threshold with which to cover fundamental internal needs'. Even if we ignore all the data which I presented in the preceding chapters, is it not true that according to CENSIS itself the level of intellectual unemployment for the graduates of 1965–6 is much higher in the South than in the North? Obviously the old belief that there must always be a positive correlation between economics and education is so entrenched that it prevents an adequate description or explanation of what happened or is happening before our very eyes.[7]

Reality is quite different. Already in 1967, while subscribing to the notion that held the 'fundamental problem of the South's development' to be 'the formation of qualified personnel, of intermediate cadres and managers', Goffredo Zappa observed – on the basis of researches carried out in Sicily on the graduates of scientific and technical faculties – that this type of qualified personnel tended to migrate North. Zappa concluded that

such a phenomenon has negative effects on the politics of development for two reasons: first of all because it drains away from the South precisely those qualified personnel which the industries settling there need; secondly, because a relevant portion of the resources allocated for the industrial development of the South goes to other areas with the drain, particularly in the Northern industrial triangle. These investments (human and technical) thus contribute only partially to Southern development, but in terms of public opinion and spending they are still perceived to be used in the growth of the Southern regions.[8]

In the last few years ISTAT has begun publishing data on the distribution of immigrants and emigrants in the different regions according to educational levels. Thanks to this, by using the data concerning the years 1964–9, one can now try to analyse in an adequate manner the phenomena which concern us. By comparing the percentage distribu-

Marzio Barbagli

Table 2. *Change of residence in relation to diplomas and geographic area,*
1964–1969, and distribution of the Italian population (over 6 years old) in
relation to diplomas in 1961

Type of diploma	Change of residence (%)				Italian population 1961 (%)
	North	Centre	South	Italy	
University graduates	1.79	2.78	2.56	2.18	1.30
High school leavers	6.44	8.65	8.86	7.49	4.24
Junior high school leavers	13.52	13.74	12.38	13.25	9.58
Primary school leavers	54.46	49.34	46.79	51.48	60.76
Literates without diploma	21.82	22.12	24.59	22.62	15.72
Illiterates	1.96	3.34	4.81	2.97	8.41
Totals	100.00	100.00	100.00	100.00	100.00
Case numbers	4,940,512	1,625,190	2,404,201	8,969,903	—

Source: Elaboration of data taken from ISTAT *Annuario di statistiche demografiche,*
vols. XIV–XVIII (for the period 1964–8); *Popolazione e movimento anagrafico dei*
comuni, vol. XVI (for 1969).

Schooling	Numbers per 1,000 inhabitants
Literacy without school diplomas	60.8
High school diploma	52.7
University degree	51.3
Junior high school diploma	39.4
Elementary schooling	28.6
Illiterate	14.9
Average total	35.0

tion in terms of schooling of the Italian population in 1961 with that of
the migrants in the period 1964–9 (Table 2), one can observe relevant
differences. We cannot calculate the derivatives, i.e. the tendency to migration of the different categories, for the last six years since we do not
know the distribution of the Italian population for this period. But by
calculating the relation for the year closest to 1961, i.e. 1964, we obtain
the values shown in the table.[9]

94

These ratios indicate that with the exception made for those who are literate but do not possess any diplomas, who constitute the strongest current towards migration, territorial mobility increases when one crosses the barrier between lower and higher schooling (the difference between high school leavers and university graduates is very small). By analysing Table 2, however, we note that these trends are quite different in the three areas of the country. The percentage of high school leavers and university graduates who changed residence is much higher in the North than in the South.

These data alone point to a strong tendency on the part of Southern high school leavers and university graduates towards emigration. In order to strengthen our analysis, if we examine the two major territorial areas – the North (which also includes the Centre) and the South – we note that, whatever the educational level considered, the current South–North prevails over any inverse movement (Table 3). Considerable differences emerge, however, in relation to schooling. The composition of net migration (column *d*) is higher both with respect to the North (column *e*) and to the South (column *f*) for the first three levels of education and for those who are literate but who do not have any school diploma, while it is lower for those persons possessing an elementary school diploma. With respect to the illiterates, column *d* contains higher values for the North but lower ones for the South. The South therefore exports toward the Centre–North *mainly* intellectual work forces (high school leavers and university graduates), or qualified workers (with a junior high school diploma) or general workers (literates without diplomas). With respect to the intellectual work force alone, in the period 1964–9 the South lost 42,000 high school leavers and university graduates.

By breaking down the data further we see that in the case of high school leavers and university graduates their migration is directed mainly to five areas of attraction: three in the North and two in the Centre, whereas all other areas have been places of 'escape' (Tables 4 and 5). In the North we find Lombardy, Piemonte, and contrary to our expectations, not Liguria which has a deficit, but the Veneto. The strongest area of attraction, however remains, just as during the Fascist period, the Lazio, seat of the political administrative capital, Rome, rather than the Northern capitals of economic life (Tuscany has a positive balance which is very modest in size).

These data give a fairly clear idea of the contradictions in the Italian educational system. The difficulties of finding a job which the young leavers from compulsory school encountered in the underdeveloped areas of the country favoured in these areas the expansion of secondary

95

Table 3. *Migratory currents North–South and South–North in relation to school diploma, 1964–1969, and composition of the population in North and South in relation to school diploma in 1961*

Type of diploma	From North to South (N) a	From South to North (N) b	Difference (N) c	Difference (%) d	Population in 1961 North (%) e	South (%) f	$d-e$	$d-f$
University graduates	13,740	24,383	10,643	1.65	1.38	1.14	+ 0.27	+ 0.51
High school leavers	44,272	76,617	32,345	5.02	4.64	3.50	+ 0.38	+ 1.52
Junior high school leavers	72,266	148,750	76,484	11.87	11.08	6.87	+ 0.79	+ 5.00
Primary school leavers	256,347	582,068	325,721	50.54	66.40	50.60	− 15.86	− 0.04
Literates without diploma	122,178	294,937	172,759	26.81	12.41	21.70	+ 14.40	+ 5.11
Illiterates	20,446	46,957	26,511	4.11	4.09	16.19	+ 0.02	− 12.08
Total	529,249	1,173,712	644,463	100.00	100.00	100.00	—	—

Source: as Table 2.

Table 4. *Migratory movement between regions of school leavers with high school diplomas, 1964–1969*

Regions	Registered	Annulled	Net immigration	Net emigration	Difference
Piemonte	64,367	58,576	6,960	1,169	+ 5,791
Val d'Aosta	1,626	1,351	278	3	+ 275
Lombardia	107,920	97,359	12,090	1,529	+10,561
Trentino Alto Adige	10,522	11,259	179	916	− 737
Veneto	47,075	45,790	2,183	898	+ 1,285
Friuli Venezia Giulia	18,892	19,306	803	1,217	− 414
Liguria	25,245	25,651	1,283	1,689	− 406
Emilia Romagna	42,414	42,927	1,691	2,204	− 513
Toscana	41,619	40,178	2,332	1,431	+ 901
Umbria	8,709	9,593	334	1,218	− 884
Marche	16,178	17,785	268	1,875	− 1,607
Lazio	74,128	56,035	18,016	13	+18,093
Abruzzi	16,360	18,463	449	2,552	− 2,103
Molise	3,644	4,969	12	1,337	− 1,325
Campania	56,638	64,580	538	8,480	− 7,942
Puglia	35,244	41,208	428	6,392	− 5,964
Basilicata	6,361	7,856	71	1,566	− 1,495
Calabria	22,731	26,982	188	4,439	− 4,251
Sicilia	53,454	62,214	—	8,760	− 8,760
Sardegna	18,673	19,178	439	944	− 505

Source: as Table 2.

education. After leaving these schools the difficulty of finding jobs pushed a portion of those with high school diplomas to emigrate to Central and Northern Italy. Despite this, however, the rate of entrance into the university of high school leavers continued to remain much higher in the South than in the North. At the end of their higher education, university graduates were confronted with the same types of phenomena: unemployment and the rush toward Central and Northern Italy. Underdevelopment therefore produces education, but it produces it for the privileged areas.[10]

Notes

[1] See the writings in 'Gli studi universitari nel Mezzogiorno', *Quaderni di 'Nuovo Mezzogiorno'*, no. 7, 1962.

Marzio Barbagli

Table 5. *Migratory movement between regions of graduates with university degrees, 1964–1969*

Regions	Registered	Annulled	Net immi-gration	Net emi-gration	Difference
Piemonte	15,264	14,236	1,413	385	+1,028
Val d'Aosta	412	342	84	14	+ 70
Lombardia	30,939	27,525	3,836	422	+3,414
Trentino Alto Adige	2,741	2,890	189	338	− 149
Veneto	14,013	13,001	1,290	278	+1,012
Friuli Venezia Giulia	4,489	4,432	340	289	+ 51
Liguria	7,816	8,639	251	1,074	− 823
Emilia Romagna	13,016	13,636	758	1,381	− 623
Toscana	13,299	12,744	1,074	519	+ 555
Umbria	2,966	3,140	167	341	− 174
Marche	5,070	5,537	168	635	− 467
Lazio	23,885	17,597	6,292	4	+6,288
Abruzzi	4,081	4,498	107	524	− 417
Molise	1,069	1,343	43	317	− 274
Campania	15,828	18,949	130	3,251	−3,121
Puglia	10,201	11,779	124	1,692	−1,578
Basilicata	1,822	2,125	52	355	− 303
Calabria	5,984	7,167	43	1,226	−1,183
Sicilia	17,778	21,010	15	3,247	−3,232
Sardegna	5,247	5,321	244	318	− 74

Source: as Table 2.

[2] M. Paci, 'Migrazioni interne e mercato capitalistico de lavoro', *Problemi del Socialismo* (Sept.–Oct. 1970), p. 769.

[3] G. Barilet & M. Paci, 'La qualificazione del lavoro nell'industria lombarda', ILSES (Milan 1969).

[4] I. F. Mariani, 'Una ricerca sulla regione di nascita e di residenza di elementi delle classi dirigenti italiane' in *Atti della XIII e XV riunione scientifica* (Jan. 1953, June 1954) of the Società Italiana di Statistica, pp. 251–70.

[5] In order to estimate the number of graduates produced by the South I have used the special samplings of the ISTAT on graduates, which have the advantage not only of reporting the distribution of graduates according to the city of their studies but also according to their parents' city of residence. By using the data for the years 1953–4, 1954–5, 1955–6, 1956–7, 1958–9, I calculated the percentage of university graduates with families residing in the South in relation to the total (38.7 per cent). For these data see the *Annuario statistico dell'istruzione italiana.*

[6] CNEL–CENSIS, *Rapporto sugli aspetti sociali ed economici della situazione universitaria italiana* (Milan 1971), pp. 103–14.

[7] It is less difficult instead to understand how CENSIS reached the conclusion on the basis of the data gathered that the internal migrations of intellectual work forces concerned only the Northwest (as a pole of attraction) and the Centre–Northeast (as a zone of exodus). In the study cited these conclusions are reached by comparing the place where the degree was obtained with the place of work of those interviewed. It is obvious that a comparison of this type is meaningless in order to quantify the flux of internal migrations because many students who reside in the South are registered in the universities of the North and especially the Centre of the country. According to the data of IS-TAT for the academic year 1964–5, only 85.6 per cent of university students residing in the South were attending South universities. The tendency of Northern students to register in universities in their own area was much higher (95.8 per cent). These are elaborations taken from ISTAT, *Annuario statistico dell'istruzione italiana 1966.* This tendency is also confirmed by the data of other years.

[8] See the presentation of G. Zappa in *Nord e Sud nella società e nell'economia italiana di oggi* (Fondazione L. Einaudi 1968), pp. 132–5.

[9] For these data see M. De Vergottini, 'Le migrazioni interne in Italia secondo il grado d'istruzione dei migranti', *Stato Sociale* (Jan. 1969), pp. 2–13. In this study the author analysed the ISTAT data for 1964.

[10] For a wider analysis of the consequences which internal migrations have had on the labour force and on the preservation of North–South differences see L. Gallino, *Indagini di sociologia economica e industriale* (Milan 1972), ch. XIV, pp. 487–519.

II: Social Classes

6. Middle Strata in the Mechanisms of Consensus*

Alessandro Pizzorno

Recent studies on the middle strata

Is it true that in Italy there is no interest for the middle strata? Ermanno Gorrieri, the author of a recent successful book, tells us that he wrote *La giungla retributiva* in order to

cast doubt on the widely held opinion that society is still structured along a nine-teenth-century division into two fundamental classes, capitalist and proletarian, since the middle strata were being progressively assimilated with the proletariat through exploitation by Big Capital.[1]

The nineteenth-century division to which Gorrieri refers is naturally that of Marxism. It is interesting, even if somewhat pedantic, to note that a similar reproach had already been made by Marx against Ricardo in an important passage of *The Theory of Surplus Value*. After analysing how productive development creates directly new spheres for unpro-ductive categories of workers whose interests tend to coincide with those of the exploiting classes, Marx adds:

What he [Ricardo] forgets to stress is the continued increase of the middle classes which stand between the workers on the one hand and the capitalists and great landowners on the other, and which feed off rent value in increasing numbers. These middle classes weigh directly on the working-class base and increase the social security and power of the ten thousand persons on top.[2]

The interest of this quotation as well as of the pages which precede it can be found in the fact that Marx posits a direct connection between the growth of the middle classes and the problem of consensus. One of the first political studies to have appeared after the Liberation in 1946, Giuliano Pischel's *Il problema dei ceti medi*, displayed exactly the same in-

---

*First published in F. L. Cavazza & S. R. Graubard (eds.), *Il caso italiano* (2 vols, Milan 1974), vol. 2, pp. 315–37.

tentions and concluded – after having presented statistical tables which were not without interest, even if rather elementary when compared to Gorrieri's diligent work (although the book was written in partial secrecy) – that 'Italy is essentially a country of middle strata.'[3] The inspiration for the book came clearly from Bernstein's work, which fifty years earlier had stressed that the capitalist dynamic did not in the least tend towards the destruction of the intermediate classes; Bernstein's theory was not unheeded in Italy. So 'who' is Gorrieri trying to convince? Three considerations must be taken into account in order to understand this problem.

First of all it is probably true that in Italian culture, among intellectuals generally, there is a tendency to base all interpretations of social phenomena on a simplified dichotomy borrowed from the sphere of production. The interesting point is that this 'dichotomized–productivist' notion prevails in two opposing camps: among the intellectuals in power and among those in opposition. We could propose an identifying label for them: the former would be 'Giolittian' and the latter 'revolutionary syndicalists', to use terms which made sense at the turn of the century. In the 1960s, the former would be called planners, while the latter would be the extra-parliamentary Left. The planners hoped to control the power of rent while the Left hoped to widen the mass movement through the proletarization of the middle strata. Both camps perceived history as moved by two protagonists: capitalists and workers. The image of society therefore remained anchored to what we would call the stable class structure (in Marxist terms found in *Das Kapital*). The empirical imperfections of real history are dismissed either in purely descriptive terms or as 'spurious' categories. No attempt is made to reconstruct a model of what we would call a 'mobile structure' of classes (even if these two terms seem in contradiction): something which for instance Marx did in his *18th Brumaire,* as well as in other analyses. The 'mobile structure' is certainly connected to the 'stable structure' and can even be derived from it, but only if such a model contains historically specific variables which are linked to the relative political traditions and to organizational specificities, as well as to given institutional structures.

In Italy such dogmatic simplifications are further reinforced by the distorted attention given to the phenomenon of the 'factory' or rather the 'big factory'. In no socialist or revolutionary ideology has the centrality of the factory, both as a locus for the creation of a movement as well as a cell for a future social order, been such a constant as in Italy. This emphasis on the factory cannot even be found among the French revolutionary syndicalists at the turn of the century. One can also find a similar attitude in what can be called the progressive ideology of the regime. As Suzanne Berger justly notes in her essay:

Planners, politicians and representatives from the major economic associations are all in agreement that in Italy's future there is no room for small-size economic units of a family character which require some form of protection. It is held that advanced industrial societies require a competitive entrepreneurship based on profit, one which is easily adaptable to the changes in technology and in markets while being structured along efficient productive lines.[4]

In referring to these attitudes, one should recall Gershenkron's reflections on the fact that those countries which were 'latecomers' to the process of industrialization needed 'industrializing' ideologies, which served to push them toward a dogged and blind concentration on one goal, that of catching up with the first industrial countries. (This notion perceives ideology as a drug: not as the opium but rather as the 'amphetamine' of the masses.) Industrializing ideologies are therefore useful for the elites, but they also influence the opposition: i.e. the Saint-Simonians in France, the Marxists in Russia, and so on. In other words, revolutionaries and planners are both more at ease in a long-term vision based on the 'stable structure' which can orient transformations rather than in a multiform vision of the 'mobile structure' which forces one to think in terms of alliances, compromises and the short term.

But there is more than merely this 'paranoia of catching up' which ultimately remains quite moderate in Italy. Italian society, the 'civilization of cities' as it was once called, not only has always known the middle strata – which were glorious in distant centuries, and far less so in recent ones – but it is out of these middle strata that the Italian intellectuals have emanated. These intellectuals, who therefore knew the middle strata intimately, are generally ashamed of them. No one described the Southern middle bourgeoisie with its *paglietta* (straw hat) better than Gaetano Salvemini; that he should have done it in such intolerant tones shows the degree of indignant shame which Italian intellectuals experience towards this social category. In Paolo Sylos Labini's recent essay, *Saggio sulle classi sociali,* which attempted to show the quantitative and therefore political importance of the middle strata *vis-à-vis* the reform movement, one can feel that before Labini enters the objective realm of statistical tables he is full of rage and indignation for these 'mice in the cheese', as he calls them. In other words, if it is true that intellectuals turn more easily towards topics of study which excite them, they must make a great effort to study the middle strata.

The second consideration is simple: if specialists and intellectuals generally are not interested in the middle strata, or are interested only halfheartedly, the opposite is true for the political sector which is only inter-

Alessandro Pizzorno

ested in them. There is no better proof of the fact that the production
of political thought in a given country has very little in common with the
ways in which politics is actually carried out; or rather it reflects politics
by contrast, by covering up or by evading the issue. The link between
political action and the middle strata will occupy us for the rest of this
essay.

The third consideration refers to the setting which provokes an interest in the middle strata: i.e. the problems which underlie such an interest. Generally one examines the middle strata in polemic against ideological simplifications. The European socialist movement at the end of the
last century is a case in point, as is Italy immediately after the war (but at
the time ideological simplifications of this type were stillborn, even if
others flourished, because the PCI made it quite clear that it had no
intention of pursuing a political line which divided Italian society into
capitalists and workers alone). Today the writings on the middle strata
combat certain simple dichotomies of the New Left. Even if this New
Left has a very hard task in redefining the lines of a new class struggle
because students, technicians, lumpenproletariats (even along ethnical
divisions), or even public employees and shopkeepers seem to take on
the most visible roles.

In the writings before us, therefore, one does not find complementary
approaches or even an accumulation of results but rather different proposals of classification or hypotheses for a theoretical breaking-down of
this heterogeneous reality alternatively called 'middle strata', 'marginal
workers', 'precarious workers', 'traditional sector', 'shock-absorbing sector' or 'rent', and which includes those social elements which cannot be
placed in the category of stable salary earners or of profit makers.

In order to understand this residual category, the most interesting
tracks to follow are the following. The first seeks to single out those
social forces which exercise a stabilizing function while reinforcing consensus in the Italian social system. The second seeks to show the internal
divisions present among those who receive dependent revenue, i.e. the
objective position of exploitation in which certain categories of 'non-
capitalists' find themselves in relation to other 'non-capitalists'. The third
analyses the repercussions of the internal divisions in the capitalist sector
on the intermediate social categories.

As an example of the first case, we can cite again Suzanne Berger's
study of the 'shock-absorbing' sector (composed of traditional tertiary,
domestic work and small enterprises, or in Berger's terms 'small shops,
small industries, small agrarian enterprises') capable of absorbing hidden unemployment, and of therefore attenuating cyclical fluctuations.
But Berger, by focusing on the political use of such a sector and its

104

strengthening, makes a point which calls for interesting further exploration, i.e. the potential solidarity of interests between certain middle strata and marginal workers.

The second point is taken by those who are above all concerned with inequalities in retribution and their consequences on the homogeneity and on the collective objectives of protest movements. The various analyses made by the trade unions on the problem of working-class skill divisions and their implications on collective bargaining fit in this category. But such a theme is limited in scope. Two other topics are more interesting in my opinion. The first is raised by Gorrieri's book which tries to establish a link between inequality and exploitation, and therefore implicitly looks at a concept of exploitation which is different from that based on the notion of the property of the means of production (to which Michele Salvati's book review gave a theoretical contribution). Gorrieri's intention is to dismantle 'the social texture of the middle and lower strata which is anything but uniform and undifferentiated in order to show that inside its ranks there are vast degrees of inequality'. He does this to stress that 'it is not only the industrial entrepreneur and the big monopolies which exploit in the widest sense; other strata also participate in the benefits of the exploitation of working class and peasant labour.' Other studies point to the fundamental disparity in the job market of three types of workers: marginal or casual workers, stable industrial workers, and intellectual workers (those with 'diplomas').[5]

The interesting category here is that of the marginal workers, which is generally defined by a process of exclusion. In it one finds all those members of the work force which for one reason or another do not have a stable place in modern industry. Their destiny is to find themselves periodically or even definitively expelled from the big productive units in times of recession, when an enterprise is restructured, or for other similar reasons. Stable workers are generally 'males who are not too young nor too old, preferably married, possessing a junior high school diploma, and already socialized in an urban industrial environment'.[6] The precarious or marginal sectors comprise all the rest: women, young and older workers, immigrants not socialized in an industrial culture, and so forth. These workers either remain in jobs with low revenue in agriculture or work in small independent occupations, in 'hidden' work or in marginal enterprises, which can pay less than the totals stipulated by national contracts, in subcontracting firms or the like.[7]

Finally, the third way of explaining the behaviour and tendencies of the middle classes is to classify them according to their links with the subdivisions of the capitalist sector. This method is chosen by Sylos Labini who distinguishes between categories which produce goods in competition with those produced by modern productive structures, such as direct growers, small businesses and the like: their fate is to be expelled from the economy. The other categories are composed instead of independent workers who produce goods and services which are complementary to those produced by the modern units: it is the situation of all the production satellites of the big enterprises, of repairing services, and so on. To these must also be added the independent professionals. When linked to the mass of salaried workers these sectors of the middle classes are in constant expansion.

Giovanni Arrighi also insists at length on the importance of distinguishing between two capitalist sectors, even if he then deals only briefly with the consequences of this division on the orientation of the middle classes.[8] The first sector is that of advanced capitalism; the second is backward capitalism. The former is capable of attaining high productivity levels and of producing goods whose numbers increase with the growth in salaries. Not only is this advanced sector capable of paying the workers more, but it also has an interest in doing so. It is therefore interested in a policy of expansion of demand, even if such a policy is eventually inflationary; above all this sector is interested in allying itself with the political and trade union representatives of the working class. The middle strata which follow the policies of this advanced capitalist sector are on the one hand the small entrepreneurs of technologically advanced industries, and on the other the managerial and technical strata which benefit from the process of rationalization of the economy. The second capitalist sector is backward and labour-intensive, and cannot therefore attain levels of high productivity; it generally does not produce goods which can be purchased by the working class. Its principal objective is to be protected against competition from the bigger sectors and against the increase in the cost of labour. Arrighi calls the portion of the middle strata destined to become faithful allies of this backward capitalist sector 'the recipient of privileges derived by the expansion of non-productive consumption'. This definition is very general, but in the course of our analysis we shall show how, if properly qualified, it effectively describes real phenomena.

Middle strata in a theory of consensus

The apparent differences in the classifications listed so far only remind us that the researcher's criteria depend on the problem he has in mind. These different analyses show, however, that the two problems around which all analyses of the middle strata turn are the traditional ones of consensus and class struggle. In other words, one is either asking how the middle strata should be treated in a strategy aimed at obtaining and enlarging the consensus surrounding a given political regime; or one is asking how the middle strata should be treated by a class opposition, in a strategy which tends to overthrow or transform a political regime.

One can say that the formation of consensus and the strategy of class divisions are simply two sides of the same coin. It is, however, useful to keep these two categories separate. In this manner certain processes which would otherwise be overlooked can be seen more clearly. By focusing only on class conflicts, i.e. the role of interested actors in the economic process, one generally overestimates their autonomy. Little attention is paid to the importance of political mediation, which is assumed to follow automatically and to coincide completely with the needs of economic interests determined prior to the intervention of political actors. There is also a tendency to look at the long term and to assume the coincidence of the stable structure with the mobile class structure.

In wishing to understand how consensus is formed one looks instead at the centres where the interest transactions take place; at the functioning of representative systems; and at how processes which develop in the political sphere tend to modify the very shape of those interests, and so ultimately the mobile class structure itself.

Let us first look at the implications which the existence of certain types of middle strata had for the construction of a consensus in Italy. Only then will we be able to understand how the acquisition of such a consensus for the regime created mechanisms which in the long run acted according to their own autonomous logic.

The middle strata generally occupy a very important position in consensus theory. One can say that there are two possible polar choices of strategies for the acquisition of consensus: the first is based on what we would call individual attraction, and the second is formed by the institutionalization of collective demands. The former is visible in a strategy which uses those very inequalities which should give rise to dissent against the system, precisely as an incentive for participation in the benefits which the system can distribute. The latter can be seen in a strategy which allows entire categories of interests to present their collective demands regularly, provided, however, they are mediated by representative structures which maintain – beyond a certain conflictual threshold – a fundamental solidarity with each other for the sake of the system's preservation. In this second case, it is precisely the process of organization of collective representation itself which acts as a mediator and moderator of conflicts and therefore as the codifier of consensus.

Neither strategy – that of individualistic inequalities and that of the institutionalization of demands arising out of collective conflicts – has ever been completely absent from a given historical situation. But, in general, the prevalence of one over the other has effectively character-ized a political regime.

In Italy it is the strategy of individualistic consensus which has practi-cally always prevailed. Exception must be made naturally for the Fascist period, when consensus was obtained through other means, and to a certain degree for the Giolittian period during which in the capitalist part of the country there was a move towards the institutionalization of conflicts, while in the non-capitalist part the clientelary system of rule prevailed. Today, as we shall see, we are confronted by a crisis in the individualistic organization of consensus.

Middle strata play a crucial role in the individualistic organization of consensus. They constitute in effect a reserve which can be dipped into to widen the area of individualistic attraction, i.e. the area of unequal incentives. In this sense the middle strata can be defined as that set of individuals who are in a position to prefer a project of individual improvement over that of a collective or sectoral improvement.

We should now examine the conditions which the Italian political class in power at the end of Fascism encountered in trying to reconstruct the bases of consensus. This political class was new, a stranger to civil society and to the state's administration. It knew or thought it knew that Fascism had been in its origins the expression of discontented middle strata. On the other hand, even the first open opposition to the new anti-Fascist regime, *Qualunquismo,* was a movement emanating from the middle strata. The path towards class agreement through negotiation of collec-tive interests was blocked, first of all because of international constraints: American tutelage had imposed the exclusion from government of the representatives of the working class. There were also internal reasons, linked to the choice of a development model, based on exports and therefore using a cheap labour force, which in effect promoted the weakening of the working class in order to neutralize its demands. In the immediate postwar period, the working class was particularly strong, both because of the industrial boom, a residue of wartime production, and because of the role it had played in the Resistance. Given these two obstacles to working-class participation, the bases of the new consensus had to be found inside the peasantry and in the middle strata.

When one wishes to obtain the consensus of certain social categories, the easiest way is through the enacting of special provisions on their behalf. Certain characteristics of the Italian social structure, however, led to the creation of a much more complex and less demanding type of strategy. Geographic, sectoral and size conflicts, along with the back-wardness of the peasant and marginal worker categories (i.e. the uncertainty of being able to draw them into a clear give-and-take exchange of provisions for votes), led to the creation of a strategy of consensus through mediation. This was economic mediation based on the solidarity of interests between certain middle strata activities and certain categories of the marginal workers; and political mediation linked to the channelling of public funds, often through 'locks' controlled by party men or allies with political connections. It is through these clientelary structures, composed first of notables and later of state functionaries, that, starting in the 1950s, a series of fractions of the middle strata acquired positions of power which, while peripheral, were iron-clad. The two most obvious characteristics of the Italian political system which manifested themselves especially starting in the 1960s – the dispersion of power and the impotence of any reform effort (in effect of all legislative activity on behalf of the general interest) – are the direct product of these clientelary developments. They are the consequence of a progressive acquisition of power by fractions of the middle strata which cashed in for the services their class had rendered to the regime.

In order to analyse more thoroughly these developments it will be best to break them down into three phases which are analytically distinct but also correspond to three successive chronological periods. First, the widening of the middle strata as a reserve for individualistic consensus; secondly, the creation of a solidarity of interests between parts of the middle strata and certain categories of marginal workers; thirdly, the formation of a clientelary system as a channel for the creation of power.

The individualistic mobilization of the middle strata

If it is true that the countryside and the middle strata were the two areas to be rallied for the formation of a consensus for the ruling class, it should be possible to find the traces of such a strategy in the measures taken in the realm of political economy. They are not hard to locate in agricultural policies and in public works projects (directed largely at the marginal workers). They are much more difficult to trace in relation to the middle strata themselves. For such an operation should be able to single out those provisions explicitly meant to reinforce specific categories even at the cost of slowing down industrial development. In many cases, however, it is not easy to distinguish between possible social components in terms of specific interests. For instance, which forces wanted the deflationary policy inaugurated by Einaudi in 1947? Up to what point did the fear of economic ruin felt by many strata of the middle classes – with all the possible disastrous implications of such a fear on forthcoming elections decisive for the regime – play a role? While leaving to future researchers the task of analysing in depth specific provisions or entire areas of political economy, it is already possible to evaluate the consequences of the fundamental choice of economic development models, adopted in the postwar period, on the future role of the middle strata.

Let us recall the fundamental alternatives available in terms of models for the material reconstruction of the economy. One could opt for a type of development in which consumption would have been relatively controlled while resources were channelled particularly towards instrumental goods, with subsequent capital accumulation and growth in agrarian production. Or one could choose a type of development preferably guided by market forces, especially those in the international market with a corresponding expansion of modern internal consumption and compression of salary goods. The social consequences of the first choice would have been the expansion of a working-class category in the industrial sector and a reduced exodus from the countryside directed towards the industrial rather than the tertiary sector. The consequences of the second choice would have led to a retarded development of the working-class categories in the industrial sector, accompanied instead by a strong exodus from the countryside and a strong development of a tertiary sector, and therefore the expansion of the middle strata both in the productive sector as well as in that based on rent.

We know that the second alternative was chosen. The role of international constraints was very strong, as we have mentioned. But it is very likely that there were other constraints deeply rooted in the Italian economic structure itself.[9] The consequences which interest us here are those linked to the expansion of the middle strata, as we defined them earlier, in terms of the widening of the reserve area for individualistic incentives. Or, more precisely, of the area in which it is possible to create incentives based on inequality, without their providing, at least for a certain period, the bases for dissent or dissatisfaction towards the regime. This individualistic mobilization through participation in the system's benefits was visible in two aspects, the first linked to production, and the second to consumption.

The expansion of the middle strata into the realm of production, i.e. the enlarging of the area of entrepreneurship, has certainly not been very widespread, but it probably acted as a model, or as a myth. 'Setting up one's own business' represented a sufficiently important individualistic alternative for many Italians, and not only for those who succeeded in achieving it. The partial rationalization, carried out by big industry on the one hand and the disorganized urban expansion on the other, provided the basis for this widening of entrepreneurial activities both in the productive and in the service sectors, and gave them credibility for a while. In terms of the diffusion of unequal incentives, the spread of mass consumerism was certainly more important. It is well known that mass consumption in Italy played both a pathological and also a functional role in the process of economic development. This double trait is clearly visible in the analysis made by those economists who stress how Italian development was in great part spurred by the export sector. According to these economists, the modern sector devoted to exports, obviously unable to export the whole of its production, was forced to sell a sufficiently large portion in the domestic market itself.

Less essential for the economists, but vital to our case, is the need to know to whom these modern goods were being sold. The thesis of A. Graziani and his group is that 'the distortion in consumption appears as the consequence of an inequality in work revenue'.[10] In other words, it should be the workers in the advanced sector who are buying that portion of goods they produce and which is not sold on the international market:

The duplicity of salary conditions produces strong inequalities in the distribution of work revenues. On the one hand, workers in the advanced sector enjoy high incomes and want consumer goods in a manner typical of industrial aggregates. On the other hand, workers in the semi-artisanal sector have much more modest incomes and cannot purchase in adequate quantities even the most elementary goods, and thus contribute to the lowering of the average level of consumption for society as a whole.[11]

From the few data at our disposal on the consumer levels of that period, it seems that the above description is not quite correct. We know, for example, that in 1957, washing machines, refrigerators and cars were owned respectively by 1, 2, and 1 per cent of the Italian working class.[12] From another source, we know that the number of dependent workers in the non-agrarian sector who in 1960 owned a refrigerator was 11 per cent, but that only 1 per cent owned a washing machine.[13] We can conclude, in my opinion, that for a long time the demand for modern consumer goods came mainly from non-industrial middle incomes, especially from the urban, bureaucratic or professional rent sector. In other words, the economic system of the miracle years (i.e. up to 1962–3), functioned by keeping work revenues low and therefore also work costs, while accepting that a portion of revenues be developed which did not bear down *immediately* on profits and which had instead the important function of bolstering the demand for that portion of 'modern' goods which was not absorbed by the export market. This trend implied the creation, or at least the expansion – largely outside the modern sector of the economy – of a group of middle strata whose existence was functional to the modern sector itself in terms of consumption. The presence of this category of savers probably had a 'demonstration effect' at a later time and stimulated the working-class protests of the 1960s.

The numerical growth of the middle strata and the functional aspect of their position in the type of economy Italy was developing thus constituted the bases of their political strength. It is on the basis of this strength that the power alliance between political forces and the middle strata was established. We can gather the political importance of these middle strata by noting that in the 1950s all the government crises were provoked by one or the other of the three lay parties whose electorate was almost entirely composed of middle strata: the Liberals, the Republicans and the Social Democrats. It is equally significant that the Christian Democrats, even with an absolute majority, as in the first legislature, always made sure that they governed with one or more of these parties. Putting it bluntly, after having controlled the peasants with a few land concessions and public works and through the capillary action of the church and of organizations such as the Coldiretti [the Association of Agrarian Owners] after having frozen the working class – or its most militant portion – in the opposition, the regime devoted its caresses and apprehensions throughout the 1950s to the middle strata.

If on the basis of this analysis we were to ask ourselves how to define these middle strata, the answer would be a very simple one: old or new, traditional or modern, in the service sector or in productive activities, agrarian or urban, these middle strata comprise all those social categories which were not ascribable either to the working class or to the peasant organizations. They also comprised that sector of society which was incapable of single-handedly taking decisions which could condition the system on their behalf, unlike the big entrepreneurs or the political class in the government. The simplified and aggregate nature of this definition warns us that this analysis is only very approximate. Furthermore, it is this non-organizational ability to make collective demands which tells us in which direction we should turn our research: i.e. towards the other social categories which remained outside any associational organizations, and which, for that matter, seem to have had common interests for a time with certain fractions of the middle strata: in other words, the category of marginal workers.

The role of the middle strata in the control of marginal workers

In order to assure consensus and to protect those enterprises which were competing in the international market it was not enough for the governing class to reinforce the middle strata. It also had to ensure order, in other words to avoid social explosions. We have seen how a series of provisions on behalf of the sectors capable of absorbing work forces were enacted precisely to keep order. Not only the agricultural policy up to the mid-1950s but also the policy of support for artisans, small businesses, small industries, construction trades, public works, and so on were only partially conceived in terms of their economic effects. Rather, these measures were implicitly linked to the danger which the insecurity of marginal workers represented to the system's political stability.

This political vision implied a strategy of alliances with the productive petit bourgeoisie in order to control social tensions. By offering politically protected solutions to the problem of precarious work, a solidarity was established between small employers and their workers, because both were dependent on a given policy rather than on the market forces directly. There was a double complicity. On the one hand the political powers were interested in making sure that social equilibria were not upset, and therefore offered their protection; on the other hand, the petit bourgeoisie was in a position to blackmail the government, which was obliged to favour it, if it wanted to prevent the social explosions which would have arisen from the excessive discontent of the marginal workers. The *de facto* alliance of the petit bourgeoisie with marginal social strata and their mutual complicity in a policy of 'precarious protection' has its roots in this logic.

One needs to make a distinction, however, between different marginal strata: some can be called traditional, or better, autochthonous; others instead arise as a consequence of social mobilization, of emigration, urbanization, or of a rupture in the traditional social equilibrium: if the word did not have unpleasant overtones, we would call these strata *displaced.*

The first example of marginal strata is to be found in precarious work centres both in the countryside and in the small cities. The second can be found mainly in the big cities. The former are kept under control in Italy by the clergy or by paternalistic employers; the latter are controlled by new clientelary situations, halfway between the labour market and the electoral market. When the former seek to improve their situation it is through associative organizations. The latter instead are marginal because they are excluded (for objective as well as subjective reasons) from such associations for collective interests. They hold towards these associations more rancour than hope (of belonging). As d'Antonio justly remarks:

Since the fundamental aspiration of these strata of the population is to find work under stable conditions, in other words, the maintenance of real earned revenue, the trade union action of the working class can be considered by them as immediately antagonistic to their interests.[14]

If this description is correct, the traditional marginal sectors are potentially left-wing while the *displaced* marginals are on the right. In Italy the strata of marginal workers belonged to the first category in the 1950s, and more to the second in the 1960s.

This phenomenon can explain at least in part the politics of the Christian Democrats. In the 1950s they had to absorb those marginal strata which were potentially on the Left. They had to respond at least partially to their need for security in order to remove them from Communist control. The consequence was a policy of alliance to the Right with, at least on the surface, progressive policies (agrarian reform, housing policies, etc.). Towards the end of the 1960s, when the problem of precarious work for the marginal strata reemerged in political form (after a phase in which these strata seemed to be absorbed by the only protagonist of collective demands, the working class), the Christian Democrats were confronted with the problem of removing these strata no longer from the Communists but from the Fascists (MSI). (In reality this had also been true for a portion of the Southern urban proletariat even in the 1950s during *Laurismo*, the phase of rule by Lauro the Neapolitan town boss, but I am concerned here with larger trends.) The Christian Democratic policy of strengthening clientelary bonds while still in the Centre–Left political phase is a result of this new political situation and has its most obvious expression in the commerce law. One should recall that this law marks an attempt to balance the consequences of the Cipolla de Marzi law on agrarian rationalization which had seriously damaged many of the rural middle classes, who had reacted by shifting their support to the neo-Fascists. One can say that the potential mass adhesion of both the petit bourgeoisie and the lumpenproletariat to Fascism constituted the nightmare of the Christian Democrats who feared that the intricate web of clientelary 'honour' and consensus which it had built up during two decades would fall apart, toppling it in the process.

The functioning of the new clientelary structure

The mediating role of the small 'private' bourgeoisie in the control of marginal strata is only one pillar in the construction of consensus in Christian Democratic Italy. The other pillar is composed of a new set of *public mediation* functions. Since the word 'public' might cause mistaken interpretations, one should speak rather of a set of public–administrative mediations. Parallel to the reinforcement of a petit bourgeoisie dependent on a politically protected market, there has also been the rise and growth of a petit bourgeoisie directly dependent on political organizations. This is an analytical distinction, because in reality not only are the interests intertwined but the functions are also enmeshed. It is, however, useful to distinguish the specificity of the two phenomena, all the more so since they did not emerge together. In the first years following the creation of the new state, when the ruling class was still primitive and in many ways, as we have seen, dissociated from the real structures of society, the alliance with the private petit bourgeoisie appeared, in addition to the use of the clergy, as one of the only instruments available with which to control social tensions. The ruling class in power, however, gradually grew stronger and expanded its authority. Its legislative instruments became more efficient and public funds at its disposal more abundant. As a consequence, it tended to perform its own controlling function, thus keeping for itself the benefits it had obtained.

The instruments this ruling class has at its disposal are essentially of three kinds: control over special credits, and in certain areas even over normal credit, and control over what we would call *interdiction and licensing*, which give it the power of granting or refusing the right to carry on certain economic activities.

In the first case (public works, special action on behalf of the Mezzogiorno, social services, etc.) the middle political levels carry out an active intervention by choosing, in the most discreet manner possible, those on whom benefits are to be bestowed, i.e. possible allies. These can be either marginal strata directly or the petit bourgeoisie. But in either case the allocation of public funds will be oriented towards the creation of new public functions or the extension of previously existing ones. These expenditures will be directed ostensibly towards controlling the use made of public funds; in reality their purpose is to expand the middle political levels.

The second case, of control over credit, is more interesting and newer because here the political class intervenes in a quasi-entrepreneurial manner. It is naturally a protected entrepreneurship since the risks are minimal: the electoral market offers few surprises. A way of measuring efficiency and the risk of sanctions still exists, however, through the size of the power network that one can weave for a given party or group. The criterion for maximization is not the productive efficiency of the credit given but the strength of the tie of gratitude which is thereby created and the type of reciprocal service which that given fraction of the political class can expect. For an economic credit there is a corresponding political debt, even if productive efficiency can be one of the elements in the growth of overall power.

115

We are therefore confronted with a small-scale phenomenon of the creation of a new bourgoisie, on whose behalf the political class first acts as midwife only to become later its ally. This process develops through the creation of a 'confidence network' (I use the term here in its structural and objective meaning: even *omertà*, Mafia honour, and complicity are forms of confidence), which brings together individuals selected by a political and administrative mechanism. Some perform roles as private entrepreneurs; others administrative roles; and still others mixed roles. One of the most important characteristics of such an incestuous mechanism is to have a positive feedback, i.e. to be able to self-reproduce. The stronger it becomes, the more this mechanism can attract public funds, which in turn will strengthen it further.[15]

Finally there is the power to license and interdict, a power which finds its utmost expression in the policy of local bodies, above all in the control and distribution networks, and over urban planning. These instruments naturally have different results and successes according to the different clients and allies they address. The projects for urban planning legislation of the early 1960s, for example, called for an alliance between the political ruling class at the peripheral level and the enlightened bourgeoisie (whose exponents were mainly professionnal urban planners), against the interests of speculators and small construction builders. Such projects did not take into account the real power base of these minor groups, which lay less in their capacity for electoral 'persuasion' (even if this was stronger than expected since it played on the irrational fears of the small home-owners) than in their existing ties with the peripheral political class, which found in their ranks both financial support and the principal terrain for its concrete exercise of power.

The law concerning the regulations of commercial enterprises, enacted in 1971, is instead the most faithful expression of the 'structural alliances' which bolster peripheral power in Italy:

Commercial licensing is a form of tutelage over a vassal; it is a feudal type of investiture over a few square metres of territory, with which one expects to protect the small merchant from competition *forever;* it is the creation of a small monopoly . . . it is in effect the reward given to a good and loyal servant by the given body which detains power.[16]

This definition, drawn from an analysis of the council-level alliance which placed Communists and neo-Fascists (PCI and MSI) in the same camp in Bologna in 1969 (the year of the 'hot autumn', the height of working-class struggles in Italy), in order to favour small businesses against the supermarkets, gives an idea of what is meant by the power of interdiction and licensing. The above definition may be somewhat exaggerated in attributing absolute power to given political bodies. In reality such power is always used as a base for transactions with another group endowed with its own power. The 1971 law reflects this system of transactions by reinforcing and stabilizing it. In many ways this law is exemplary because it brings together some of the typical ways used by a system which above all fears the threat of instability. By reinforcing the alliance between peripheral political classes and the small commercial bourgeoisie, and making it practically indispensable (the arbitration power of the political class is partly limited while the positions of the established interests become virtually impossible to assail), this provision tries to counter the threat of a mass movement of those middle strata which are losing their relative status (i.e. movements of the Poujadist type). Such a provision at the same time prevents the possible surge of new concentrated interests – which would be difficult to control at least at the local level – by implicitly stipulating short-term advantages for other 'big interests' (those of the producers who are no longer confronted with the threat of protests or with the revision of the 'imposed price').[17]

These two, practically automatic, reactions of the system – the reinforcing of existing alliances (and therefore of the mediating functions of the political class) and the granting of short-term advantages so as to avoid a clash with potentially innovative interests – are particularly visible in the areas of rent and reform.

Rent and reforms

We have so far described a consensus strategy which uses the middle strata as buffers where incentives toward inequality can operate, by offering as a reward either access to economic benefits (modern consumer goods) or to political ones (protected entrepreneurial fiefs and clientelary power) which the system can provide. We have even begun to see one consequence of such a strategy: the rooting and self-feeding of a new public–private class which has a strong, even if diffuse, power of veto and blackmail.

We can further note that such an exchange (of participation in benefits for consensus) can only function if there are some who are either excluded from such benefits or who at least receive less in a period of growth. (Otherwise the sum of inequalities would equal zero and would thus cease to produce incentives, unless one were to assume the existence of a general illusion.) The excluded in Italy were the unemployed and the salaried workers, agricultural as well as industrial, as long as their contractual power remained low, i.e. until the early 1960s. The development of the middle strata in Italy took place under the shadow of export policies and unemployment, and we know that the former was possible only because there was the latter.[18]

Major problems arise when the prerequisites for such a strategy of individualistic consensus begin to disappear. Once unemployment diminishes (or when owing to particular geographic and cultural reasons of the labour market it ceases to act as a deterrent to collective demands), and when consequently the industrialists' capacity for obtaining higher real salaries increases, entrepreneurs have different alternatives for keeping the cost of labour low so as to remain competitive in the international market. One such solution is to alleviate the pressure which rent exerts on such labour costs. This is done through a struggle on behalf of reforms against rent. The issue of a reformist alliance against rent has been at the centre of political debates in the last few years (I say 'debates', more than politics as such). The hypothesis behind these debates and around which the political forces of the first Centre–Left governments rallied is that there exists in Italy a sector which can be *clearly singled out* and labelled generically that of 'rent', and which a series of reforms (in urban affairs, the bureaucracy, in the health sector, etc.) could at least reduce in weight, if not entirely eliminate. The economy would thereby be rationalized, thus permitting a major share of the national income to go towards salaries and profits.

What is exactly meant by the notion of 'rent' in these debates is not altogether clear, because here also, as in the case of the middle strata, the definition given depends on the problems one confronts and on the issues one seeks to defend; and for those who carry out a responsible political line on the type of alliance sought. Besides landed and urban rents – rents in the strict sense of the term – most debates on the topic tend to label as 'rent' professional and bureaucratic revenues as well as those produced by the distortion of the distribution system. According to certain authors (Napoleoni for instance), one can classify as 'rents' even those revenues in big organizations of the modern sector which seem wasteful expenditures, for instance the advertising services. In other cases, the emphasis is placed not on waste but on protection. All the protected industries are placed under 'rent'. Recently the political debate surrounding work costs has drawn attention to the weight of social security costs, which have also been included in the category of rent. 'Social security rent acts as a differentiating element between salaries and the cost of work, and is one of the factors which have weighed most in the fall of profits', asserted Agnelli in an interview with Scalfari, a most authoritative voice on the question of profits and work costs.[19] At the other pole, as if in reply, the PCI in the person of Luciano Barca also raises the problem of rent in general terms:

We too are preoccupied by the discrepancy between salary and work costs linked to the current social security system, but we feel that this is only part of a wider problem: that comprised by the ever-growing portion of surplus value which is absorbed by rent – (urban, agrarian, monopolies in production and distribution, bureaucratic and speculative) – which prevent what is accumulated from becoming a productive investment; it is rents which prevent further accumulation.

There probably was never a political negotiation which was treated with such care for definitions. The concept of 'rent' became a bowl which the different dinner guests wanted brought to the table if they were to dine together. Each wanted it to be as full as possible. Some even wanted it to be too full (perhaps so as to break the eggs), such as Cesare Zapulli in 1972: 'Industry is not capable of paying rents to everyone: state employees, businessmen, agrarian workers, electricians in ENEL, railroad workers, postal employees, municipal workers, etc.'[20] In other words, the concept of rent used here bears no kinship to that of economic theory: it has become a way of singling out a series of 'enemy' categories to single out in charting a new direction for the economy.

The interview Agnelli gave Scalfari raised a storm. It seemed that in order to hasten bargaining Agnelli was adopting the language and even the analyses of left-wing intellectuals. Castronovo reminds us that the substance of the proposals, if not the language, was already advanced by the Agnellis in the 1930s – unfortunate proposals, just as these will be.

Why? Why is it that such a strong alliance on behalf of reforms cannot succeed, Magri justifiably asks in the opening article on the debate over reforms.[21] Why cannot the combined forces of Big Capital, reform-oriented politicians, working-class trade unions, disarm Rent?

Our analysis of the consequences of a given type of consensus strategy on the changes in the relationship between public and private power, especially at the peripheral level, sought to formulate precisely an answer to such questions. But it is only a partial answer which must be expanded. The new class of public–private bourgeoisie embedded in the 'locks' of public expenditure and protected rent comprises only one wing of this class formation. The role it performs is more defensive than offensive; it is more capable of blackmail than of conquests. Next to this wing of the bourgeoisie there is a mass wing, composed of the petit bourgeoisie and of marginal groups. The capability of mobilizing such a mass is linked to the degree of nurtured common interests between certain fractions of the middle strata and the marginal workers. It is this potential mobilization of the masses which constantly threatens to break the original consensus, thus 'stepping out of the system'. It is an offensive threat because it is capable of proposing an alternative to the regime of a Fascist kind (and can be seen as a more serious threat than *Qualun-*

quismo, Laurismo or Poujadism). This is true even if such an alliance of middle strata and marginal populations needs to win the support of at least one portion of the industrial bourgeoisie in order to become politically relevant.

Peripheral veto power and the threat of a Fascist-type mass movement explain why the opponents of the reformist alliance are so strong. But the alliance is weak in itself. Two considerations will suffice: one referring to the type of advantages which the subjects of the alliance can expect to obtain; the other to the nature of their relations.

The advantages which workers and industrialists can expect from a reform policy are linked to the reduction of the role of rent in national revenue. It is not only difficult, as we have seen, to obtain such a reduction, but, even having obtained it, any advantages would only become visible over a long period of time. In the short term, given the situation of the international market and the difficulty of acting on prices, the costs of work must still be kept down. The effects of the reforms will only be visible with time. Who can be the guarantor of the future behaviour of one or the other partner? The industrialists certainly cannot make definitive plans, since the essentially international factors that determine their actions are almost entirely beyond their control. Nor can the trade unions programme a line which can take for granted the future actions of their adherents, since the nature of their representative mandate is increasingly more difficult to conceive over long periods.

This last remark leads us to an examination of the second factor in the weakness of the alliance: the types of relations which exist between the two halves of the industrial system. In recent years industrial clashes in Italy have been particularly intense. Such intensity was partially derived from contingent reasons, such as the long preceding period of repression and trade union weakness; the authoritarianism in hierarchical relations inside firms, which was probably exceptional for an advanced industrial context; and the composition of the working class in which the 'new' forces, of recent immigration, not socialized in the traditional working-class culture, had become prevalent. Of these motives, the first certainly, as well as the second and third, have lost their thrust. Other conditions are still present and will continue to remain. One is the increased international competition Italian firms have to face, with the subsequent need to extract the maximum labour from the working class. The other is the increased contractual power given to workers, even if they are not many, in a situation of ever-stronger industrial interdependence in organizational terms, and in all economic organization in general. The first condition shows us with what little security Italian industrialists (and not only the Italians) can enter into political alliances which take for granted future advantages. The second condition shows us that the trade unions are less than ever capable of guaranteeing working-class demands in coordinated strategies over a long-term period.

Given the above, we can fully see the intrinsic weakness of the reformist alliance.

The new contradictions

The organization of consensus postulated in Italy in the 1950s, which relied basically on individualistic competition and on inequality as an incentive, thanks to the repression of collective demands, no longer works today.

The clientelary structures, even if they are still tied to those in power, are less capable than previously of guaranteeing the acquiescence of marginal population groups. Blackmail, which lay at the basis of the exchange of consensus for influence, has become a real threat, and in some cases has even been carried out (cf. Reggio Calabria). Furthermore, the groups of marginal population have become too mobile to be solidly controlled by clientelary mediations.

The explosion of working-class struggles has provided other social categories with an example of how to organize collective demands. Many of these categories are typically composed of middle-class elements: state or state-affiliated functionaries, workers in the banking, insurance, hospital sectors, and so on. The conditions of close interdependence and subsequent organizational vulnerability are not unique to the factory but pertain to all economic organization in general. When a category which holds the partial or total monopoly of a service can organize collectively, it also becomes capable of paralysing, more or less seriously, the entire economy. The sanctions which a democratic government has at its disposal against such a threat are very weak. The result is a system of 'sectoral catching up', in which every category or group of specific workers is sufficiently strong, when organized, momentarily to carry out its objectives, but not strong enough in the long run to maintain the positions of relative advantage which it has acquired. The only way of obtaining a certain level of consensus is by institutionalizing the negotiations at the most centralized level possible. The more centralized the negotiating process the greater the possibility of coordinating gains by category in terms of predictable effects. Conversely, the more a class action is dispersed (within certain limits) the greater its incisiveness. In Italy, paradoxically, the high degree of politicization and centralization of the trade union forces offers a favourable setting for a *de facto* consensus towards the existing regime. Both politicization and centralization became increasingly weaker in the years 1968–72, but they are now reconsolidating their strength, just as PCI control is once again increasing. It is still not clear to what degree political activity can reabsorb trade union negotiations.

Besides the attempt to resolve politically the problem of repeated trade union demands by category by bringing in the PCI in its tradition of opposition, the only means which those in power can use – if one excludes the creation of emergency situations (which are increasingly tempting) – is that of redressing short-term and conjunctural equilibria. Political action is becoming one of ever shorter small-term operations. This is the only manner in which one can satisfy the 'big interests'. Having proven itself incapable of coordinating and favouring long-term ends for the big economic interests (for instance through anti-rent reforms), those in political power can only support such ends in immediate terms, by giving in to the demands for political services which such interests and their representatives can make from time to time.

It is precisely when they are most often cited that the concept of the 'middle strata' loses all significance. The middle strata, as we have seen, have never constituted a united category. But one could find in their midst those internal strata through which the organization of consensus on behalf of a given regime was taking place. These processes could either be found in the clientelary structures, on which a portion of peripheral and party power is still based today; or in certain collectively organized categories; or even inside the big business sector for which they provided a recruitment base for the leadership of the public or private economy, through the traditional mechanisms of mobility or career. In all three groups, but particularly in the first two, a centrifugal process of disaggregation, i.e. of moving away from the rules of political complicity (in the case of clienteles), or of institutional negotiations (in the case of sectoral organizations), can favour the formation of reactionary mass movements.

Notes

[1] Ermanno Gorrieri, *La giungla retributiva* (Bologna 1972), p. 14.

[2] Direct translation by the author from the German, K. Marx, *Theorien über den Mehrwert* (Berlin 1967), ii, 576.

[3] Giuliano Pischel, *Il problema dei ceti medi* (Milan 1946), pp. 16–17, 203. For an attempt to propose an articulated classification of social strata in Italy see Luciano Gallino, 'L'evoluzione della struttura di classe in Italia', *Quaderni di Sociologia*, xix, 2, 1970.

[4] Suzanne Berger, 'Uso politico e sopravvivenza dei ceti medi in declino' in F. L.

Cavazza & S. R. Graubard (eds.), *Il caso italiano* (2 vols, Milan, 1974), vol. 2, p. 292.

[5] Gorrieri, *La giungla retributiva*, p. 8; M. Salvati, 'Note di lettura su *La giungla retributiva* di E. Gorrieri', *Quaderni Piacentini*, no. 50, July 1973; M. de Cecco, 'Un'interpretazione ricardiana della dinamica della forza lavoro in Italia', *Note Economiche*, 1, 1972; M. Paci, 'Le contraddizioni del mercato del lavoro', *Inchiesta*, ii, no. 6, 1972.

[6] Paci, 'Le contraddizioni del mercato', p. 7.

[7] For a somewhat different, even if non-contradictory classification, cf. P. Calzabini, 'Problemi per un'analisi delle classi in Italia', *Inchiesta*, iii, no. 11, 1973.

[8] G. Arrighi, 'Una nuova crisi generale', *Rassegna Comunista*, i, nos. 2, 3, 4, and 7.

[9] M. D'Antonio, *Sviluppo e crisi del capitalismo italiano, 1951–1972* (Bari 1973), p. 170.

[10] A. Graziani *et al.*, *Lo sviluppo di un'economia aperta* (Naples 1972), p. 49.

[11] *Ibid.*, pp. 48–9.

[12] F. Momigliano & A. Pizzorno, 'I consumi in Italia' in *Aspetti e problemi dello sviluppo economico in Italia* (Bari 1959), p. 198.

[13] ISTAT table in P. Braghin, *Le disaguaglianze sociali: analisi empirica della situazione di diseguaglianza in Italia* (Milan 1973), i, 235.

[14] D'Antonio, *Sviluppo e crisi del capitalismo italiano*, p. 35.

[15] G. Ruffolo, *Rapporto sulla programmazione* (Bari 1973), p. xii; G. Amato, *Il governo dell'industria* (Bologna 1972), p. 27.

[16] T. Torrato, 'Valvassori e valvassini: Comuni e Bottegai', *Il Mulino*, 207 (January 1970), p. 116.

[17] R. Ariotti, 'Pretese corporativistiche ed esigenze di sviluppo nella programmazione del commercio', *Il Mulino*, 216, 1971.

[18] D'Antonio, *Sviluppo e crisi del capitalismo italiano*, p. 20.

[19] *Espresso*, 19 November 1972.

[20] C. Zapulli, *Il Corriere della Sera*, 17 November 1972.

[21] L. Magri, 'Spazio e ruolo del riformismo', *Il Manifesto*, 26 April 1973.

7. Uneven Development and Social Disaggregation: Notes for an Analysis of Classes in the South*

Carlo Donolo

Premise

This contribution to a social and political analysis of the South constitutes a first presentation, in problematic and approximate form, of categories and hypotheses which require deeper theoretical elaboration and the investigation of concrete situations. Its schematic and incomplete nature reflects the initial phase of research but it has been made possible thanks to the recent accumulation of interpretations of the Southern situation which radically modify the theoretical paradigm used hitherto.

The theoretical and political context of discussion in which this analysis should be placed needs to be specified. In the last few years significant steps forward have been made in relation to: (1) an analysis of the economic, social and political tendencies operating in the South; (2) a reflection on the new contradictions brought about by the type of development encouraged in the recent past; (3) and our understanding of the particular forms which social conflicts have taken. These analyses are still partial and tentative, but they have the advantage of posing the problems of the South in their true light, i.e. as those of unequal and dependent capitalist development. In so doing, such analyses mark a theoretical break from the more classic interpretations, including Gramsci's, and even more radically in terms of the neo-Southern approach of the last twenty years based essentially on the models of development inspired by the sociology and economics of modernization. The presuppositions of this modernizing approach – which justified for such a long period the ideology of special intervention in the South, and which now

---

*This work was written in collaboration with Riccardo Scartezzini and published in *Quaderni Piacentini*, no. 47 (July 1972), pp. 101–29; also reprinted in M. Paci (ed.), *Capitalismo e classi sociali in Italia* (Bologna 1978), pp. 115–48.

appear to belong to a historically superseded phase – must still be critically reexamined. More recent analyses (such as the writings of Collidà, Foa, Ferraris, Mottura and Pugliese, or the contributions of the Campanian coordinating centre[1]) stress however that the contradictions present in the South today are those of the capitalist development which began after 1950 both at the national and European level. In this context the Southern Question becomes a particular case in a more general phenomenon of unequal and dependent development. Its historical specificity – linked to pre- and post-unification developments, which were given such a priority in the traditional analyses of the South – thereby loses significance with respect to the general mechanisms of capitalist accumulation in its oligopolistic phase. In reality the Southern Question has been liquidated as an historical problem by the developments of capitalism itself, and not by the politics of intervention. This, too, is a contradiction worthy of analysis.

In addition to providing a critical contribution against a dominant interpretative tradition, these new approaches to the South gather their significance from the fact that they arose out of the urgent need to understand new, little-known phenomena in the social and political realm. These phenomena can be summarized in one term: 'new social disaggregation', which is responsible for the failure of all strategies, aiming either at modernization or revolution. The conflicts and revolts which have exploded recently have abruptly drawn attention, even on the part of the Left (which is always lagging behind), to the social structure of the South and to the new power structure which developed there in recent years. This structure hitherto condemned in terms of moralistic categories linked to the notion of a *buongoverno* (good civic government), has never been understood in terms of a theory of Italian capitalist development. In such a situation of theoretical abandon, the South represents both a source of hope and a threat: hope because of the nature of its potential contradictions; threat because the mediations between contradictions and real conflicts generally materialize in deviant, desperate, populistic forms instrumentalized for struggle around false objectives. The very nature of Southern contradictions is contradictory: the potential mobilization of the masses arises out of profoundly contrasting causes and motives which are almost always undermined by particularism, localism and corporatism. Political unification is sabotaged by the permanent processes of disaggregation of the social structure. Nevertheless there is hope in the fact that in the South the accumulation of all the mechanisms of disparity, inequality and dependance are very clearly visible – even if they are not yet fully accessible to the consciousness of the great masses. There are both advanced and backward contradictions, corresponding to the most developed productive forces and modes of production as well as to the most *apparently* traditional.

It is our purpose to show that backwardness is a phenomenon produced by development itself: regardless of how one defines pre-capitalist and pre-modern social forms – in terms of poverty, mass unemployment, illiteracy, or levels of infant mortality – while characterizing backwardness these forms are integrally linked to a process of development. This process hides behind the appearance of historical residue: from agricultural modes of production to the 'trachoma' at Palma di Montechiaro. Illiteracy coexists with a very strict educational selection, yet there still is manual and intellectual unemployment. Overabundant work forces still yield the overworking of a few 'privileged' producers. Metropolitan consumer patterns exist without the least presence of a capitalist industry.

This appearance dominates even those objects of development, the dominated classes. Dominance manifests itself not so much as the hegemonic capacity of the ruling classes but as the apparently natural consequence of underdevelopment, in continuity with past backwardness.[2] Thus the dominated classes tend to interpret their needs and interests in categories linked to a tradition of misery and personal dominance. They are unfortunately encouraged along these lines by the manner in which the slogans (criticizable in themselves) of the organized Left are presented. This analysis is based on the belief that only large-scale collective movements – which are fully articulated and capable of pursuing middle-range objectives, while led by a conscious and organized avantgarde – can transform contradictions into social conflicts which will produce effective change rather than modernization at their expense, refinancing of old structures, or desperate revolts. Precisely because the problems of the South are the problems of capitalist development in Italy, no policy of intervention and industrialization can solve them, whether it is separate from or in opposition to these movements. In reality the policy of intervention is increasingly fulfilling the function of conflict-containment while supporting the aggressive expansion of monopoly capital. In assuming the point of view of the collective movements we do not presuppose a great faith in the possibility of their success and growth. On the contrary, such a faith must be evaluated on the basis of a structural analysis of tendencies and contradictions, which must still be carried out. But if one does not assume such a point of view, one would not see those problems which lie between contradictions and conflicts – and which are the correct ones.

The new terms of the Southern Question

Any contemporary social analysis of the Italian South must take into account a few facts which should be obvious by now. First, during the post Second World War period the Mezzogiorno has undergone, both in its economic and social structure, profound contradictions which have essentially done away with the Southern Question in its traditional historical terms. Secondly, tendencies in the national economic system in the past twenty years have produced a steady accumulation of new types of contradictions in the South, turning it into an area of potentially very serious social conflicts. Thirdly, implicit in what has just been said above, the declared objectives of Southern policy, bent on narrowing the gap between North and South and setting up the bases of self-propelled development, have visibly failed.

The need for adequate interpretations of Southern problems has made itself increasingly felt in the South itself especially after the explosion of new types of conflicts, such as the recent mass movements and popular revolts, with all their ambivalences and weaknesses. These new conflicts are the only source of hope for the South, the only justification for an attempt to single out its 'correct' problems at present. In order to analyse these struggles correctly one would need to possess a theory of development for Italian society in the postwar period. Such a theory exists currently only in a fragmentary and hypothetical form. Our contribution therefore cannot go beyond a general and at times abstract level of analysis. We must run the risk of schematism if we wish to produce a systematic interpretation from which hypotheses and trends for crucial questions can be derived.[3] In programmatic terms these are the key questions: (1) what is the nature of present-day contradictions in relation to the prevailing tendencies?[4] (2) through what processes are social classes formed and which mechanisms produce aggregation or differentiation (e.g. how is the specific type of 'Southern disaggregation' produced)? (3) under what conditions do contradictions explode into social conflicts, and what structural forms do these conflicts take? (4) what are the objective and recognizable interests of these political actors, and around what objectives can they be rallied?

These issues are relevant for the subordinate classes, and any social analysis which assumes such a viewpoint has the task of redefining the demarcation line between those who suffer from unequal development and those who impose it.

Before elaborating on our schematic outline, let us briefly recall the principal current tendencies of Southern development:

(*a*) The historic dualism between North and South, which used to include also other dualisms such as city–countryside, industry–agriculture, working class–peasantry, is being replaced by the new dualism of centre–periphery, by the polarization into developing areas on the one hand (either urban or industrial) and marginalized, stagnant or degraded areas on the other (this process has national and even European dimensions).[5]

(b) One of the structural manifestations of unequal development described in (a) is the 'scissor' effect of industrialization–urbanization: i.e. the disproportionate number of persons living in urban areas compared with the real possibility of their obtaining revenue from productive activities, especially in the industrial sector.

(c) A second result of unequal development, strictly connected with (b) is the differentiation inside the proletariat between groups which are more or less integrated in the productive process (especially in the crucial sector for the formation of the working class, the capitalist factory), more or less integrated in socially 'transparent' relations of production and more or less capable of aggregating and organizing themselves into a class.

(d) There is a specific type of social disaggregation which manifests itself through the polarization of productive and territorial situations and which culminates in the inability to form a working class. This disaggregation is equally present, however, on the other side of the social and political barrier, among those intermediary strata which profit from the management of unequal development (and its products) and from its socio-economic consequences (hypertrophization of the tertiary sector, urban rent, speculation, etc.).

(e) The current power structure in the South is composed of three elements: a capitalistic 'modern sector', political–administrative apparatuses (especially those of the special intervention) and the new middle strata. In the South this historical bloc is the enemy of the subordinate classes. It no longer has an effective hegemony over them, but it can disaggregate them either by controlling the conditions of economic development and therefore those of their subsistence or by repressing their weak manifestations of autonomy.

Elements for an interpretative analysis of unequal development

The interpretative scheme proposed here tries to conceptualize certain aspects of unequal development with the Southern situation in mind. This situation is characterized by processes of differentiation and polarization in the productive structure (both industrial and agrarian), in the territorial distribution of industrial and residential areas and in the occupational structure (more precisely in the labour market).[6] The more general categories with which to interpret such phenomena are those of *centre* and *periphery*.[7] They are formal and descriptive and therefore unsatisfactory, but they can be gradually substituted – after they have pointed the way to greater social knowledge – by a clearer understanding of the specific contradictions belonging to each pole and phase of unequal development. 'Behind' these categories one can find specific capitalist economic laws at work, in relation to industrial locations or to urban rent as well as to the structure of objective class interests and their interaction, the distribution of institutionalized political power, the system of social inequality, and so forth. The heuristic value of the 'centre–periphery' categories lies above all in the fact that they draw attention to the processes of integration–exclusion inside the realm of development.

The centre–periphery category (which is derived from a political model, even if it is mediated by the function of economic interests), covers a series of relations of superiority–subordination at the territorial and institutional level. It permits the singling-out of asymmetrical relations between institutional spheres in different sections of the economic base, in the spatial distribution of economic activities and residential areas, and therefore in the unequal distribution of resources as well as life chances among different sectors of the population. This model tallies the different mechanisms of inequality which accumulate in certain regions or social classes. When analysing unequal development, the categories of centre and periphery shed light on the tendency for different parts of the social system to polarize in terms of functional relevance, with a subsequent disparity in the distribution of resources favouring certain social groups.

The use of such categories in essence brings to light those relations of *dominance* – which are more or less institutionalized and which pertain therefore to the political aspects of development – such as dependence and the political–administrative management of underdevelopment as a paradigm for the relation between state and economy in advanced capitalist societies. Using these categories it is possible to interpret contradictions which are not immediately linked to the social relations of production but pertain instead to the wider mechanisms of development in its economic and political dimension. They can therefore serve as a way of demarcating a new line between those who profit from underdevelopment and those who suffer from it.

Carlo Donolo

Centre and periphery in the South

If we apply these categories to the South, we see first that the old opposition North–South, which used to also include the oppositions of city–country and industry–agriculture, tends to be substituted by the polarization between those areas which are already industrialized or undergoing further industrialization, and those areas which are either not industrialized or which have industries in crisis and are thus heading towards marginalization, depopulation and stagnation.

Such a process takes place through the further concentration of investments and industries in areas which have already experienced industrialization, either by expanding to immediately adjacent areas or by creating new industrial islands inside regions which belong on the whole to the industrialized portion of the country – even if they are divided by marginalized or stagnant areas or if they include on the margin entire areas which are abandoned or which are in a phase of socio-economic degradation. During the 'economic miracle' and in a more limited manner later, the industrial base was definitely extended territorially. In the South this process took the form of macroscopic implantations (the 'cathedrals in the desert') and of a minor industrialization which was territorially dispersed, while however remaining inside the more urbanized areas (especially along the coast). Such a process is linked to the constant restructuring of the Southern industrial sector which often replaces diffuse small and medium-size enterprises by a big industrial plant or even contracts the absolute number of quasi-industrial forms of activity. The extension of the industrialized area in the South appears to be less significant than in the North. It is accompanied by territorial and sectoral contractions in economic activity and by processes of simple substitution or concentration. This territorial extension can even be accompanied by a relative and at times absolute contraction in the number of employment opportunities. Such processes become more visible if we substitute the dichotomy 'urbanized–non urbanized areas' for that of 'industrial–non industrial areas'. In the South the processes of urbanization have been significantly more intense than those of industrialization; there is no significant relationship between the percentage of the population living in urban areas and the percentage that has a chance of obtaining revenue from productive activities. In the North the spread of urban areas has been more consistently accompanied by the implantation of industries, so that one can truly speak of the extension of developed areas. In the South, by contrast, this phenomenon took place on a much smaller scale with a parallel sharpening of the polarization between developing areas (more urban than industrial, however) and marginalized areas.

By using the category 'centre–periphery' in relation to the social system we also obtain a profound reorganization of the notion of marginality and its differentiation. Under the term 'centre' one can find not only the traditionally more developed areas but also all those new areas or islands where an industrial base has been established. They are distinguishable from the non-industrial areas as well as from the urban areas which are not sufficiently industrialized. In the South especially it is important to consider as 'centre' even those poles of population attraction with continued urbanized growth, and where relevant activities linked to the circulation of goods and to administration are concentrated, even in the absence of production. A similar process takes place in the countryside with the polarization between areas of high or increasing revenue (occupying increasingly narrower portions of the territory covered) and areas of stagnant productivity in the process of being abandoned.

It is important to stress that the 'centre' not only includes the majority of the population, thus making the traditional clash of city–countryside meaningless, but is also the seat of the most important contradictions, which are capable of being translated into social conflicts. The 'periphery', contrary to the traditional role it played in the historical Southern Question and in other situations of underdevelopment, is no longer that area which contains the bulk of the population, thus harbouring the potential of conflicts and social movements. The contradictions of the marginal peripheral areas are now secondary because they comprise relatively irrelevant portions of the social system, both as a potential market for output or as a source of work forces. As a consequence this area even lacks the power of exerting sanctions, which would imply the possibility of refusing relevant services for the system or threatening its social and political stability.

The 'periphery', now emptied of its population and of any essential functions, is no longer capable of independent political action. It is more interested in obtaining marginal concessions than in solving its contradictions. A guarantee of a minimum yearly increase in the standard of living can ease the sense of relative deprivation, even if the process of further marginalization continues, thus leading to a relative worsening of living conditions. Such a solution is possible with the use of minimal resources and is indeed carried out, especially in the presence of clientelary or electoral needs.

In what we have called the 'centre', i.e. those urbanized or industrialized areas in the making, one is confronted, however, with the dichot-

131

Carlo Donolo

omy of integration–marginalization. In the North such a contradiction is channelled into the objective integration (Mallet) of the working class through its social and cultural subordination inside civil society and in urban life. In the South, given the previously mentioned distortion between urbanization and industrialization, a growing mass of the population is placed in a position of marginality with respect to industrial relations of production in the strict sense. This mass is not objectively integrated. It is subjectively integrated insofar as it is permeated by consumer society models, while being constantly confronted with its social, political and cultural marginality. This is why the urban areas of the South are potentially explosive since they can threaten political stability (public order, electoral shifts, crisis of clientelary systems).

It is this marginality inside the developed pole, varying whether it is urban and industrial or merely urban, which provides the *principal contradiction* of the process of development.

Having sketched this general overview, we can now examine some of the differentiations which arise inside it. First there are the processes linked to the division, polarization and disaggregation of the Southern population with respect to the *functioning of the labour market* (these can best be suited by using the categories of relative overpopulation, industrial reserve army and marginal mass). Secondly, there are the distinctions linked to stratification or the *structure of inequality,* which are particularly relevant for an adequate interpretation of the nature of the *new* contradictions in Southern underdevelopment (the categories to be used here are those of proletarization, pauperization, marginalization, marginality and relative deprivation). Finally, there are the peculiarities linked to the *formation of a working class* in the South in the postwar period (here one is assuming that certain characteristics of economic development and of industrialization yield a differentiation inside the proletariat itself and thus render political aggregation difficult).

Let us first examine some of the differentiations inside the labour force itself.

Overpopulation, industrial reserve army, marginal mass[8]

By integrating certain Marxian categories, one could define *relative overpopulation* (RO) as that part of the work force which is in excess of the average amount needed for the correct valorization process of capital in a given phase of its development.

Inside the RO one can distinguish a fluid, a latent and a stagnant sector. The *fluid* sector corresponds to that portion of RO which in periods of expansion tends to disappear, only to reconstitute itself rapidly in periods of depression or stagnation. This RO also includes that portion of the work force which is rendered momentarily superfluous by the processes of sectoral restructuring (technological or attritional unemployment). The fluid RO can be associated with *unemployment* as it is calculated by ISTAT (i.e. the work force which is unemployed and looking for a job along with the work force in search of a first job). The *latent* sector of the RO includes structural underemployment ('hidden unemployment') in low productivity sectors such as agriculture and small tertiary activities. This latent sector performs a structural role because it absorbs ('hides') a portion of the objectively superfluous work force thanks to its economic organization. Indeed productivity could only rise in these sectors if this superfluous work force were reduced. One of the main characteristics of this latent sector is that its members are open to any potential job offers which provide better pay than the previous ones. Workers consolidated in areas of low productivity are not part of this sector. Finally, the *stagnant* sector encompasses workers with short-term work contracts or with sporadic or precarious jobs, who are therefore underemployed or partially employed, often both at the same time, while being both overworked and underpaid (in terms of working hours, salary and job regulations). While the latent sector is comprised mainly of formally independent workers (poor peasants, artisans, small shopkeepers), the stagnant sector is composed instead of dependent workers, i.e. proletarians in the strict sense of the term totally separated from the means of production. Part-timers cut transversely across both these categories.

To these three sectors of the relative overpopulation envisioned by Marx we can add today other categories which are assuming increasing weight. If we take the Italian situation into account, given the new role which the working forces have assumed in relation to the population as a whole, we see that there are new categories comprised essentially of former work forces either expelled from the productive process or discouraged and slowed down in entering it. They can be broken down in the following manner:

(1) *the 'discouraged' female work force*, which takes on the role of housewife. This category obviously does not include all women of working age but only those who would present themselves on the job market if jobs were available, offering a reasonable salary and adequate social services (which could replace some domestic tasks such as child care and reduce the social cost of being outside the home, i.e. proximity to the work place, adequate transportation, etc.).

Carlo Donolo

(2) *'discouraged' unemployed youth* in a student or post-student category. The continuation of studies can be seen in many cases as an 'anticipated discouragement' (after a period of active job-searching) or as a 'waiting period still as a family dependent' (e.g. waiting to gain a job through civil service examinations).

(3) *elderly persons* (whether retired or not) who could compete on the job market if it could provide adequate jobs, even with lower incomes than the average.

These three groups together form the *unemployed mass* which could be employed under given conditions.

The RO includes, then, all the unemployed, the underemployed or semi-employed; as well as those without an occupation. The size of this RO varies according to the different phases of the economic cycle (besides seasonal variations which we will overlook here). The RO, to use Marxian categories, attains *acute* levels in periods of depression when there is either an absolute diminution in the number of jobs or a relative slowing down in employment with respect to the growth of the population. The link to the population can be of two types: either the population increase can be in absolute terms and occur at age and sex levels which will produce an immediate growth of the work force available, or there can be a growth in the active population which enters the job market as a consequence of the elimination of its old jobs in crisis-ridden sectors (as the result of a capitalist-provoked relative overpopulation). The stabilization at *chronic* levels represents that 'normal' RO residue which is present even during periods of significant job increases.

Inside the relative overpopulation one should distinguish analytically between the *industrial reserve army* (IRA) and the *marginal mass* (MM). These two categories perform different functions in the process of capital accumulation, and have increasingly different sociological characteristics.

First, the IRA contains that portion of the RO which has real chances of finding jobs with average salary levels during high conjunctural phases and periods of structural economic growth (i.e. with the widening of the industrial base and increase in the scale of production). From the point of view of capital this 'army' represents that portion of the work force which is kept available for development. In periods of relative underdevelopment or of slow growth this IRA acts as a competitive pressure against the employed work force, thus increasing the discretional powers of those controlling job offers (through salary or work conditions), as well as weakening the organizational capacities of the trade unions.

Secondly, the MM is instead that portion of the work force which would remain unemployed, partially or precariously employed, even during periods of high economic growth (always inside the sphere of capitalist organization in a given international setting). From the point of view of capital, the MM represents that portion of the work force which has been rendered superfluous by the inner logic of development. The MM can be considered as a *consolidated overpopulation* (CO) at least with respect to the volume and nature of predictable investments (in the South the majority of investments are in capital-intensive forms of production).

One can create a further distinction inside the marginal mass between the pauperized marginal mass (PMM) which includes the chronically unemployed, with no job prospects either because of their out-of-date qualifications or because their work is so precarious that it is a very secondary source of income with respect to family or state financing; the *strictly unemployable* (because of age, illness, geographic remoteness or sociocultural marginality); and the *lumpenproletariat* which does not include those deviant groups who are capable of guaranteeing for themselves higher living conditions than the proletariat even if they are subject to social and cultural discriminations.

We can elicit some hypotheses concerning the relations between the different categories outlined above:

(1) As the proportion of RO increases with respect to the employed work force so does the CO;

(2) as the IRA increases, the MM mass and PMM increase accordingly and at times in even greater proportion;

(3) with the lowering of activity levels the MM will increase with respect to the IRA;

(4) the greater the rapidity and violence of the process of unequal development (whether sectoral or regional) the greater the increase in PMM;

(5) when the new productive investments are capital-intensive and consist of 'substitutions' rather than 'additions' to already existing initiatives the mass of unemployed workers which could be potentially employed increases (the discouraged);

(6) when industrial interventions are concentrated territorially (in the poles of development) the MM in the excluded areas increase;

(7) with the increase in the urbanization-industrialization 'scissors' effect there will be a concentration of the PMM in the urban areas (e.g. ghettos in the old historical neighbourhoods);

(8) with the growth in consistency of the migratory flux and rural exodus from the internal areas the fluid sector of the RO will tend to bi-

Carlo Donolo

furcate into an IRA in the industrialized areas and into a marginal urban mass in the others.

The categories we have presented here are of course also applicable at the national level. The specificity of the Southern situation can be found in the quantitative relations present inside the different sectors of the work force, and even more in the social and political relations which arise from these differentiations. It is precisely in trying to isolate the conditions which permit subordinate classes to form a sociological aggregate which then will lead to a united political stance, that we need to reconstruct in greater detail the differences produced by unequal development. Only by precisely identifying the contradictions which oppose different social groups, including the sectoral conflicts inside the subordinate classes themselves, will it be possible to develop a strategy which is neither abstract nor voluntaristic, with which to give political weight to these classes.

The distinctions we shall make should serve to identify better and more precisely the subordinate classes present in the South today and in particular those groups which are the most available and vital for a struggle against the social bloc in power. As we shall see, there are relevant differentiations inside the 'army' of the active work force itself.

Proletarization and pauperization

Separation from the means of production is the necessary precondition for proletarization, but it must also be accompanied by the presence of a 'free' work force on the market which can be exchanged for capital. If such an exchange does take place we witness the transition to another type of worker, the salaried dependant who exchanges his work for a salary in a position of subordination inside the productive organization. Unequal development entails the proletarization of vast groups of the population who shift from one sector to the next, from the countryside to the city but also from one region to another (in the South the process of effective proletarization often took place outside the area itself). Such a process of proletarization was particularly relevant for the old middle strata who controlled means of production such as land, artisanal capital and small industrial and commercial enterprises. There is no phenomenon of proletarization instead for the old strata of employees and 'traditional' intellectuals, even if these groups have experienced objective *déclassement*. The decline of these strata has been more than compensated for by the rise of 'new' middle strata. The risk of proletarization continues to exist for some of these forces (or at any rate for their children), but it is delayed by the swelling of ranks in the tertiary sector (public and private). One should not confuse *social degradation* (the loss of status or of prestige) or the loss of an independent economic base (without the loss of property over the source of revenue) with the process of proletarization. This term should be reserved exclusively for those processes which immediately precede the formation of a working class (either industrial or agrarian, or even in the tertiary sector).

We use a restrictive definition of the term 'proletarization' in order not to run the risk of interpreting the new contradictions of the traditional middle strata according to a classic model, which is not effective in the current context. This is particularly true for categories such as youths with school or university degrees. If used in too wide a sense proletarization would imply the potential polarization of society into two conflicting classes and the subsequent possibility of interpreting the contradictions of the subordinate class according to the model of the working class in the factory. It is both unreal and politically problematic to draw such a similarity.[9]

Pauperization denotes the inability to obtain revenue above the average subsistence level (which is culturally defined), and in ways which are not derived from work, but rather from forms of assistance or different sorts of precarious activities. One should not therefore confuse pauperization with proletarization, even if the inferior strata of the proletariat are constantly running the risk of falling into pauperization. Most pauperism is to be found concentrated in urban areas as the necessary result of the phenomenon of attraction–repulsion (i.e. intense urbanization in the absence of or with scarce industrialization). Whereas traditional pauperism (misery) was produced by the lack of resources, today's pauperism (neo-pauperism) is produced by the lack of job and revenue opportunities to replace those which have been destroyed. Poverty can be defined as the inability to satisfy the most elementary needs, even with respect to the reduced standards of a pre-industrial situation: in such a case even survival is not guaranteed, for one is below its level. Neo-pauperism, instead, can be defined as the satisfaction of needs *below* the institutionalized average level of aspiration (defined by a 'realistic' normative reference group), and/or the distorted satisfaction of elementary needs (mediated through consumer mechanisms, mass media, processes of imitation, etc.). The crucial element in neo-pauperism is its development in a situation in which a portion of the population, and not only the upper classes, begins to participate in the consumer society. As a consequence, the excluded inferior levels – who cannot keep up or who are in effect excluded through more or less formal mechanisms from participation in the process of development – assimilate the levels of aspiration of the population which can guarantee for itself, even if only gradually, the satisfaction of both the old as well as the new needs. Even if it is nearly impossible or very difficult to determine where such levels begin one can decide to define them in the following manner: school attendance for the required number of years, housing which is not over-crowded and possesses sanitary facilities even if in deteriorated con-dition, a balanced diet, decent clothing, some participation, even if at a reduced level, in cultural consumption, etc.

A portion of this excluded population tends to develop deviant ways of guaranteeing satisfaction, according to a Mertonian version of *anomie*. Such mechanisms work most intensely in urban areas for obvious rea-sons (e.g. higher revenue levels, greater dependence on consumer and service structures, greatest collective visibility of participation–exclusion effects, etc.). Pauperism in the countryside is kept under control through the extension of social services (social security and pensions) to those groups of the population which are below subsistence levels. In the cities it is handled through a welfare–clientelary–police network, which sees pauperization above all as a problem of public order.

Historical marginality, marginalization in development, relative deprivation[10]

In assessing the differences between the 'classic' South and the South in the process of development after 1950 one of the key is-sues which must be precisely defined is the altered nature of the integration–exclusion process of inequality.

Historical marginality came about during Unification and through the rise of an industrial economy in Italy. The creation of a national market meant the end of isolation and segmentation, but it also implied the loss of relevance of certain markets and the dependence on a 'central' mar-ket for all types of resources, i.e. the end of self-consumption. In this process the local community loses all functions and becomes part of a national and regional hierarchy over which it has no influence. Histori-cal marginality implies that development takes place elsewhere (in the centre), and that at the same time the traditional community (the periph-ery) experiences its destructive consequences (ceasing in effect to be a community). The only response to historical marginality has been emi-gration, in other words the shifting toward the centre. It is in the frame-work of historical marginality that the culture of misery develops. Con-trary to poverty in a pre-bourgeois society this type of misery is already relative, since it is measured in terms of a capacity concretely emerging from it in other places (i.e. in the centre). The only type of integration is through national unification in the shape of the centre's administrative and political control over the periphery. This situation, which lasted up to the Second World War, is characterized by the separation between centre and periphery in terms of territory as well as population, between city and countryside, North and South.

This type of dualism ends about 1950. Historical marginality receded thanks to the war itself, and effectively ended with the accelerated rhythm of development. While centred in the Centre–North of the country, this development still pulled along all the other regions. In the beginning and throughout the first postwar decade domination of one part of the country over the other prevailed, through the despoliation of the Mezzogiorno. The channels used were: emigration, growing penetration of consumer products (from the North) into the Southern market, the channelling of products especially from agriculture for external processing, and absorption of accumulated savings to be invested in the most industrialized regions. In a second phase the Mezzogiorno definitively ceases to be a homogeneous reality and is polarized into extremely differentiated economic, social and territorial realities, especially through the extraordinary public intervention (which was supposed to provide political stability while enlarging the industrial territorial base). The new differentiation which emerges from this process of unequal development redefines the notion of marginality and of privation, i.e. the system of inequalities and contradictions. Historical marginality is replaced by what we could call 'marginalization through development', a product of participation in unequal development as well as in the compensatory administration of marginality. In this process part of the periphery is absorbed by the centre while remaining excluded from an effective participation in the advantages of development. If the appearance of participation is obtained in some areas (always in a subordinate capacity) it is generally at the expense of a greater exclusion–deprivation in others. In such a case privation becomes truly *relative deprivation,* mediated by the mechanism of reference groups.

In juxtaposing the neo-pauperism produced by the destructuring of the periphery and the 'scissors' effect of urbanization–industrialization to traditional misery, and historical marginality to the marginalization of development, we only want to underline the specificity of current contradictions and the necessity for new interpretations of the needs and interests of subordinate groups. All analyses which do not recognize this specificity tend to overstress the continuity with the past, contributing in effect to the appearance as well as to the ideology of backwardness, and therefore proposing objectives for struggle which are inadequate for the current level of contradictions. Such analyses are incapable of bringing

139

Carlo Donolo

about the bonding between the most advanced and the most under-developed sectors: between workers and peasants, North and South.

Relative deprivation tends to reduce potential conflict because it lowers the horizon of aspirations to a series of requests for gradual improvements along a relative participation–exclusion scale. But relative deprivation also exacerbates the feeling of having missed out on participation with respect to development, as well as the awareness of the necessary costs an effective participation would entail. It provokes reactions not only to absolute variations in need-satisfaction levels but also to relative levels. The transition from countryside to city generally entails an increase in life changes, through the reduction of absolute deprivation, but it also results in an increase in relative deprivation. It is in this feeling of participation–exclusion, being marginalized while being at the centre of development, which produces the type of social conflicts which exploded recently in the South.

Labour market and unequal development

In order to single out the characteristics of the Italian labour market with particular emphasis on the Southern situation and its transformation since the postwar period, it is important to distinguish two phases in Italian economic development:

The first is the phase of extensive and repressive development (1948–1963)[11] characterized by the mobilization of all available resources particularly in terms of the work force, which was almost totally available on the market. The still relevant mass of urban unemployed (caused by industrial reconversion or destruction of production plant) as well as the mobile labour force from the countryside (rural exodus), constituted the bulk to the labour supply. Agrarian labour came especially from those areas where the population level was too high in relation to the possible increases in productivity of scarce resources, given the capitalist restructuring process. These areas therefore hid an enormous amount of unemployment. The labour market thus became homogeneous and undifferentiated, if one excludes the clear division – pertaining to a backward phase of development – in job markets between an unskilled work force and a work force in possession of formal school diplomas.

This work force is also available because it can be displaced geographically according to need, thus doing away with practical as well as cultural obstacles (communications and isolation). The elimination of legal obstacles will take place when the process is already well under way. In this manner a great labour force is created which is 'free' from local ties, from means of production of low productivity and from control over the conditions of production. During this phase the greatest demand is for unskilled labour to carry out simple tasks. The numerical increase in the industrial proletariat is due almost entirely to such a force and it is at its expense that capitalism brings about the unification and the visible homogeneity of the national (as well as the European) labour market.

The second is the phase of 'precocious maturity' (1946–1972), characterized by the growing differentiation (in tendency) between a market which provides the nucleus of a numerically stronger working class (which includes generally all urban salaried workers) and an additional market which provokes a 'peripheral' work force, the so-called weak component of the work force.[12] In a parallel manner, the divisions between a skilled and unskilled labour market begin to blur, through the diffusion of minimum schooling and the increasing inability of finding adequate jobs for those who possess diplomas. From a social and statistical point of view the 'strong' and 'weak' components of the labour force correspond fairly evenly to a male work force of average age (20–40) already working in an industrial–urban environment, for the former, and to a female work force, whether young or old, from a prevalently rural environment for the latter.

The weak, secondary component of the work force is concentrated in productive activities characterized by: unstable and precarious work relations, which are either short-term or part-time; below-average wages, disrespect for work norms and trade union rights; and the lack of a factory environment (as the rational capitalist organization of work) which by physically concentrating the work force, while forming social relations, permits the roots of social conflict to become clearly visible, even transparent, in the social relations of production. This type of work is exemplified by work performed at home or domestic work, services of a 'personal' nature, promotional and sales activities in the tertiary sectors, etc.

Job-market differentiations essentially reflect analogous processes in the productive structure itself. In the phase of precocious maturity, with its restructurings and concentrations, the distinction between 'modern sector' and 'relatively backward sector' takes on an ever-increasing importance (based on differences measured with the following criteria: type of technology, organizational methods and administrative productivity). In order to analyse the formation of the working class in all of its manifestations it is important to formulate a more complex typology of sectors of activity than the one currently used by economists (for instance in the Southern case by Vera Lutz).

It seems necessary to distinguish between the following sectors:

Carlo Donolo

(1) The *modern sector:* besides the big oligopolistic enterprises this sector also includes minor ones which are integrally linked to their productive cycle as subcontractors, and thus vertically integrated with respect to the big enterprises, even if formally autonomous. One should also place in this sector those small and medium-size enterprises which operate on a non-local and at times foreign market with products of high technological content;

(2) the *'competitive' sector:* enterprises which operate almost exclusively on the local market with low-technology products or even on the international market with simple goods, such as clothing, shoes or artisanal products;

(3) the *politically guaranteed sector:* includes small and medium-size enterprises with low productivity which survive only through political credit or through orders obtained on the basis of political accords, and generally through high-level agreements between political and administrative actors. These enterprises do not survive inside the market;

(4) *'service-oriented' competitive sector:* includes mainly subcontracting enterprises which are often marginal and crisis-ridden, and can only guarantee their survival by establishing 'exclusive' links with major enterprises or by carving out a restricted market for themselves in a subordinate manner.

That portion of the work force which has average or higher than average salaries, contractual guarantees and so forth is concentrated in the modern sector. The 'weak' portion of the work force is to be found instead in all the other sectors, especially those with low productivity. In the phase of 'precocious maturity' the relationship between these sectors has attained stability. The modern sector is very restricted even in terms of the percentage of work force it employs, while the other sectors harbour most of the workers. One should also keep in mind the sector of pre-industrial, artisanal and commercial activities which are often conducted at the family level.

One must above all take into account, especially for the South, the 'public administration' sector, defined in a large sense, which assumes increasing relevance in a period of relative decline of productive work places, and in the presence of a superabundance of a qualified work force.

In this phase of precocious maturity we witness an increasing differentiation of the labour market, with the subsequent stratification of the work force. The divisions which emerge inside the proletariat and in general inside the subordinate classes constitute the principal political and trade union problem for the working class and the principal cause of its weakness.

142

Unequal development produces a specific type of *social disaggregation* in the phase of precocious maturity, linked to the following processes with respect to the work force structure: the contraction in the rate of activity, the distinction between the strong and the weak component of the work force, the concentration of 'peripheral' characteristics on certain groups of the population and on certain sectors and regions, and finally the growth of social and economic disparity and the sense of relative deprivation. In order to comprehend fully the contradictions of uneven development all these processes must be seen as a totality.

Class interests

We shall now examine some of the implications of what has been said above with respect to the formation and aggregation of working-class interests. We can distinguish three preliminary components or strata inside the working class: the 'central' working class, the 'peripheral' working class (with precarious employment) and the marginal mass (when it is employed). We shall leave aside other considerations such as those linked to skill structure, revenue, etc.

The 'central' working class

This sector is concentrated in the building, metal and steel industries, as well as in the construction of transport vehicles, petrochemicals, textiles, ceramic and glass production, etc. It enjoys relative advantages in terms of salary levels, job regulations and trade union activity, but it is also exposed to the most intense forms of rational capitalist exploitation. The following strategic interests can be attributed to this group:

(1) The pursuit of a guaranteed, continuous work relationship.

(2) salary increases which are not inferior to the rise in productivity of the given enterprise or to the average growth of the sector as a whole;

(3) a guarantee of some type of career pattern or at least of cumulative advantages due to seniority;

(4) avoidance of all job dequalification processes;

(5) avoidance of the consequences of excessive work loads or nefarious working conditions (this strategy is subordinate to the other objectives).

These objectives are all centred on a factory work experience with industrial entrepreneurs and management as negotiating partners in the struggles and bargaining processes. One should note that some of these objectives are formulated in a positive manner in terms of increases in available resources, while others are phrased instead negatively in terms

143

Carlo Donolo

of a desire to reduce the negative consequences of work in the 'modern sector.'

Other objectives of a more general nature not centred on the 'factory' but on the 'city' presuppose bargaining with the public authorities for the following aims:

(1) The desire not to fall into the inferior proletarian strata, by pursuing some form of social promotion for the family, through the indirect path of schooling for the children;

(2) avoidance of an excessive ghetto-like existence, through the positive demand for social services (including housing) and the demand for reforms.

The 'peripheral' working class

This group is concentrated in the building trade, in subcontracting companies and in small and medium-size marginal industries operating on a regional market, often run on political credit and with a speculative mentality. Its interests can be described as follows:

(1) To reduce to a minimum the precarious nature of the work relationship or at least to guarantee a minimum global yearly revenue (either through further part-time work or through welfare-type revenue guarantees);

(2) to obtain salary increases which cover the rise in cost of living, independently of increases in productivity; to attempt not to lose ground in relation to the higher strata of the working class;

(3) other objectives are entirely subordinated to the first two, even if there is an increasing desire to avoid falling definitively into the marginal mass, as well as a demand for essential social services, even without specific qualitative standards such as the demand for housing.

The marginal mass

This sector is underemployed and is dispersed in semi-industrial, artisanal or tertiary activities carried out in an organizational work setting which is different from that of the capitalist 'factory'. Its interests are:

(1) To guarantee a short-term subsistence revenue from any type of source (work, personal services or 'deviant' activities), including public welfare or resources distributed through a clientelary network, etc.;

(2) to attempt to enter the peripheral working class.

It is difficult for more structured objectives to emerge for this group because it is strongly trapped in the condition of marginality, and in its accompanying subcultural interpretations.

We can sum up the attributed interests of the three strata of the working class in the following manner. The central working class wants increasingly to participate in the advantages of economic development but with fewer physical, psychic and social costs. The peripheral working class is interested in a stable occupation with revenues which are somewhat higher than the subsistence level (defined culturally and in terms of a given context). The marginal mass is interested in obtaining by any means available a subsistence revenue.

The central working class lives its contradictions inside the social sphere of production. The worker feels them in terms of the high costs (work hours, heavy tasks and a toxic or harmful environment) he must bear in order to guarantee for himself an 'adequate' living condition. The increasing impossibility of obtaining through work, i.e. through a salary, essential goods such as decent housing and schooling for one's children, etc., places the very mechanism of social–economic capitalist development under fire as a source of increasing conflict. In these new conflicts the bargaining adversaries are now both capitalism and the state (defined loosely as the political administrator of development).

The peripheral working class experiences a complementary situation. It must first of all defend the very bases of its subsistence (its work place even if it is precarious and underpaid, the possibility of part-time work, etc.). This stratum of the working class must bear even higher costs than the central working class in order to enjoy the right to work so as not to fall into the marginal mass. It is therefore much more interested in job and revenue stability than in changing working conditions. These objectives have the state as a counterpart more than the capitalist class, relying on the mechanism of development more than the relations of production. The differences between these two strata are naturally only relative because there is a link between these two forms of contradictions (even if this link must still be understood by the proletarian masses, as the events of Reggio Calabria proved), and also because the passage from one stratum to the other in the industrial proletariat is very gradual.

All the objectives outlined above necessitate by their very nature collective action on the part of the interested strata. In the case of the peripheral working class, however, there seem to be greater possibilities for an individual solution to the subsistence problem (either because there still has not been a complete detachment from the means of production or because of a greater reliance on clientelary mechanisms). Because of its relative peripheral position this stratum is forced to fight for immediate and defensive objectives (i.e. a work place). Taken singly, the peripheral working class is therefore incapable and not even interested in liquidating the conditions of its own deprivation through collective

Carlo Donolo

trade union and political action. It can remove its 'peripheral' condition only if it is allied with and guided by the central working class. One should not exclude, however, especially in periods of recession, that the central working class will tend to defend its own privileges with respect to the other proletarian strata, limiting itself to generic manifestations of solidarity on their behalf. One should not forget that the central working class – through its greater trade union affiliation, the centrality of its productive function and the type of economic production in which it is placed – is much more capable of translating into positive results the objectives of any joint struggle. We are currently facing a crucial test for the establishment of a non-casual link between these two strata: in the struggle against the phenomenon of subcontracting.

Conditions in the formation of the working class

Finally, we must underline one fact mentioned previously: the *relative absence of capitalistic factories* in the process of unequal development in the South. An essential condition in the formation of the working class as a class – as was often underlined in the Marxist classics – has been its forging in the factory experience as a rational organization of production with its technological binds, its technical division of labour, its functional hierarchy of authority, and above all its great transparence in terms of the social relations of production which permitted the clear identification of the 'other side' in conflicts of interest.

Certain socio-economic mechanisms must prevail in order for the proletariat to become a class: (1) the physical concentration of workers in productive structures as well as in living areas (factories and neighbourhoods); (2) the process of homogenization derived from common work, struggle, social life and experiences as well as relations with other classes; (3) a drastic limitation in the possibility of coping on one's own and a complementary development of class solidarity as the only way with which to defend common interests; (4) having salary as the only source of revenue, without momentary or provisional alternatives at hand (with no possibility of 'regressing' to activities in other sectors or to autonomous activities). If these conditions are not present the proletariat will tend to disaggregate itself into a series of strata and groups based on socially limited and particularistic experiences – unless it is united and integrated in socio-cultural terms through the mechanisms of urban integration–exclusion or through exposure to mass manipulation and penetration by pseudo-universal petit bourgeois values aimed at consumption. One can also add, as an aside, that the absence of the factory as the centre of experience for productive work greatly facilitates the

146

manipulative adaptation to consumerism and explains many of the distortions in the structure of consumption which can be found in those areas condemned to underdevelopment.

One can advance the hypothesis that in those areas of relative underdevelopment and in the presence of a strong unemployed unskilled work force it is the 'regressive' type of industrial organization which is most favoured. Modes of production which today appear as 'premodern' – given the current level of productive forces – are once again 'made fashionable': domestic work, subcontracted work given to small semi-artisanal enterprises and concessions. Advanced technological levels and 'primitive' work organization can coexist in these situations even if technological innovation is indeed discouraged with the possibility of using decentralized forms of organization. In such cases it is the labour market which shapes the organization of production rather than the reverse, even though it seems that such an inversion also took place in certain phases of the industrial revolution.[13] Such an outcome is reasonable when the population is pushed out of the countryside by prevailing living conditions and is attracted to the city by its consumer possibilities rather than by its productive job opportunities. The existence of a semi-proletarized fluctuating work force, willing to perform the most undesirable and precarious jobs, encourages the creation of industries which exploit precisely these social characteristics while at the same time strengthening them. Domestic work, subcontracting, the exploitation of an under-age and female work force in pre-industrial enterprises – a series of speculative economic activities – all play determining roles in the formation of a proletariat by causing its disaggregation. It is a well-known fact that an excess of work force supply renders any effective defence of the peripheral workers by the trade unions impossible. And the lack of trade union action and adherence is in turn the precondition for the persistence and reproduction of 'regressive' work activities.

The relative absence of the factory as a rational system of social relations and the subsequent dispersion and multiplicity of work experience hides the relations of production and the nature of interest conflicts between classes. Precarious, occasional and discontinuous work experiences (in the sense of a non-cumulative work experience) also impede the development of a work commitment (according to Morse's definition) without which there can be no objective integration of the working class into the productive system.[14] Such an integration forces the working class to confront directly all problems linked to the relations of production and to the global mechanism of development.

In what we have said above we do not intend to deny the proletarian nature or political centrality of the peripheral strata of the proletariat.

147

Carlo Donolo

Rather we want to underline the problems which must be confronted both theoretically and practically in the current phase. We are convinced that the process of 'disaggregation' must be understood before we can know where to look for the bases of aggregation and political unity.

On the bourgeoisie of underdevelopment

Without pretending to be exhaustive, we must mention here the complexity of those middle and high strata which flourish by underdevelopment, by extracting from it both job possibilities and sources of revenue while managing it against the interests of the subordinate classes. We are dealing here with that portion of the middle and high bourgeoisie which provides the social basis for the new power structure in the South – even if for major decisions it is in turn bypassed and dominated by the predominant fractions of national and international capital. This Southern bourgeoisie does effectively manage local and regional power on its own behalf as well as for others. All the interests of the subordinate classes clash against the barrier of this bourgeoisie's constituted interests. The groups which compose the medium–high social structure are both compact and complex. Despite internal contradictions and variations in this bloc it remains remarkably stable, precisely because it is articulated along economic, political and administrative lines.

We will leave aside those strata engaged in minor activities in order to concentrate on certain key sectors: the construction industry, small and medium-size enterprises focused prevalently on the local market (in certain rare cases as purveyor of goods to national industries implanted in the South) and the new professional classes.

The construction industry

One can assume that it received its initial push from the investment of agrarian capital into a sector for which there could be no Northern competition. The North also approved that such capital be invested in the production of goods, which were not competitive to its own, while even generating additional demand for prevalently Northern products (such as cement, supporting pylons, electrical networks and piping). Given the technological level of the construction industry, this was a productive activity which required a minimal outlay of capital per worker, minimal organizational capacities for the 'enterprises' and permitted minimum salary levels for an unskilled work force. The construction industry was the road of least resistance. Furthermore, the mechanism of speculation in urban areas fostered the development of advantageous

148

links between the political class and these new entrepreneurial groups. In exchange for economic advantages (participation in the profits), the political class protected and still protects (thanks to the failure of urban planning legislation) the construction industry from political and administrative controls.

Such deals also occurred in the North, to the point that a new fraction of the political class in the big cities emerged out of the building speculations. In the South, however, given the disproportion between this industry and other sectors of activity, the development of the construction industry corresponded in effect with the politics of development as they were effectively carried out (in the big urban areas). This equivalence produced two results: either the renewal of political personnel or its reorientation on behalf of this productive–speculative activity. In recent years a new restricted fraction of medium–large size entrepreneurs has emerged out of the competition, at the economic level as well as in terms of different political machines among different construction interests. These new larger entrepreneurs tend to rationalize productive activity through the creation of larger enterprises with greater capital (and with the subsequent expulsion of the work force). This new productive activity is oriented away from individual housing or small complexes towards entire large urban areas. At such a level this fraction of the construction industry will run straight into the growing competition of the large Northern enterprises as well as those of the state itself. New and important occasions for mediation by the political class (both local and national) are thus emerging in this context of partially conflicting interests.

One of the 'latent' political implications of the growth of the construction industry in the South is its territorially diffuse nature. It is locally based and does not presuppose great exchanges of resources or communication with politico-administrative actors at the non-local level. Economic and political interests (clientelary and local) can thus embark on a 'happy' fusion: hence the functional collaboration between the new entrepreneurs and the political class and its persistence (reinforced by the great resources made available by the collaboration itself). One should also remember that the construction industry is a major contributor in the creation of that 'precarious' proletariat we have mentioned earlier.

Small and medium-size manufacturing enterprises

Just as the construction industry received legislative favours, the survival of these enterprises would be unthinkable without political credit, i.e. privileged access to financial resources (as well as sponsor-

149

Carlo Donolo

ships) which have been politically mediated. This enmeshing of interests allows one to assume that there is very little role-differentiation between entrepreneurs and politicians (in relation to the North), since both roles are complementary and equally necessary, or at least advantageous, for the same person. The issue of political credit brings us to that of public intervention in the South. In reality it is an alliance between two groups coming from the same social class, carried out through a partial exchange of personnel and through the simultaneous filling of both roles. This phenomenon does not imply that there are no independent entrepreneurs in the South; it only points to the weakness of a politically autonomous entrepreneurial stratum capable of negotiating with the political class from a position of hegemony. It is this weakness which makes for the strength of the entrepreneurial–political bloc (to which must be added the personnel of the bureaucratic apparatuses) which is endowed with a strong veto power and a remarkable capacity of diverting public capital for 'welfare' or speculative purposes. This bloc also conditions the national political leadership itself in relation to urban planning legislation, with chronic cases of spillover of resources initially intended for specific delimited projects and blackmail against reforms in the last administrative elections. Not even the increase in large public and private capital can destroy this bloc, which at most will be internally restructured since it continues to remain vital thanks to its capacity to preserve order and political stability through the global mediations which take place inside Christian Democracy (even if there are conflicting interests between this bloc and Big Capital).

The Southern economic bloc is composed of an alliance between these small and medium-sized industrial and construction entrepreneurs (leaving aside the agrarian component). It is facilitated by the social homogeneity between these two groups and by their similar 'organic' relation to the political class.

The new professional stratum

This stratum is directly rooted in the most 'gaudy' and visible aspects of distorted Southern development: building speculation and the rush towards a consumer society in a social structure which for the greater part does not participate in its production. (One can speculate that it is precisely the relative absence of places of production, the factories and their accompanying social and cultural relations, along with the relative prevalence of the moment of consumption, that open the way for the 'irrational' interpretation of individual and collective needs and even facilitate social integration.) The new professions fulfil the role

150

of mediating different aspects (and different social groups) in these activities: construction, granting of credit, loans, draft notes, technical (as well as 'political') assistance and consultations, pensions, jobs, etc. What counts is that all these activities swell the ranks of a non-productive middle stratum oriented towards speculative activities. This stratum is more interested in exploiting revenue and power possibilities linked to a development judged as inevitable than it is in participating effectively in this development in an autonomous manner. This social group is not only closely linked to political personnel; it is actually an integral part of it. The traditional social form of the Southern 'intellectual' can be found in this stratum: i.e. the mediator and subordinate holder of political power. These are the three most important components of the dominant class in urban areas. One can assume that these groups are on the same social and political plane and that there is no social and political hierarchy among them, except in terms of individual or family differences in revenue and power. These groups also share another characteristic with respect to the past: they are no longer restricted to the top of the pyramid but are composed of a relatively numerous group (which becomes even larger if we add to it the middle-level commercial bourgeoisie). Given all these reasons and because of its material location inside the political class and the public bureaucracy, one can say that this power bloc is very compact. It even thrives on the mediation between internal conflicts of interest; it is 'dominant' almost everywhere, no longer having the need to be 'hegemonical'.

From contradictions to conflicts

We finally come to the crucial point for an understanding of current tendencies and for the elaboration of a politically adequate strategy, given the current level of contradictions. We must first take into account the variety of social conflicts which have exploded in the last few years; and, secondly, the specific difficulty, amply documented by experience, of adequately and efficiently translating contradictions into conflicts.

From what we have said it is clear that in the South, more than in the North, the contradictions provoked by a distorted development take on mediated or 'deviant' forms. On the one hand we have the emergence of clear conflicts linked to the modern capitalist factory; these conflicts, however, only concern a small portion of the subordinate classes and even of the urban proletariat itself. On the other hand, we have the growth of conflicts linked to the process of relative marginalization within urbanized areas and in which the 'scissors' effect of urbanization–industrialization is accentuated. These conflicts are linked to the

151

problem of the labour market, i.e. to the structural impossibility of finding jobs for the growing masses of urbanized population. Furthermore, since heterogeneous social groups have a personal negative interest in distorted industrial development, conflicts necessarily take on an 'interclass' quality, mobilizing 'territorial' solidarities. These conditions give rise to political instrumentalization and deviant integrations of struggle objectives. But they also hint at the emergence of new types of conflicts which are much more linked to the model of unbalanced development than they are to the immediate contradictions in the modes of production. These new conflicts are not tied to the factory (which is often nonexistent) but to the territory (neighbourhood, city and area). Community identities are quickly rekindled and instrumentalized even when the effective issue of conflict is certainly not the traditional community. Nevertheless the territorial reference is real, because the global marginalization into a 'periphery' is real.

The social demand behind these territorial conflicts focuses on the desire to become direct participants in the development process rather than administered subjects in the 'periphery' to whom marginal quotas of the resources of development are meted. This type of conflict has an interclass nature and tends to be confused with a more traditional form of different origins, linked to the weak articulation of classes in society as a result of the lack of a capitalist factory or even urban setting, with their clear-cut social relations and neatly differentiated social and political identities. The crucial fact that must be underlined is that class conflict and 'territorial' conflict are often carried out by two different social groups who do not communicate in the current urban structures: the industrial working class and the urban masses who are more or less proletarianized, and at any rate not integrated in a stable manner in industrial work or in the capitalist 'factory'.

Current contradictions and conflicts are not complex to analyse if we realize that they are the product of three different types of conflicts: *class conflicts* in the strict sense; *pluralistic conflicts,* according to the model of advanced capitalist societies, which are oriented toward the problem of the distribution of socially produced resources as well as the exercise of veto powers; and *particularistic conflicts,* based on the mobilization of personal clientelary or local loyalties, either external to or in the absence of civil society. These three types of conflicts break out both against the contradictions produced by the social relations of production as well as against the disparities produced by the model of development. It is against this background that the social bases of Southern politics must be interpreted: in the interaction between horizontal organizations for the structuring of interests (parties and trade unions) and vertical structures for the 'particular satisfaction of demands' (clientelary systems), or better yet in their interpenetration.

The central problem of any social and political analysis of the South lies precisely in understanding systematically the obstacles to an adequate translation of contradictions into conflicts. Any research that limited itself to underlining the dramatic dimension of the contradictions produced by unequal development in the South and to cataloguing them objectively would greatly overestimate the amount of political conflict present. Some of the processes which prevent the translation of contradictions into conflicts are:

(1) The very nature of certain contradictions: one need only think of those present in the intellectual work force or in the teaching corps (for the contradictions to explode here, the common political will must be created from scratch, and this can only be done insofar as expectations and social identity are changed), or in those areas which are being abandoned, where the contradictions which indeed prevail destroy by their very existence the potential subject for structured conflicts.

(2) The prevalence in the social structure of processes which encourage social disaggregation. We saw some examples with respect to the work force and the working class. In such a case it is the formation of a subject or a class which is impeded. Consequently, even the aggregation of a political demand is made more difficult, not to mention the political and trade union organization necessary to convert this diffuse conflictuality into an appropriate vehicle for the existing contradictions.

(3) One should not underestimate the cultural and psychological destructuring produced by the violent transition from countryside to city (especially if accompanied by an urban marginalization), along with the changes in family structure, in social habits and interpersonal relations.

(4) The operating of compensatory mechanisms for the costs borne by the subordinate classes in unequal development: consumerism, mass manipulation, urbanism itself and the 'revolution in aspirations' including the satisfaction projected from one generation to the next, as in the case of schooling, etc.

(5) The systematic use of interventions designed to contain and compensate tensions by those apparatuses meant to manage underdevelopment (welfare politics, political credit, local politics of public welfare and 'special' revenues whose total expenditures often approximate the amount of all salaries combined).

(6) All these tendencies foster the disaggregation of potential subjects and/or contain the negative consequences of destructuring, while eroding the social and organizational base of those parties and trade unions

who have traditionally interpreted the demands of the subordinate classes. One need only think in terms of the loss of the traditional category of the agrarian labourer which is disappearing as social figure, as a group, as a subcultural island and as an economic function, while no new alternative social base is being rebuilt (this rebuilding is made all the more difficult by emigration, defined often as the creation of an industrial proletariat *elsewhere*, by urbanization and by depopulation).

(7) Finally one should mention the obstacle arising from the apparent continuity in the passage from backwardness to underdevelopment in the conscience of the masses. The tendency to use traditional interpretations of the contradictions prevails even inside political and trade union organizations (and thus facilitates the particularistic instrumentalization of social conflicts, such as those of Reggio Calabria). Populistic and paternalistic interpretations persist, only slightly modernized by technocratic overtones. We will only signal here the 'cultural lag' in political–trade union structures and in their slogans even if the link between this 'lag' and a comprehensive strategic choice is obvious. Some of the slogans in question are the Italian parliamentary road to socialism, the strategy of reforms and the hope of local autonomy. This strategic choice, especially when brought down to the level of bureaucratic inertia, in reality acts as a further obstacle in the translation of contradictions into conflicts.

All these difficulties must be underlined, because they are the ones against which all anti-capitalist political action runs. Without a better understanding of the difficulties it is not possible to develop a reasonable long-term strategy or even intermediate objectives.

The 'social disaggregation' which we have underlined should not make us forget that the same mechanisms which produce underdevelopment also form the profile of that portion of the Southern population which, even if disaggregated and divided and far removed from any political unity, still bears the costs of this uneven development. These are the groups which would be interested in upsetting the dominant mechanism of development and the social means of production on which it is based. The components of this 'anti-capitalist' camp must still be identified: one cannot trace the demarcation line without knowing the contradictions, tendencies and specific interests which can be attributed to each different group. Above all, one must try to implement unified objectives in concrete situations based on true common interests as opposed to generic slogans or instrumental alliances (even though these can be at times useful) among the different sectors of the anti-capitalist camp.

Many problems persist: in the unification of the different sectors of the urban proletariat, in the creation of links between the urban and the rural proletariat (salaried workers, agrarian labourers and poor peasants), in the linking of these proletarian components to those sectors of the middle strata (intellectual petit bourgeoisie, students and teachers above all) who are not implicated in the 'new power structure'.

In analysing objective class interests through the singling-out of specific contradictions and the interpreting of concrete behaviour it will be possible to determine the bases for a possible convergence. It is important to single out those groups who will consider themselves (*a*) *interested* in an alliance with the working class; (*b*) *capable* of mobilization/ organization; (*c*) *capable* of provoking the explosion of social conflicts which will bring into question the structure of authority and the equilibrium of alliances in the institutions and the structure of local powers, as well as the mechanism of development.

Synthesis

One can summarize in the following manner the logic of what has been proposed here:

(1) In the postwar period the South experienced a mechanism of unequal and dependent development which was politically administered through the apparatus for extraordinary public intervention and further aggravated by the criteria of industrialization followed first and foremost by state industries.

(2) This mechanism produced a polarization between 'centre' and 'periphery' (in terms of productive and occupational structure, the territorial distribution of residential and productive implantations, resource distribution, etc.).

(3) Through this polarization obstacles emerged which prevented the subordinate classes from developing into classes, i.e. collective political subjects, even in the presence of accumulated inequalities derived both from the relation to capital and the global mechanism of development.

(4) This type of development and the accompanying administration of 'social disaggregation' have strengthened an entire system of political mediations (non-traditional clientelarism, linked to politics and the state), inside the dominant class and between it and the subordinate classes. This mediation was meant to prevent the explosion of grave contradictions between different fractions of the bourgeoisie and dominant groups, even if the dominant class no longer possesses hegemony but simply controls the material conditions for the reproduction of the dominated classes and the means of repression of all conflict. In this respect, however, the relation between antagonistic classes has become much

Carlo Donolo

more visible than in the past; this is an important anti-capitalist resource.

(5) The difficulties entailed by an efficient translation of contradictions into conflicts are many and complex. They are entrenched in prevalent objective processes which tend to sabotage all efforts towards a political unification. These difficulties must be evaluated with respect to the acuteness of the existing contradictions in order to derive strategic criteria which are not based on wishful thinking or on resignation.

In relation to the more traditional interpretations, our interpretation like others listed in the Premise seeks to stress the shift away from:

(1) The Southern Question as a historical and national question to the more general problem of unequal and dependent development at the Italian and European level;

(2) the traditional alliance of peasant–worker hegemonized by organic intellectuals to the formation of a united anti-capitalist camp held together by common motives and interests;

(3) slogans such as 'rebirth' or 'agrarian reform' to slogans against the mechanisms of development and the capitalist organization of work.

Notes

[1] In *Vento dell'Est,* no. 22.

[2] For the distinction between underdevelopment and backwardness see F. H. Cardoso & E. Faletto, *Dipendenza e sviluppo in America Latina* (Milan 1971), pp. 25ff.

[3] Cf. Giovanni Arrighi, *Sviluppo economico e sovrastrutture in Africa* (Turin 1969), pp. 26ff.

[4] Among the principal tendencies let us recall, for example, the concentration of production as well as social investments in limited areas of the territory, the disequilibrium between levels and rates of urbanization and of industrialization, the strong differences in productivity between different sectors and inside the same sector, and the growing bifurcation between supply and demand of the labour force both in relation to size as well as skill.

[5] Even though the historical contradiction in the development of Italian society which goes by the name the 'Southern Question' now tends to be substituted by the centre–periphery/development–marginalization polarity, it is still true that the South preserves its own specificity in many aspects. The principal ones are: (a) the weight of the population in relation to the possibility of employment with revenues approximating the national average; the growing concentration of this population is in urban areas (thus augmenting the possibility of turning the contradiction into conflicts threatening the political stability of the system); (b) the necessity of further restructuring in low productivity sectors (agriculture, but also certain branches of the tertiary sector and of small and medium-size enterprises) with the subsequent accelerated expulsion of the labour force which is unemployable in the internal sector of the Southern regions; (c) the particular sensitivity of the South to the conjunctural situation: in the last few years, the fall in industrial investments, not compensated for by the investment decisions of oligopolistic private and public enterprises, had an

even stronger impact on the South; (*d*) in the South the marginal areas, and in particular marginality inside the poles of urban development, is especially unstable (through low levels of integration of marginality, at the level of social structures and of 'subcultures'); in the North by contrast the fact of being integrated in a stable and stabilizing context prevents the consequence of *anomie* and of conflict which is more likely in the South; (*e*) finally, in the South, unequal development is often the result and specific consequence of an *extraordinary public intervention* over many years. This intervention is so relevant that one can sustain the thesis that an entire subsystem of the political system is devoted to the management of internal underdevelopment. This last point is treated here only in passing, but not because it is underestimated. On the contrary, I feel that the theme of the interventionist policies and the role of the state in the process of underdevelopment is so crucial that I wish to reserve it for another systematic analysis.

[6] These themes are now at the centre of political and scientific debates on the Mezzogiorno; cf. G. Mottura & E. Pugliese's contributions in *Inchiesta*, no. 5 (1972).

[7] On the use of these categories see the recent sociological literature from Latin America and in particular the writings of Frank, Stavenhagen and Nun; see also J. Galtung, 'Teoria strutturale dell'imperialismo', *Rassegna Italiana di Sociologia*, no. 3 (1971) especially in relation to 'centre' and 'periphery'; these themes are also discussed in L. Gallino, 'Le migrazioni interne: problemi sociali delle "zone di attrazione" ' in *Indagini di sociologia economica* (Milan 1962). A similar debate which touches on the question of the compatibility of the centre–periphery scheme with Marxism is going on in Germany cf. K. Offe, 'Struttura di classe e dominio politico', *Rassegna Italiana di Sociologia*, no. 4 (1971); Bergmann, Brandt, Körber, Mohl & Offe, 'Dominio, rapporti di classe e stratificazione' in *Verhandlungen des 16 Deutschen Soziologentages* (Stuttgart 1969). For a critique of these positions see Wolfgang Müller & Christel Neusüss, 'L'illusione dello stato sociale e la contraddizione di lavoro salariato e capitale' in *Sozialistische Politik*, nos. 6–7 (1970). From another point of view, in terms of analyses of the social system, the theme was treated by A. Gouldner in his articles on 'Functional Autonomy' and 'Norm of Reciprocity', and by David Lockwood in 'Social Integration and System Integration' in G. K. Zollschan & W. Hirsch (eds.), *Explorations in Social Change* (London 1964). On the issue of comparison between the Latin American situation and that of the Italian South in relation to the validity of similar conceptual schemes see the chapter on 'Class and Politics in Latin America' in James Petras, *Politics and Social Structure in Latin America* (New York 1970), substituting the Mezzogiorno.

[8] For a recent application to the Italian setting of Marx's concepts of 'relative surplus labour' and 'industrial reserve army' (to be found in *Das Kapital*) see L. Meldolesi, *Disoccupazione e esercito industriale di riserva in Italia* (Bari 1972). For the concept of 'marginal mass' see J. Nun, 'Proposte per lo studio della marginalità e della participazione in America Latina', *Community Development*, nos. 25–26 (1971), pp. 175–212, for an introduction to the problem see Desal, *Marginalidad en America Latina, un Ensayo de Diagnostico* (Barcelona, 1969).

[9] For a different approach to the topic see Gruppo A. Gramsci, *Crisi del Capitale e compiti dei comunisti* (Milan 1972), part I.

[10] On the concept of marginality see Nun (note 8 above) and for the Italian case A. Pizzorno, 'Familismo amorale e marginalità storica, ovvero perchè non c'è

Carlo Donolo

niente da fare a Montegrano', *Community Studies,* no. 15 (1966), pp. 55–66. For the concept of a relative deprivation see W. G. Runciman, *Relative Deprivation and Social Justice* (London 1966).

[11] For this terminology ('phase of repressive development', 'phase of precocious maturity') see Michele Salvati, 'L'origine della crisi in corso' in *Quaderni Piacentini,* xi (1972), no. 46.

[12] For the concept of 'peripheral' work force see Dean Morse, *The Peripheral Worker* (New York 1969).

[13] Cf. Marshall's observation on the 'residual' population cited by and discussed in Morse, *ibid.*

[14] On the concept of 'work commitment', see Morse, *ibid.;* on the idea of 'objective integration' see Serge Mallet, 'Integration objective et integration subjective' in G. Balandier (ed). *Sociologie des mutations* (Paris 1970).

III: Social Actors and Politics

8. The Trade Union Movement, Social and Economic Crisis and Historical Compromise*

Emilio Reyneri

All commentators agree that the new season of trade union congresses which has just ended had as its focus the change in political line; inside the trade unions, by contrast, such a change has been denied (Lama, the CGIL leader, said so openly, claiming that the political change took place four years ago). In this game of words one finds the key to the problems which the trade union movement is currently facing.

In order to understand these problems one needs to turn briefly to the last trade union congresses, even if congresses of big political organizations or trade unions often only ratify changes in line which have been decided long before. The congresses of 1969 were certainly not of this kind. Working-class spontaneity and the aggressiveness of the federation of industrial branches turned these congresses into the least predictable since the war (speaking for the CGIL, Novella said, 'we walked out far different than we had entered'). The change in line was marked in 1969: leaving aside the debate over planning and the politics of income, great attention was placed on the demands and struggles going on in the factories. The bases were therefore laid for the profound renewal of trade union action in the 'hot autumn'. The congresses of 1973 also marked a turning point, even if a clear change of tack had already been planned a few months earlier. The 'pansyndicalist' management of struggles for reform and for centralization as well as the control of the demands at enterprise and branch level was abandoned. The 1973 congresses were those during which the different trade unions confronted with the greatest resolve the problems of the Italian economy. What emerges is a clearly articulated hypothesis of a new model of development; neutrality in relation to the political setting is considered an essen-

*First published in *Il Mulino* (July–August 1977), pp. 501–13.

tial condition for any united and effective action by the trade unions for a plan for national economic policy.

Both at the CGIL and the CISL congresses of 1977 many held that the line of 1973 was still valid. The only thing at stake in 1977 was a discussion of the new instruments necessary to carry it out, since the traditional contractual approach had proven ineffective. This is why after ten years there is talk again of planning and the theme of industrial democracy has appeared in the Italian setting. Regarding the internal structures there is a greater prevalence of horizontal organizations over vertical forms of branches (even inside the CISL, a sign of a radical revolution away from its federative and industrialist traditions).

Even if all these themes were indeed discussed, a completely different question monopolized everybody's attention in practice: the change in political line and role of the trade unions in a political setting which was profoundly transformed by the elections of 20 June 1976 and the agreements between parties, which, during the congresses themselves, were changing their line of 'no distrust' into one of active consent *vis à vis* the government. Conversely, other crucial questions for the trade union movement disappeared, as if they could be satisfactorily discussed in pre-congressional meetings. I am referring to the debates on the role of youth, on the unemployed, whether in intellectual or other fields, on the school and its students, on women and on internal democracy inside the trade union.

After many years trade union congresses have returned to the open with prevalent discussion of politics and political formulas. Has there been a change with respect to the position of neutrality *vis à vis* the political setting or of autonomy with respect to the parties, which were both decided at the preceding congresses? Has the change in political line with the entrance of the PCI in the area of government marked a change in the trade unions, despite all affirmations to the contrary? Before tackling these questions, I would like to deal with a preliminary issue: in what changed conditions do the Italian trade unions, after a long immersion in social and economic questions which profoundly renewed them (some have even spoken of their recasting), return to the sphere of politics and to the relations with the parties? What are the factors which explain such a return?

Let me be allowed to make a brief methodological transgression, almost a personal aside.

It is a vice of Italian culture, derived from the ever-present idealist framework, to prefer the analysis of ideology to the analysis of behaviour. Consequently, economics is sublimated in philosophy, history becomes a detailed chronicle (based only on written sources, of course) and politics becomes an art. In the study of the trade union movement this tendency becomes almost a paroxysm. Reality is confused with what 'should be', the real effects of a given action are confused with the objectives set forth by the trade union, and actual behaviour is confused with the image which the trade union has of itself.

This vice is further helped by the fact that it is a nuisance to get up from one's own desk, to leave behind the glossing of documents and congress reports, in order to go into the factories and in the trade unions in compliance with the inaccessible hours of the proletariat. Those who are used to such a militant activity are unfortunately also likely to bolster massively their analyses with a dose of personal ideology and voluntarism, often deformed unintentionally by their own role as trade union or political 'operators'.

There is also another hindrance, feared by Italian intellectuals young or old alike, that of appearing to be critical of trade union organization, of not being 'organically' tied to the movement, of being isolated individuals who do not comply with the 'ought to be', i.e. with the typical dimension of the trade union or political activist but who instead want to look behind the ideological facades and barriers so as to reconstruct those factors which really determine action.

It seems especially necessary to raise such problems at present when the trade unions are sponsoring a dialogue with the intellectuals: Lama speaks of their 'constructive' contribution towards an Italian 'New Deal'. The danger of a new cultural conformism, this time coming from 'the Left', looms on the horizon. In his introduction to the series of essays on the trade union movement in the Feltrinelli *Annals* Accornero reminds us opportunely that 'to raise criticism or to carry out verifications *vis à vis* the trade unions does not mean that one is speaking badly about Garibaldi'. I would add that precisely at a moment when many intellectual circles have become advocates of the trade unions, of their strength and their responsibilities, the trade unions need instead critical contributions. These contributions would address the fundamental problem of how to make those who act reflect on their actions as well as on the structural determinants which condition them well beyond the role of intentions, that is of ideologies. For example, one should finally confront the problem of why Italian trade unionism produces perhaps the greatest amount of ideology in the capitalist world, without however falling into the sociologism (which is truly negative) of explaining the phenomenon in terms of the strong presence of intellectuals among the leaders of the trade unions. One should instead begin by concretely analysing at specific moments the role played by ideological 'caricatures' on trade

Emilio Reyneri

union action, while keeping in mind the different functions which ideology can have: these range from subverting consolidated behaviour to satisfying the need for identity, as well as displacing the conflict from immediate problems to ultimate ends. It is my intention to analyse the ideological writings of the trade unions in relation to the organization of labour, a theme to which I have personally contributed. The field is wide open and it is unfortunately significant that those who have ventured in it, even if in a gauche manner such as Pipau and Salerni (*Il sindacato come oggetto di equilibrio*), have been surrounded by silence.

There are two significant questions one can ask concerning the Italian trade union movement. First, is it an entirely atypical movement or is it instead progressively adjusting its actual behaviour to the model of more industrialized countries with a social-democratic tradition? This question has been treated by A. Pizzorno in his contribution to the Feltrinelli volume ('Fra azione di classe e sistemi corporativi' now in *Movimento sindacale e società italiana*). Secondly, in recent Italian trade union history have the unions always gone toward new solutions or has there also been a return to choices of the past, i.e. are there also cyclical phenomena next to the unilateral tendencies of trade union action?

Inside trade union organizations there is always the tendency to underline the specific and innovative character of trade union actions ('we are the Vietnam of the trade unions' is a recurring phrase). Nevertheless, in an interview which introduces the special number of *Quaderni di Rassegna sindacale* devoted to the CGIL Congress of 1973 Lama has made a specific reference to the cyclical pattern of trade union policies.

The trade unions and the CGIL in particular seem to have a cyclical behaviour with respect to the relationship between wage and union demands and political–economic action. Lama stated essentially that the unions had experienced a period in the 1950s when all trade union actions were centred at the level of the national economic system. In the early 1960s an 'industrial' line emerged which placed emphasis on strong wage demands for the major working-class categories. During the economic recession of 1964–7 the trade union line returned to the problem of economic planning when the issue of economic development was once again discussed. In 1968–9 trade union emphasis was transferred to the factory level, with wage and work-organization demands. In 1973, Lama concluded, the trade union line had stabilized itself, no longer oscillating in tune with the economic cycle, because the trade unions were now capable of acting simultaneously on both the industrial level and the national economic and political system (the 'global proposals' of the Bari Congress).

Unfortunately, this conclusion has proven to be too optimistic. After a brief period of equilibrium the close ties between factory struggles (centred around salaries and work organization) and those struggles aimed at the institutions, at unemployment and the problem of the Mezzogiorno, broke down. Trade union action swung once again to an emphasis on political and economic issues as during all moments of crisis and recession. Not everything has been repeated, of course. Negotiations at the local industry level have not disappeared and have even met with constant success. They have however become defensive in nature (especially in relation to employment, since wage demands are linked to the centralized mechanism of the cost of living index). Similarly, the struggle for the organization and division of work has been replaced by approaches to production which are increasingly less 'alternative' in nature (mobility, absenteeism and new individual professionalism). The only vestiges of a past season are the summit negotiations of the big industrial branches, the fixed reference point of all trade union interventions during the confederal congresses. If such actions still exist at the level of the major industries (Fiat, Olivetti, etc.) the final aims and time delays have acquired a more generic and abstract nature.

The economic cycle has produced another cyclical phenomenon, this time inside the trade union organizations, and one which is even more misunderstood: the alternation between centralization and decentralization in decision-making. If one were to briefly consider the prevalent decision-making levels in the trade unions one can see that in the 1950s it is only the confederations which count in practical terms. In the early 1960s, with the first wave of working-class struggles, after years of sterile theorizing, the branch federations assert themselves, especially in industry. Not coincidentally, after 1963 there is a return to the confederation level which once again stipulates important agreements also in terms of a 'framework' with which to structure contractual procedures and therefore control the lower-level trade union deliberations. One needs the wave of trade union struggles of 1968–9 for the decentralization of decisions concerning demands to reach down to the enterprise and even the shop level.

But this dispersion of trade union initiatives, which is accompanied by a 'permanent conflictuality', does not last long. Already with the first signs of economic crisis in 1971 the long process of progressive recentralization of decisions begins. This recentralization appears to be completed with the formal choice made in the last congresses to reduce the field of action and of autonomy of the branch organizations in favour of the territorial organizations, i.e. the confederal ones (and implicitly to reduce the role of the factory councils in favour of the territorial ones,

Emilio Reyneri

which could be more easily controlled from the higher bodies). One cannot list here all the numerous phases of this process; the last will suffice: the choice to defend salary demands only with the mechanism of the cost of living increase which gives the confederations once again the management of this fundamental bargaining instrument.

Since these different tendencies are after all represented by men, Giovanni Russo is right when in the *Corriere della Sera* he affirms that the transfer of Bruno Trentin from the FLM (Federation of Metal Mechanics) to the CGIL marks the end of an epoch. This epoch was characterized by the largely autonomous role of the branch categories which therefore needed to be 'overrepresented' by high-ranking personalities.

Another phenomenon also seems to follow a similar cyclical pattern, even if in a less evident manner: the relationships between the trade unions and the parties. This link is strongest in unfavourable economic periods and weakest when the labour market is structured and 'industrial' demands prevail. Nevertheless, there have been deep structural changes in trends in this aspect of the industrial relations system, and any analysis must be necessarily more complex, as will be seen below.

Up to now I have underlined the cyclical components of recent Italian trade union history. I have done so purposefully to counter the prevailing tendency of seeing the present situation as entirely new and unique, a tendency which ignores all that is structurally determined in the behaviour of trade unions when faced by similar economic circumstances. The cycle, however, is never repeated in the same manner because certain deep changes are irreversible.

To ask the question in somewhat simplistic and even provoking terms, what distinguishes the present situation from that of the 1950s and from the recession of 1964–7? In a more complex and articulated form the question would be: what socio-economic conditions have changed and what irreversible transformations have taken place in the trade unions themselves for the trade union movement not to return to its earlier behaviour?

The economic and social aspects which characterize the present crisis are well known. It will suffice therefore to recall their important consequences for the trade unions themselves. The labour market is profoundly divided: there is no marked unemployment for the urban–industrial areas of the North, whereas there is a great prevalence of marginal and precarious employment, and the number of youths looking for a first job has reached exceptionally high levels, even among those with advanced schooling. By remaining strong the 'guaranteed' working class has provided an element of security for the trade unions, but at the same time this class does not understand the unions' defensive strategy. It has proven much more difficult for the trade unions on the other hand to organize the marginally employed and the unemployed intellectuals than it had been to organize the 'normal' unemployed of the 1950s.

Precisely at the time when the trade unions have decided to sponsor the development of the economic system, thereby recognizing the need to increase the resources destined for productive investment, there is a strong pressure – camouflaged in various ways at the ideological level – to spread welfare services and subsidies as well as to swell the ranks of the public sector and the tertiary sector which carries out public services. Furthermore workers in the public and service sector, whose job security is not threatened by the crisis, have embarked on a series of ever-increasing spontaneous wage demands which have been supported both by the Right and by the extreme 'autonomous' Left (hospital workers, railway workers, public transportation workers and non-teaching personnel at the university). So far, these have been the sectors in which job offers have created job demands, and many hope that such a trend can continue. The trade unions on the other hand are not sympathetic to the problems of these workers; they have their network of influence in the 'productive' working class.

There is also another condition which is different from the past. The working class in the large industries, either because of its diverse composition or because of the struggles waged, no longer experiences its traditional deference towards the factory system. The period of struggles against forms of work organization has certainly passed, but I think that phase has definitively marked the new unskilled working class. Every hypothesis of a new productive effort cannot be formulated therefore in terms of efficiency and rationalization alone but must also take into account the problem of work quality and above all the problem of the workers' own control of their tasks and the flow of production. All those inside the trade unions and the parties of the Left who think in terms of a new development model based on the old use of the work force will have to confront this new working-class attitude.

The most important 'residue' of the phase of struggles inside the factory, however, is the remaining presence of a capillary trade union organization with a high local-level participation. This grass roots trade unionism wants to and must survive as an autonomous factor, because it is mainly composed of militants and leaders who have no links with the political parties and very little in common with the trade union leaders of the confederations. It is a little-known fact, but in the last few years, while membership in the CGIL has increased by more than 80 per cent, PCI membership has remained nearly stable. The existence of a diffuse trade union militancy which is autonomous from the parties is further confirmed by the evolution of the CISL and not merely the FIM, along with other institutions mainly in the North.

This non-political trade union militancy, which has often been accused of being pansyndicalist when not corporativist or salary-oriented, has been lately on the defensive for two reasons which are closely interconnected. The first reason for this weakness is linked to the very origins of the militancy: born and formed at the factory level around the issues of salary and work organization, this non-political militancy has met with notable difficulties when it has sought to translate its local-level energies into a more general economic vision. Many attempts have been made to 'go outside the factory' while preserving the characteristics of a refusal of party mediation and the desire for direct and immediate links with the working-class base. These attempts have met with little success. Examples include the 'contractual' management of the reform struggles as well as the experiences of self-proclaimed price reductions.

The other source of weakness of these forces is precisely the lack of a political hinterland which can guarantee their survival when the trade union struggles touch the loftier realm of economic development and the political system itself. Attempts were also made in this direction but they only reproduced the same mistakes made earlier by the small ultra-Left parties (the MPL and the PDUP).

This diffuse grass roots militancy, however, to which must be attributed not only the episode of the Lirico [manifestations at a meeting held in Milan] but also heated debates in many trade union congresses and in the recent delegates' assemblies, constitutes a strong brake against any choice towards centralization as well as against the delegation of power to the parties. Such a militancy, however, is not capable of indicating alternative solutions, beyond the essentially methodological one of local-level democracy.

A new element and one which can come into effect in several and contradictory ways must be underlined. In recent years the trade unions have become big organizations, with millions of members (half of all those who could be unionized) and tens of thousands of cadres. Few have noted recently that certain internal divisions in the trade unions did not reflect political or cultural realities but realities of organization: for instance between the FLM delegates of Turin and Milan, and inside the CGIL between the trade unions in the North and those in the South (the same division also exists inside the CISL but there it carries stronger political connotations).

Although favouring centralization, the abandonment of the principle of 'no delegation of powers' (to which the trade union movement owed so much of its fortune) and extreme caution, if not wariness, towards the unorganized sectors of society, such as the young and the unemployed, the organizational force still pushes the trade unions to remain on the political scene as autonomous actors, clearly undermining the hypothesis of becoming in fact pressure groups or consensus-producing machines for any given political line.

And this brings us to the last new element: the political framework which is no longer one of more or less bitter contrast but of *rapprochement* and agreement, even if only partially, among all the parties with which the trade unions are affiliated – with the exception of course of those who recognize no 'political head'. We shall see later on the consequences of these new factors on the trade unions. First, however, I would like to unearth an old debate which centred on the parties and the trade unions as channels for the formation of collective demands, and which can help us to understand the current situation.

According to certain scholars, inflation is also the result of the explosion of social conflicts when the hegemony of a class collapses without the hegemony of another having affirmed itself in its place. There are certain economic and political systems in which the rules of the game no longer hold once all the actors are obliged to play with their cards on the table. In other words, when all forces succeed in being fully represented and are therefore free to express their demands, a mechanism of 'catching up' develops whereby each group discovers the advantages earned by the others and demands even more as a consequence. The outcome is a diffuse behaviour aimed at seizing as much as possible without worrying about what will eventually happen to the economic system as a whole. This 'take the money and run' attitude produces an ever-increasing inflationary process.

What are the consequences of such a situation for a group which is interested in a radical transformation rather than in a simple adjustment of the system? We in fact know that such a transformation is only possible when interests are aggregated in a stable manner and with the least amount of divisions. The divisions which exist should be very marked and the lines of caesura of different conflicts should not be superimposed.

The aggregation of interests and the polarization of conflicts constitute a problem which should be naturally avoided by those who hold power, but it constitutes above all a problem for the working-class movement. In a situation where social demands are fragmented along particularistic lines and in which interest conflicts are dispersed the social system is certainly managed in an efficient manner and enters a phase

167

of crisis. But such a crisis cannot easily precipitate or give birth to a radical transformation.

I remember the criticisms addressed seven or eight years ago against the parties for being inefficient transmission channels of collective demands. What was the basis for this criticism? The parties were seen as composed of many classes, as 'catch-all' parties which tended not to dissatisfy anyone and therefore refused to become the expression of a single set of aggregate interests. Instead it was held at the time that the trade unions were capable of expressing such an aggregate demand, since they (as organizations of dependent workers) did not have to take into account the interests of the lower and middle classes.

It seems to me that the argument is now being reversed. The trade unions no longer appear to be capable of carrying out their role because of the particularistic pressures which are unleashed inside them: the public sector, shop levels and even sectors of the central working-class protest when their economic demands are sacrificed in the name of employment and of investments. On the other hand one discovers that wage demands, which the trade unions are best equipped to control, have not brought about any changes, while those investments which are agreed upon at the enterprise level have not been made and the strategy of reforms supported by the trade unions has exhausted itself in fatiguing negotiations with the government.

There has been a tendency on the contrary to rediscover political parties as the instruments best able, thanks to their ideological characterization, to define and to aggregate interests over a long time period. The parties are not only seen as capable of aggregating interests but also of transforming them into finalized interests, i.e. interests which can be 'self-containing' in the short run in the name of longer-ranging ends. In substance one hears on the Left the following reasoning: this is no longer the moment for the distribution of resources because there aren't any; one should instead get the mechanism which produces resources running again while trying to make it better than the preceding one. To do this one needs sacrifices, and only political parties can ask them of the popular masses because they can offer in exchange not only the 'golden eggs of tomorrow' but also ideological rewards, that is, the entrance of the popular parties in the government area. This is precisely what is meant when one stresses the notion of 'accord' in mentioning the agreement between parties.

It is this discrepancy between immediate concessions and future rewards which requires the mediation of ideology and the total identification with the party which reaches power. At the same time such a discrepancy provokes discussions and divisions within the trade unions, which by their very nature, besides raising questions of structural change, need to obtain immediate concrete results.

We will trace the problems which the present political attitude of compromise raises in the different sectors of the trade unions, while trying to transcend the verbal subleties which cloud the Italian trade union setting as well as its political life. We will also confront the paradox of a political framework which appears to be devoid of conflict but which is accompanied by an increasingly more manifest crisis in trade union unity.

First of all one must recall a well-known fact which is often forgotten, thus giving rise to confusion. The change in political line does mean the end of a historical discrimination against the entry of the PCI in the area of government. But it also implies that the parties of the Left have entered into an agreement with the Christian Democrats and opened the way to that politics of 'historical compromise' which can lead to anything except the alternative of a Left in power. This dilemma explains the contradictory behaviour of the Socialist trade unionists. Inside the CGIL, who first appeared as the most fervent advocates for a trade union that would abandon its agnostic attitudes *vis à vis* governmental programmes (of which they had been the strongest supporters during the Centre–Left). Once the Communist contingent inside the CGIL also chose to accept the end of trade union agnosticism, the Socialists in the CGIL fell back on the same fear expressed by the Socialist Party of being squeezed out by the agreement between the two 'giants', the PCI and the DC. They therefore insisted in a polemical manner that in the new political situation the trade unions must preserve their autonomy, upholding with firmness their programme of economic demands. Soon afterwards, while the agreement between the parties has been finally reached, the Socialists inside the UIL (the trade union which is neither Communist nor Catholic inspired) proposed to become the pole of attraction for all those dissatisfied by the PCI–DC compromise.

The Communist trade unionists had the clearest behaviour of all even if one could already discern more than a few differences in their ranks. At first they were wary of going beyond the formula of a government without discrimination on the Left, both because of their traditional moderation on the tactical plane *vis à vis* changes of line and probably also because they wanted to keep good relations with the CISL (the Catholic derived trade union). But at the congress the Communist trade unionists came out in favour not only of a direct Communist participation in the political running of the country (because only such a government could realize the planning policies which trade union objectives had demanded); they also affirmed through Lama that in the changed political context the autonomy of the trade unions needed to be redefined, while denying that in recent times autonomy was already being reduced (something which was affirmed at the FIOM congress). In reality, by placing the emphasis on the contents of the economic programme and – as Trentin did – on the problems of the transformation of the state towards a new power of the workers, the Communist contingent of the CGIL showed its fear that the DC would make the PCI pay for its government recognition by a serious delay in planned reforms.

This hypothesis is explicitly formulated by the 'trade union Left' (Lettieri) as well as by Benvenuto. The *compromesso* is not at all liked by this portion of the Left, which is, however, aware of the dangers of corporatist and *qualunquista* demands (such as those which took place in Chile) against a government which includes the strongest working-class party. Therefore the 'trade union Left' rtepresented inside the CGIL underlined at the congress its refusal to become a consensus-producing machine, as well as its refusal to accentuate further its conflictual position by indiscriminately welcoming all discontented forces.

This second type of refusal appears to be less explicitly stated in the majority of the CISL as it tries to mediate with its right wing. The Right defines the notion of autonomy from a political framework which has moved to the Left, to mean precisely the unleashing of those particularistic tendencies in certain categories of the public sector. The ambiguity was resolved in the conclusions of the congress, which underlined above all the fear, shared by all the elements of the trade unions without party allegiance, that a government composed of 90 per cent of the parties with no open conflict, would not only suffocate the role of the trade unions but would also stifle the more general social and local-level debates which have their own autonomous dimension, and one that cannot be immediately resumed under a political heading.

All of the above problems have drawn the attention of the press and of those commentators who are always inclined to translate all developments in terms of party politics. There is one problem which, however, was not raised or only tangentially discussed through the deforming lenses of political analysis: I am referring to the very real step backwards which trade union unity has experienced at the cost of a resurrection inside individual trade unions, even inside the FLM, of a spirit of organization which until recently would have been unthinkable.

Precisely at the moment when the process of *rapprochement* between parties in the 'constitutional area' is concluded with the signature of the government agreements, the divisions between the different confederations are once again reappearing and the objective of trade union unity vanishes for the long term. This development may appear as a paradox for those who made the long process towards trade union unity depend simply on the evolution of the political system. It is not a paradox if one assumes that the present accord is a very unstable event and that the mental reservations of all parties are coming out in the open in the trade unions, now seen as the new battleground for clashes while the parties wait for the present state of emergency or of impotence to come to an end so that the battle can once more take place openly in the political arena.

There are also other motives with which to explain the recent aggravation of divisions inside the trade unions. First of all, as Manghi has underlined, the external difficulties have produced a 'feeling of death' inside the organization. But this is not enough to explain why the principal divisions are once again along confederal lines rather than inside them as had been the case until recently.

The organizational spirit has reappeared once more because, with the grass roots level movement having abated, different ideas on how to organize the trade unions have emerged, each based on a different concept of class. The CGIL has returned to a reflex of class defence based on a fully ideological vision of the working class, which is assumed to have demands and needs that can only be mediated through the trade union as a 'transformer of reality'. The danger in such a concept of class is that collective demands are divided according to criteria which remain fundamentally economic in nature.

The new CISL, on the other hand, has always had a much more sociological vision of the notion of class, one which advocated conforming to demands and needs rather than preachings from above. The danger here is the opposite of the CGIL case, i.e. of not selecting among the various needs raised, so that the consequence is one of generic protest without any hypothesis for the transformation of reality.

The period in which class demands appeared as a compact and unanimous bloc, thus obliging all organizations to redefine their interpretations, has ended. We are now witnessing an increasingly deep division between those who would run the trade unions along directive lines and those who oppose any such direction from above. A further division can be found between those who look at the role of the trade union militant (and the distinctions he makes between public and private) rather than at the role of the organization and are more interested in the worker as

171

Emilio Reyneri

protagonist of trade union and productive life than in the democratic management of the institutions of the state or in economic planning. The recent 'critical comments' of Manghi, the newly elected secretary of the Milanese CISL, symbolize perfectly this problem by their title: 'To decline by growing' (*Declinare crescendo*).

9. Ten Hypotheses for the Analysis of New Movements*

Alberto Melucci

The debate surrounding recent aspects of youth protest movements points to the lack of analytical tools for an understanding of their meanings and purposes. The debate also reveals the need for a theory that will be able to interpret the facts. I propose ten hypotheses as a brief contribution to such a theory. They form a set of questions intended for reflection so that both the debate and the confrontation will not fall within the commonplace juxtaposition of extremism and rationality.

1. A social movement is an object created by analysis; it does not coincide with the empirical forms of collective action

The current approach to phenomena of collective action, including those of youth protests, consists in assuming the empirical manifestations of these movements. They are perceived as objects of analysis which are meaningful in themselves and capable of conveying the general meaning of the action in question.

When trying to classify forms of protest, one achieves at best the building of typologies which contain those common and recurring characteristics of the phenomena studied as general categories. One speaks of the student movement, of the feminist movement, and so on by assuming their historically observed behaviour, i.e. the emergence of student or women's protests carry a homogeneous meaning as well as determined structural characteristics. Not only in current political language and party debates but also in intellectual analysis, the 'women's question' or the 'youth question' are considered as meaningful objects in themselves.

From an analytical point of view I do not believe that such 'general' questions exist. Rather, within historical phenomena of collective action, one should distinguish a plurality of analytical meanings which eliminate the apparent unity of the empirical object and yield a different evaluation of its structural components as well as of its political implications.

* First published in *Quaderni Piacentini*, no. 65–6 (February 1978), pp. 3–19.

Feminism, for example, is a heterogeneous collective process in which multiple drives for equal rights and equal status for women coexist: through the overcoming of century-old discriminations; through the creation of new integrative mechanisms with the marketing of 'feminist' items and symbols; and through the emergence of demands in relation to intrapersonal relationships and the definition of the individual's emotional and sexual identity. Obviously, the meaning of each of these components is quite different. One can single out multiple meanings even in a phenomenon as apparently remote from conflictual mobilization as youth fashion. Next to the aggregation of atomized consumption patterns and market manipulation there is in youth fashion a cultural content and symbols which give rise to conflictual behaviours.

No phenomenon of collective action can be considered in its entirety because it never speaks in a single language. Any analytical approach to social movements implies their being broken down into different levels, according to the system of social relationships involved in the action and the orientation which such an action assumes. A strike is never a homogeneous phenomenon because within it demands of a conflicting nature coexist: some affect the organizational system of the enterprise, others the political system and finally still others are linked to elements of the class struggle which attack the capitalist system of production *per se*. The meaning of the phenomenon varies according to the system of social relations to which the action refers. It is not the same thing to ask for a different functioning of an organization or to question its power.

The general proposition I have spelled out may seem abstract; as we will see in the following passages, however, it is fundamental. Indeed, only by distinguishing the different levels and meanings of collective action will it be possible to understand the content of a concrete movement which carries numerous and often contradictory requests. Only by starting from this complexity will it be possible to achieve a thorough and non-ideological political evaluation.

2. A social movement is not an answer to a crisis but the expression of a conflict

'Bourgeois' sociology and political science have always linked the appearance of collective action to a crisis of the system in one of its aspects. Collective action is seen as pathological to the social system. This general approach is found in many recent interpretations of youthful phenomena: not only in the quick diagnoses made by the ideologues of the regime but also in the more thoroughly meditated analyses made by the Old as well as the New Left. By reducing the phenomenon to a position of marginality these interpretations deny all conflictual significance to current collective processes. Constant reference to the Italian crisis, whose importance cannot be denied, often hides the existence of new conflictual contents. I will return to this point later on.

In theoretical terms, I wish to stress the structural correspondence between a social movement according to my definition and a conflict. The importance of crisis factors in the appearance of collective behaviour is not at stake. One must distinguish clearly, however, the structural character of a conflict affecting a certain system from the factors which in a given situation activate the conflict. A conflict presupposes the struggle by two social actors for the appropriation of resources valued by both. The actors in a conflict fight in the same field for the seizure and control of the same resources. For conflict to exist one must define the actors in a common system of reference. There must also be a stake to which both opponents either implicitly or explicitly refer. If in the history of capitalism class struggle had been a simple reaction to economic exploitation and to cyclical crises it would have been solved by the social-democratic conquests of better wages and working conditions for the workers. The struggle is to be found instead in the system of production itself which divides the opponents who define antagonistically the conditions, the means and the objectives of social production.

The presence of such a structural conflict within a system can be activated and brought to the surface by peculiar crisis situations within the system itself. It would however be an error to confuse a movement, which is the expression of a structural conflict, with a simple response to a crisis capable of conjuncturally facilitating or accelerating its activation. A crisis always refers to the process of disintegration of a system such as: dysfunction of the mechanisms of adaptation; imbalance among different portions or subsystems; paralysis or blockage of some parts; difficulty in integration, etc. The breadth and quality of a crisis vary according to the levels of the system which are affected. A crisis sets in motion processes of disintegration and also creates reactions which tend to re-establish an equilibrium. A conflict, instead, conveys opposition to the control and use of certain resources. In the concrete history of society these two dimensions are often interwoven, thus making the analysis of collective mobilization all the more difficult.

If it is true that the ideology of the ruling class has always sought to reduce social movements to simple answers to a crisis the differentiation we have outlined above is not of minor importance. To admit otherwise would be to acknowledge the existence of collective demands which attack the legitimacy of power and the use of social resources.

Alberto Melucci

3. A social movement is a collective action expressing a conflict; it implies a break in the limits of compatibility of a system

A movement is the mobilization of a collective actor defined by a specific form of solidarity. It struggles against an adversary for the seizure and control of valuable resources. The collective action of a movement manifests itself through the breaking-up of the system's limits inside which the action takes place. A movement not only reveals the presence of a conflict; it pushes it beyond the limits of compatibility with the system in question, i.e. it breaks the rules of the game, puts forward non-negotiable objectives, questions the legitimacy of power, and so forth. The above conditions must exist in order to identify a movement first as a category of analysis then as an empirical phenomenon. The presence of a conflict and the breaking-up of the limits of compatibility to which it refers are both necessary conditions for the discussion of a *social movement* in a strict sense.

When confronted by a conflict which develops within the institutional rules and the operating limits of a system, we can speak of *conflictual action*. The action of trade unions in the highly institutionalized industrial relations systems of advanced capitalism fall increasingly into this category. The clash of interests and the conflict which follows take place within the partners' common preoccupation to guarantee the compatibility of the system and to abide by its negotiating rules. If one is faced with the simple breaking-up of the rules without clear identification of an adversary and a common field of struggle then it is legitimate to talk of true *deviance*. All those behaviours which detach themselves from the rules of the social order without questioning its legitimacy can be considered deviant. The fruit of the breaking-up of an order or of the insufficient assimilation of its rules by individuals, deviance produces a search for particular compensations beyond the accepted norms and behaviours. Finally, there is one last category of behaviour which must not be confused with social movements and which I will call *crisis behaviour* or *aggregate behaviour*. It refers to collective phenomena produced by the aggregation of atomized individual behaviours. Crisis behaviour consists in the repetitive multiplication of individual actions which are in themselves separate. They answer to a crisis in an area of the social system through the creation of a generalized belief. This belief, which is not a system of solidarity but an object of affective identification, unites a plurality of atomized behaviours. Panic, a new fashion or the diffusion of certain collective rituals contain predominantly, if not exclusively, these characteristics.

Social movements in their literal sense should then be considered in relation to other behaviour categories and differentiated from them.

Conflictual action, deviance and aggregate behaviours often coexist in the historical practice of a concrete movement. Hence the need to define social movements first for their analytical characteristics (conflict and rupture of limits) and later for their empirical features.

4. *The nature of the social movement depends on the system of relationships in which the collective action is situated*

Social movements can refer to at least three types of situations and behaviours. If conflict and breaking of the rules occur within an organizational system, i.e. one which is characterized by roles and functions, it is appropriate to speak of a *movement of demands*. The collective actor claims a different distribution of the resources within the organization, fights for a more efficient operation of the apparatus and finally clashes with the power which imposes both the rules and the forms of the division of labour. A large part of the unions' demands belongs to this category, especially when they are beyond the control of the organization and beyond the limits set by the negotiations. The fact that the mobilization is intense and the forms of action aggressive does not indicate *per se* that there is a class content. Such action can in fact safeguard the advantages of a given category; it can mobilize a group of underprivileged workers; it can claim a different distribution of roles and rewards, without attacking the class relationship or the manner in which resources are produced.

A *political movement* expresses a conflict through the rupture of the boundaries of the political system. It fights for the widening of political participation and struggles against the prevalence of the ruling interests within the representative systems. Many of the urban struggles for the decentralization of political decisions belong to this category. Social groups or interests which are excluded from participation request the broadening of the limits of representation through a non-institutionalized action. Another example could be women's action on behalf of real equality to be reached not only through parliamentary steps but also through direct action.

A *class movement* is a collective action which affects through conflict the mode of production and the appropriation of a society's resources. It fights not only against the manner in which resources are produced but it also questions for whom they are produced and the trend of development. In terms of definition, class movements constitute the most abstract category discussed so far since no movement can be only a class movement. In a real society, a movement runs into organizational systems and forms of representation as well as political decisions. What, then, is the purpose of such a distinction?

I believe there are two reasons for which it is important. First, the ideology of the ruling class tends to negate the existence of class movements which attack both the mode of production and the appropriation of resources. At most a ruling class acknowledges the existence of demands or of political problems, and it always tries to keep each conflictual phenomenon within these limits. At the same time it is necessary to recognize the existence of collective actions which are not carriers of class conflicts. Even when violent, not all types of protest attack the class relationship in a society. Affirming the existence of class movements and distinguishing them from other types of movements implies fighting against the reductionist action of the ruling class. It also implies not falling into the illusion that all types of collective protest mark the beginning of a revolution.

5. Each real movement always carries a plurality of analytical meanings

Notwithstanding the brief examples I have used intermittently, all the distinctions suggested so far are purely analytical. They are conceptual tools to be used in the analysis of empirical phenomena. A real movement is always a complex and heterogeneous historical reality. Within it one finds meanings for actions which refer to the different analytical categories mentioned above. A movement operates within diverse organizational systems; it is situated in one or more political systems and it acts within certain class relationships. Its scope covers many problems, actors and objectives. One aspect may prevail over the others and thus characterize specifically a given movement. Conversely all actions can combine in different ways.

In a movement the different levels of marginality and deviance which are present in a system often merge; aggregate collective behaviours coagulate. All these behavioural fusions must be broken down by analysis and reconstituted in a system of meaningful relationships in order to single out the meaning and the direction of a movement.

This is not an easy task. The rough tools at our disposal are a first obstacle. A strong resistance can be found, however, in the movements themselves, given their immediate need to project a global and united image of themselves in order to secure the mobilization of their own base. The real conditions under which the movements operate, especially in Italy, and the restrictions to which they are subjected make this situation almost inevitable. As a consequence collective mobilization is fragile, since it often holds together around general and confused objectives a heterogeneous 'base'. I am convinced that reflection, even when it is theoretical, on the structural components of new movements plays an important role in the growth of collective action.

I will cite just one example which will be discussed later on. The abuse of marginality as a concept in recent debates does not help to clarify the real actors and possible outlets of the 'movement' in our country. The term 'marginal' has become alternatively synonymous with the terms 'opponent', 'excluded', 'revolutionary' and 'unemployed', with varying consequences on the movement's practical stance. A clarification on this point is less an academic question and more a necessary condition enabling the movement correctly to single out its base, interlocutors and opponents.

6. *New class movements are born in advanced capitalist societies*

Collective phenomena which emerge in advanced capitalist societies cannot be regarded as simple reactions to a crisis or as the result of marginality and deviance. One should realize that they are the symptoms of new class movements, even if this is not their only significance. I speak of class movements because the new forms of collective action affect advanced capitalism in all its productive systems. These no longer concern the sole production of economic resources but also the production of social relationships, symbols, identity and individual needs. The control of social production has little by little shifted away from the middle classes' simple ownership (as a real social group) to the large apparatuses dealing with economic and political decisions. Capitalist development can no longer be guaranteed through the simple control of workers and the transformation of natural resources. It requires a growing intervention in social relationships, symbolic systems or identity, as well as individual needs. The refusal to have their identity and needs manipulated, the request for a balanced relationship with nature and with one's own body and the will to control development in all of its social and cultural implications, are the emerging contents of these new movements. They demand a different direction in society's transformation as well as a different orientation of production.

Characteristics common to many recent forms of collective action in mature capitalist societies underscore the novelty of these conflicts. One is impressed at first by the generalization and lack of concrete bargaining issues of the struggles. Beyond the conflicts linked to occupational struggles, mobilization and collective protests touch upon other apparently heterogeneous social areas: student struggles, feminism, sexual liberation, urban movements, ecological struggles and consumer mobilization, as well as issues linked to ethnic and linguistic minorities, community and counter-culture movements and the struggles on health issues, as well as against different types of segregation. As I have already stated, all these struggles do not carry the same meaning nor are they the expression of class struggle. They are nevertheless important signs of the qualitative change of collective action. These struggles mobilize social groups around scarcely negotiable objectives because they cannot be reduced to political mediation. Indeed, the second characteristic of these movements which many observers have noted is precisely the limited focusing on the political system and the scant interest shown for the question of the seizure of power. The conquest of political power as well as the conquest of state structures seem to be replaced by the desire to control living conditions directly, to demand an autonomous space independent from the system. This characteristic, often defined as an element of political weakness in the movements, raises important questions concerning the meaning and future prospects of the new struggles. The end of the separation between public and private areas can be regarded as the third characteristic which closely follows the two mentioned above. Public and political relations are enmeshed with questions concerning the affective, sexual and biological identity of the individual. 'Private' areas, where traditionally the affective exchange took place and where individual rewards were given as well as claims made, are now invaded by media manipulation, thus becoming the place where resistance begins and conflicts emerge.

The realm which permeates daily life as well as existential choices is generalized, thus making it empirically more difficult to differentiate between protest and marginality, between deviance and social movements. The silent majority is not only a ghost created by authoritarian politics but a reality which threatens mature capitalism. The system multiplies the ways of 'treating' all forms of an opposition defined as 'difference' or as social pathology. Dissent becomes a disease; struggles are relegated to the realm of phenomena to be cured either by behavioural therapy or by repression. A further feature seems to characterize the new movements: the search for a community identity and the return to primary affiliations (in terms of sex, age, place or group). The struggle always has an instrumental aim; it also, however, wants to strengthen the solidarity of the group, its symbols and the affective exchange which characterizes it (to be 'comrades' after 1968 means much more than belonging to the same organization or holding the same political aims).

The group centres on its own solidarity and resists the 'rationality', the decisions and the aims imposed by a distant and impersonal power. The search for participation and direct action is the last relevant characteristic: the refusal of mediation or of delegation expressed in a non-negotiable form, i.e. 'wild', the opposition to a control or to decisions which are imposed by various authorities. The spontaneous and anti-authoritarian character of many recent struggles together with their distrust for political mediation constitute factors of fragmentation, organizational weakness and discontinuity in the new movements, as many critics have stressed. These traits, however, should not prevent one from apprehending the originality of the new demands and should not be used as a pretext for denying their conflictual potential.

To analyse these demands as the expression of new class conflicts means first of all to cease considering classes as empirical social groups defined both by a culture and a way of life. It means instead focusing on *class relations* as a system of oppositions for the control of social production. It also implies realizing that the production for whose control the classes wage struggles cannot be arbitrarily relegated to the 'economic' sphere.

In a society which produces increasingly through total control on the systems of social relations, ranging from large organizations to emotional relations, class conflicts and collective actors are transformed, making traditional categories of analysis inadequate. If classes are increasingly less real groups to be identified by recognizable social signs or a common culture, does it still make sense to talk of class struggle? Yes, providing one considers conflicts as a network of oppositions for the control of development rather than as the antagonism between two groups, two languages, two ways of dressing or of living. While classes understood in these traditional terms tend to dissolve and are replaced by a multiplicity of groups, stratified and crossed along complex lines, the importance of *class relations* remains. The control of certain groups over social production (even when the public apparatus is used) continues just as does the struggle by other groups for a different direction in development. Undoubtedly their identification becomes more difficult. Class domination becomes impersonal, and it becomes 'public' through the large planning and decision-making apparatus. Through the action of social groups more directly affected by the consequences of a manipulated growth class opposition becomes fragmented and scattered.

To consider this analytical perspective seriously means in effect to cease supporting the myth of a compact and homogeneous working class on its way toward a bright revolutionary destiny. In advanced capitalist countries the working class is increasingly differentiated and shifts its action more and more towards concrete demands and the political arena. Complex systems of industrial relations regulate the negotiations between management and unions. Systems of representation and political mediation interpret the demands of professional groups which have increasingly become pressure groups. It would be meaningless, given the above, to conclude, however, that workers' action no longer expresses class content. This has been disproved by the intense social conflicts of the last decade. In the advanced capitalist countries the role of the working class remains central for any political change, given its electoral weight as well as the strength of its organization. Its role in the class struggle, however, remains tied to a certain form of capitalism which is far from being overcome, although on the way to transforming itself.

The hypothesis of new class movements is much more than a political sign. Intellectuals of the Old and New Left who emphasize their Marxist ties, in order to take the new movements into account dust off an old functionalist armature which has fallen into disuse and which explains collective behaviour in terms of marginality or of deviance. Confronted with this late rediscovery, which was to be expected of the most primitive functionalism, the hypothesis of new class movements takes on not only theoretical but also political value in the redefinition of the field and of the instruments for analysis.

Marginality and deviance are concepts which only make sense in a theoretical context which assumes consensus to be the condition for the integration of the system. This perception eliminates the problems of domination, conflict and class relations. Functionalist or neofunctionalist empiricism spreads under the cover of formal adherence to sacred principles. Few take the time, however, to check the correlation between categories worshipped in the abstract and their application to concrete analyses. As during all great moments of crisis we see the blossoming of a scholasticism which interprets and explains the forefathers' texts. This purely intellectual exercise which has no connection with what is changing in advanced capitalism covers in practice the instrumental use made of 'bourgeois' social sciences in their most ideological but also most operatively useful elements. One can witness therefore the transfer into the language and practice of the Left of concepts and research methods deprived of any reference to their theoretical origins.

The success of concepts such as marginality and deviance in the analyses of recent youth phenomena can be explained as follows: functionalism is rediscovered in the vacuum left by the crisis of traditional categories confronted with newly emerging phenomena. This is a meaningful coincidence for those who are transforming Marxism into a doctrine of order; it is less meaningful and more dangerous for those who, wishing to side with the move ents, harbour the illusion of increasing the onrushing 'wild' impact of the struggles by assigning a central role to the 'marginals'. According to functionalist tradition, marginality does not produce conflicts; rather it produces social disintegration.

While we witness the growing use of Marxism as a functionalist theory of order, the analysis of new class relationships and of new conflicts is relegated to the area of intellectual and social marginality. I believe that the time has come to face in a systematic manner the hypothesis of new class conflicts and to derive all the theoretical implications. In essence such a step implies questioning the conceptual apparatus of codified Marxism which is increasingly becoming the ritual repetition of formulas.

7. We are witnessing in Italy the grafting of new class movements on the structural distortions of economic development, on the degradation of the social system and on the crisis of the political system

This general hypothesis, which covers chronologically the last decade of Italian history, can appear too summary to take fully into account the surge of the various collective phenomena during this period. As we will see, such a hypothesis does not deny the specific causes which have produced the different movements and protests which our country witnessed in the last ten years. Rather it offers a key with which to explain what is common beyond these differences and what is permanent beyond the conjunctural variations. New class demands are carried by new collective subjects, representing those social groups touched most by the transformations in the forms of social production and in the modes of domination. They are collective actors fighting against a development which implies the increasing manipulation of identity, of social relations, of daily, private and body life as well as the relation with nature. But these questions and actors are intertwined with the special characteristics of our social system and with the vicissitudes of our political life.

The explosion of 1968 represented the meeting point of a new class movement in the making and of an important process of institutional modernization. After ten years, one can judge the importance and the amplitude of the role of modernization, while giving a new dimension to the expectations and the enthusiasms and the myths linked to that mobilization. The struggles which characterized the end of the 1960s and the first half of the 1970s acted as factors in the transformation of Italian society notwithstanding the growing crisis. These struggles functioned as the only or at least the principal channel of expression of new demands by exercising a real pressure on the political system and imposing limited transformations. The role of these struggles was the product of the substantial failure of a reform policy due to the blockage of the political system and the crisis of institutional mediation. The modernization which ensued was obviously contradictory. It resulted from the necessity of controlling the explosive potential of certain conflicts while not touching pre-existing assets. This modernization was not managed by an innovative elite but by an old dominant class trying to stay in power with the least possible cost.

The contradictory character of the transformation should not make us forget, however, the real changes in Italian society. Without taking into account the innovations in culture and in mores, one has to admit that there has been a definite modernization in the political system, despite its crisis, through the widening of representative and participatory channels. The modernization of the political system has taken place in a reductive and unstable form through such new elements as: the *Statuto dei Lavoratori* which substituted traditional relations of authority and the refusal of trade unions by a negotiated system of industrial relations; urban decentralization which institutionalized spontaneous forms of mass mobilization concerning territorial problems; and the delegated decrees which codified in rigid formal mechanisms the participatory thrusts inside the school. The Communist Party received the most important benefits from this push towards modernization both at the electoral level and also in the renewal of its base and its cadres. At the same time, by becoming the most qualified and influential interpreter of this modernization against the tendencies to reduce its innovative aspects, the PCI emphasized its institutional role and its integration in the political system (in the same manner as the unions have tended to become the institutional actor of a modern system of industrial relations).

The year 1968 began a modernization process in Italian society which changed, even if in a contradictory manner, its institutional level. In saying this, one does not have to endorse a policy of 'normalization' which is taking place with the interpretation of the cycle of struggles. One cannot reduce these struggles to a temporary and casual outbreak, or at best to 'growing pains'. 1968 also marks the first appearance of a new class movement on which modernistic trusts are pitted against the resistances and the archaisms of traditional Italian society. The embryonic content of the new movement is the same as that which characterizes the collective mobilization in many advanced societies and reappears in the most recent youth struggles, with different overtones. In the meantime Italian society has partially modernized in a chaotic manner because its transformations have been kept within minimal limits compatible with the assets of established interests. This explains the fragility of the equilibrium reached at different stages and the multiple effects of the crisis. The recent forms of collective mobilization reflect the change in structural conditions which are more worrisome than those of 1968.

The crisis which seized the more advanced capitalist countries struck Italy with massive disruptive effects. The impact of the crisis has been worsened and multiplied by the structural distortions of a dependent development which creates a rich society while generating underdevelopment, the degradation of the social system thus bringing out its deep disequilibria. We do not need to recall phenomena which are so intertwined with our daily life such as: the contradictions of an urban growth guided by the anarchy of speculative interests; youthful unemployment; the disruption of public administration and of its elementary mechanisms without which the system cannot function (one has only to think about the ridiculous and tragic problem of small change and the lack of coins in circulation). To these processes of social disintegration one has to add the closing-off and the immobility of the political system, the inability of institutional channels of representation adequately to treat ever more pressing and diffuse demands. The failure of reform policies, the inefficiency of public intervention and the fragmentation of legislative action dictated by clienteles and pressure groups are among the most visible signs of institutional blockage and inadequate representation.

This intertwining of conflict and crisis marked in a special way the new forms of collective action in our country. While living through the changes of advanced capitalism, Italy bears the weight of its archaic productive and social structure and its marginal position in the international division of labour. While it witnesses the birth of new movements tied to the most advanced processes of capitalism it must also confront demands arising from its specific crisis as a dependent society. This situation explains the difficulty of representation and of the political mediation of heterogeneous demands, and accentuates the fragmentation of collective protest. With respect to the movements it is very difficult to identify the new elements in their contents and their actors.

8. *Violence is the result of the specific combination of conflict and crisis characterizing the new movements in Italy*

Given specific conditions, collective action takes on violent aspects. In Italy the new movements have focused on the political system which became the real and only target of collective demands. The crisis and the closedness of the political system combined with the relative decomposition of the state's administrative apparatus made the latter incapable

185

of dealing with the new demands and of opening new channels for the expression of new conflicts. This situation intensified the focus on 'politics' in the emerging forms of protest. The strongly politicized character of the collective struggles in our country derives from this situation, even when the specific contents of the new movements do not refer to the political system or to the state apparatus but address the defence of identity, of social relations and of daily life against their manipulation by large decision-making apparatuses. The closing of the political system coincides with the growing disaggregation of the daily social fabric, of the systems of solidarity and of the elementary functional equilibria needed by society. Violence is the symptom of the prevalence of crisis over conflict. The answer to the processes of decomposition and to the institutional rigour of the system prevails over the struggle to affirm a different orientation of collective resources.

The desperate choice of terrorism signals the limit of the decomposition of a movement and the prevalence of its crisis element. As signs of a collective action which is now defined uniquely as reaction to the crisis and to its institutional blockage, incapable of generating objectives for struggle or mobilization, one can indicate: (1) the illusion over the efficacy of clandestine struggle which is isolated and without any base; (2) the choice of an exemplary gesture; (3) the faith in disaggregation as a factor which accelerates change; (4) the permeability to infiltration and manipulation. Terrorism in mature capitalist societies cannot be liquidated, however, with a few passing remarks. Clandestine groups choosing violence as a means of struggle appear even in societies where the crisis is less evident than in Italy. The use of violence and of 'wild' behaviour are not only effects of the crisis and of the closing of the political system. In mature capitalist societies there are some collective demands which cannot be reduced to political mediation but which the system nevertheless tries to integrate and to manipulate through various agencies for the creation of a more powerful consensus. The rationalization imposed by the great apparatuses chooses repressive tolerance and reduces every form of opposition to marginal behaviour. The 'wild' reaction to the limit of exemplary action of minorities becomes an ever more frequent way of answering which tends to multiply in advanced societies. Violence becomes a sign of the non-reduction of some social demands and terrorism a hopeless indicator of the critical points of conflict.

In the case of Italy, once again it seems to me that the elements of crisis and disaggregation of the system prevail. This makes the choice of terrorism even more desperate but it also brings out its disruptive effects. The important presence of right-wing violence is once more a symptom of the increasing effects of crisis, beyond the complicities and protections it still enjoys. I do not intend to analyse Fascist violence on which so much has already been written. I wish only to remark that violence from the Right is always a form of counter-mobilization guided from above and manoeuvred by dominant interests which feed on the generalization of the crisis. The 'wild' radicalization of minorities, the counter-mobilization from the Right, the intervention of provocateurs and infiltrators become impossible to distinguish when the movements for struggle are obliged to adopt a role of defence and reaction in a time of crisis.

If terrorism indicates the limit of a process, there is in Italy an overload of deviance and of anti-constitutional struggles in the new emerging class movements. By deviance I mean the marginal, atomized response to the decomposition processes tied to the economic crisis and to the contradictions of our development (urban ghettos, youth unemployment and the South). The anti-institutional struggles are the visible sign of rigidity in the decision-making apparatus and in the mediation channels as well as those of political representation. As these channels become increasingly closed and incapable of handling demands, collective action is increasingly dominated by the struggle against institutional archaism. The same can be said against the obtuseness of the command apparatus and against the inefficiency of the organizational functioning. This explains the difficulty of singling out a new class movement beneath the weight of circumstances.

Anti-institutional struggles risk playing exclusively on the lagging behind of the adversary without making use of their new content and of their new thrusts which are the product of new circumstances. In the field of psychiatry or health, for instance, much has been done in denouncing the inhuman character of psychiatric institutions, the inefficiency and the falling apart of hospital organization, and the relationship between sickness and the organization of work, between economic interests and medical practice. The growing awareness of these problems and the resulting important debate have played a fundamental political role. One must understand, however, that the focus of collective mobilization has been around the problem of delays, the closing and inefficiency of the institution. The hidden concepts of this mobilization concerning the relationship between madness and identity, the right to dispose of one's own body against medical practice which treats it as an object, the meaning and the instruments of therapy in society, which increasingly tends to 'cure' away every diversity, have remained in the background. What is madness, what is sickness? How are the categories of medical and psychiatric practice to be redefined in a vision of medicine which acknowledges the rights of individuals to dispose of their own bodies and their own identities? These are some of the questions concealed in the mobilization process around health problems. The relationship between sickness and social structure and the repressive character of the therapeutic institution are elements in a necessary consciousness-raising, but they leave many fundamental questions unanswered. A reforming modern ruling class can very rapidly coopt at the institutional level many years of struggles by using them as a platform for a rationalizing project. For this reason it is very important to pull out the more radical even if latent content of these struggles, even if it is still hidden. One must go beyond the singling-out of the external enemy (capital, Christian Democracy, institutions, etc.) to attack the categories, the conceptual apparatus and the techniques supporting medical and psychiatric practice.

The difficulty of singling out a new class movement is increased by the fact that a new ruling class in the making and a new class opposition are united on many points and objectives, such as: (1) the struggle against the resistances and the archaism of Italian society; (2) the struggle against elites and the most entrenched institutional interests; (3) the struggle against the closing of the political sphere and economic crisis. Temporary allies against the past and against the crisis, these groups stray apart as the new conflictual contents become more specific. Inside the confused flux of a militant movement new power bases coexist: radical elites struggling for a technocratic transformation and new competing demands fighting against the expansion of control and manipulation. The crisis keeps these disparate groups united while slowing down any clarification of positions.

One last element increases further the complexity of current phenomena. Advanced societies show an increasing tendency for marginality and social movements to coincide, inasmuch as the increasingly remote and centralized power tends to reduce every opposition to a marginal phenomenon. The class significance of certain conflicts nevertheless cannot be eliminated. One must make a clear distinction between the marginality imposed by the system in order to eliminate all opposition and the marginality which derives from the disaggregation processes of the system itself.

To talk about marginality in the first case means to accept an ideological use of the concept in a way which is useful to the dominant interests: every form of collective action hindering development directed from above while questioning its logic becomes marginal. The label of marginality is useful to hide the class struggle. It is important to resist such a subtle but powerful operation in which the intellectuals play an increasingly important role. The marginality which derives from the disaggregation processes is instead of another nature. It would be mere illusion to think that the protest of these marginals can nourish a collective action going beyond the simple, often violent answer to the crisis.

In the recent debate on the 'youth question' both equivocal stances are present. Whenever the prevailing interest is to control the 'movement' and reduce it into the channels of a well-regulated participation the analysis in terms of marginality is used to deny the presence of new forms of class conflict, going far beyond youthful unemployment or the university crisis. The shadow of a new power is already visible behind such a use of marginality. On the other hand, almost as a defence of the actions and perspectives of the 'movement', the term 'marginal' is overloaded with conflictual meanings and all marginals become potential actors in a revolutionary conflict. One thus runs the risk of no longer distinguishing between the processes and the actors who are the product of the crisis from those who are the carriers of new conflicts. Their interests might coincide for a brief moment, but this does not imply that the meaning, content and perspective of the protest are not destined to diverge widely. It is in the functional use of marginality that Fascist groups always found their base.

The complexity which I just described sends us back, therefore, to the plurality of the analytical meanings present in the new movements. A few examples will illustrate this multiple interpretation. The women's liberation movement naturally operates as a modernization factor in interpersonal relations, and in sexual relations in a direction which is compatible with the more innovative interests of the dominant class against the resistance of more traditional groups. At the same time, however, the movement struggles to affirm the right of individuals to dispose of their own personal identity and their relationship with others quite beyond the simple claim of equality of rights for women or a generic sexual liberation. The various student movements are at the same time processes of formation of new radical elites and of their intellectual cadres, movements struggling for the modernization of academic institutions against archaisms and restrictions; but they are also the expression of new youth demands affirming cultural stances which are incompatible with the models of technocratic development. The neo-religious movements promote a repressive utopia of identity but also operate as modernization factors in the clerical institutions and as channels of adjustment and integration of protest, deviated towards merely individual or mystical–ascetic attitudes.

The recent phenomenon of autonomy brings together new youth conflicts tied to the need for identity and expression, processes that are the answer to the crisis and to the productive social marginality of large numbers of young people, as well as phenomena of refusal to the growing institutionalization of the trade unions and the left-wing parties. The core of a rising social movement, the thrust of marginality produced by the system but no longer controlled by it, the grafting of fundamentalist sects of militants deceived by an increasingly institutionalized Left – these are the three different components brought together in the so-called 'autonomous' area. The university whose functioning is in deep crisis but which is also transformed in a mass university becomes a meeting place for these heterogeneous realities. Its increasingly serious condition coupled with the dramatic situation of the job market strengthens this juncture and makes it all the more homogeneous. Such a phenomenon, however, can only subsist in times of crisis.

Each one of the components mentioned above must be analysed separately in order to understand its role inside the collective process and to predict the possible differing outcomes of apparently homogeneous phenomena.

9. The new movements cannot survive without the mediation of political actors, but cannot be reduced to them

Current collective movements can only precipitate if they emerge out of the crisis. The collective action of movements, confined to violence or to social disaggregation, can affirm itself with its own content only when society finds a working equilibrium and if the political system becomes truly representative and capable of mediating interests.

The new class movements require political mediation and can only survive if the demands they carry are interpreted and mediated by the political system. Such a mediation cannot, however, absorb the entire charge of the demands, which express themselves through collective action. The struggle against nuclear plants is efficient only if taken up and interpreted by the political system. Energy policy decisions, however, do not absorb entirely a collective demand which attacks the logic of development itself, the decision-making aspects of development, the use of resources and the link with nature. The movement continues to exist beyond its political mediation.

Divorce and abortion struggles become efficient only when transformed into institutional movements on behalf of divorce and abortion legislation. The mobilization linked to these themes went well beyond the legal results and touched upon man–woman relations, issues linked to the body, the role of medicine, life and death and the right to choose one's identity. The movement carrying these collective demands reconstructs itself well beyond the mobilization on behalf of divorce or abortion.

The link between movements and parties thus becomes the central knot for any project of social transformation. A truly socialist transformation of society, in my mind, finds its preconditions in the ability to represent the new class thrusts while also pursuing the dualism between power and collective demands. Collective control of development can only be secured by keeping open the space which separates a movement from a decision-making apparatus. The myth of a transparent society has already been dearly paid for in the history of the working-class movement and of the Left in general. The dead who burn most in the history of this century's struggles are not those killed by capitalism but the victims of other 'comrades', in the name of a power which pretended to be the transparent expression of a peaceful and conflictless society, having become once more a community (by decree).

Power cannot at the same time be the administration of society through the mediation of interests and conflict itself. The space for the expression of conflicting demands and for the organization of unrepresented interests must be guaranteed beyond consensus. The survival of the movements and their possibility of action are the measure of a democracy which can assure collective control over development.

The Left has timidly begun confronting the debate on Eastern European societies, without having the courage to push its analysis to its most rigorous consequences, i.e. to the critique of Leninism, up to the discussion of the myth of a transparent society without classes and of a party which is its interpreter and guarantor. By constantly shifting its references, the Left in the West has saved its good conscience with respect to the possibility and the models of socialism without ever grappling with the theoretical roots of the problem. The last version of this conscience can be found probably in the analysis of Eastern societies as those of 'state capitalism', as if the keeping of the term 'capitalism' allowed one to attribute to the enemy, to the residue of the old system all the contradictions of these societies. It is impossible to avoid the fundamental problems which hide behind this formula, such as the formation of a new dominant class, the specific characteristics of the mode of production of these societies and the links between class dominance and institutional forms. Years ago this ideological operation was carried out in relation to Stalinism, rapidly liquidated as a deviation, without any analysis that went back to its structural and political roots, thereby addressing

Alberto Melucci

the tie between Stalinism and Leninism. Today it is no longer possible to confront this type of good conscience with analyses which skip over the problems I have mentioned.

Criticisms inside the Left can no longer be meek and reticent. The stakes in our country and in Western Europe concern the type of development of social relations and of power on whose behalf one should fight. The attitudes and choices made with respect to the new movements therefore become central for the entire Left.

10. *Knowledge plays a fundamental role in the process of transformation and in the development of social movements*

Knowledge, especially sociological knowledge, acquires a central importance for the collective phenomena before us. The opening-up of puny controversies over the superiority of this or that discipline are not at stake here. One must acknowledge the need for a theory of social action which can account for the transformation of systems and the formation of collective action. Let us free ourselves from the heritage of the philosophy of history and think of social systems as the product of collective actions. Critical reflection on classes and movements should first of all facilitate the analysis of the transformation of the mode of production in advanced capitalist societies in order to define better the novelty of what is at stake in the new conflicts. More importantly, one needs further knowledge on the possibility of transforming class relations. We must ask ourselves whether it would be possible to think scientifically, not of a mythical classless society, but of a conscious intervention on the mechanisms which shape and reproduce social classes. The sociology of collective movements cannot overlook the task of anticipating future movements. If an intellectual does not wish to be the prophet either of the defeat or the institutionalization of these movements, quickly transformed into new forms of power, he must then scientifically raise the problem of the changes in class relationships, the control over productive and reproductive processes of classes and of the actors responsible for this change. Between the utopia of a classless society, without conflicts, pacified and transparent (and therefore inevitably totalitarian) and the realization of the reproduction of class systems there is perhaps room to ask the scientific and political question of the possibility of a society which acts on its own class relationships in order to decrease their negative consequences and therefore control their reproduction.

Knowledge plays an important role because it finds itself at the centre of the new conflicts: when the problem is one of controlling symbols, language and identity; when it is no longer a matter of obtaining the assignment of work forces but rather of consensus, the manipulation of symbolic systems becomes *the* condition for the system's survival. Opposition therefore becomes all the more 'cultural'. It is made up of antagonistic languages and symbols and it is built on the ability to apprehend a non-manipulated knowledge. In the past ideology was perhaps an important element in the mobilization of subordinate classes to counter the dominant ideology. Subordinate class ideology was the expression of the proletariat's separate culture and way of life, always in some measure the antagonist of bourgeois values, language and symbols. In mass society, where the separation of culture and way of life is no longer present, ideology tends to become the privileged medium of the dominant interests. A non-illusioned opposition can be built by stepping out of ideology to produce knowledge. The collective action of movements does not need to strengthen its convictions through ideology. Rather, it needs to free itself from ideology. It must refuse the exclusion from knowledge because through this exclusion new forms of domination try to control class opposition.

The need for new forms of knowledge comes from the quality of the new conflicts which are increasingly concerned with the individual, his profound dimension, his needs and his unconscious. The need for control over the development and technical rationality of structures takes on routine and affective features. Problems concerning the individual and the unconscious become collective problems because they refer back to the identity manipulation by the ruling class or to the cultural form with which new needs are defined. Ruling-class ideology moves towards a growing lack of differentiation between problems, language and techniques of manipulation. Collective problems are brought down to the individual level and rendered private, through affective gratifications as well as symbolic compensations. The ruling class tries to psychologize and doctor away the 'social', thus absorbing all conflictual potential linked to the problems of identity. What is needed instead is a 'socialization' of the individual, of affection and of social relationships. Furthermore, one should give the proper status which they deserve in a planned capitalist society to the problems of daily life, of expression and of the unconscious; these problems should become the stake of new class conflicts.

The task ahead necessitates considerable work on a theoretical plane as well as the elaboration of methods of analysis and of social intervention. It is in this direction that critical knowledge becomes an essential component of the non-utopian growth of new movements. The real

193

drive towards irrationality and towards individual evasion threatens these new forms of protest. Ruling-class ideology has a vested interest in relegating these protests to an individual level in order to legitimize repression. Critical knowledge must confront its responsibility by giving depth to the new demands and breadth to the actions expressing them.

IV: Dualism, the Welfare State and Market Economy

10. A Case of Welfare Capitalism: Italian Society*

Laura Balbo

From the data given above one can form a picture of a society in which people are assiduous workers and perform many tasks in different roles and manners. They organize their activities, bustle about and try to cope by producing creative and enterprising answers to specific external conditions. The situations which we have described are truly significant. The system of the family enterprise found in the Marche region centres around the productive organization of small or medium-sized enterprises in a peripheral situation (in relation to the more important industrial areas and to the central seats of political power). Public resources play a minimal role, and the entire system is built around the maximization of the work role and the resources which are derived from it. The family system in the areas of subsidized economy gravitates entirely around the resources of the public structures and their multiple 'fallouts' of personal and clientelary contacts. The patient putting-together of these casual fragments of distributed income allows the family to survive and even to be relatively well off, provided its roles are organized as a function of this structural element of the local economy. The system to be found in the metropolitan areas, comparable to situations studied in the urban areas of advanced capitalist societies, is based on a characteristic fusion of resources derived from roles in the labour market and resources from the public sector, generally in the form of services.[1]

In welfare-capitalist societies, as has been suggested initially and as the data prove, adequate living standards cannot be reached without disposing of work revenue from the labour market, of resources transferred from the public system and of resources produced through domestic

*Inchiesta (July–August 1977), pp. 11–16. This is a portion of a longer article which also contains detailed case studies of families.

195

work. The resources available to the family unit are therefore maximized, so long as the individual performs various types of activity, by compounding 'specialized' roles.

One can observe that in the life of the people studied there is a tremendous amount of commitment and fatigue involved in order to obtain resources. There is the vast quantity of work performed by women to handle family tasks. There is a mass of work produced in conditions which heighten its waste, in the bureaucratic apparatuses ranging from the school to the sanitary and welfare sectors and other public offices. There is the work of those who are looking for work in a labyrinth of recommendations, contacts to maintain, applications and waiting periods.

The organization of society as it is described does not allow (except for a minority, a social class we are not studying here) a respite from a life of constant work and tension. Everyone is heavily implicated in these conditions which are not chosen but assigned: youth in precarious work, women mainly in household work, men in the central age brackets and in the developed areas, in industrial work; in the Mezzogiorno in precarious activities financed by public funds, or in emigration. It is not that people work little; those who speak of a 'work dissatisfaction' in Italian society should reflect on these data. People work, but with low productivity and high waste margins, if one thinks in traditional terms. Conversely, there is an extraordinary flexibility in these work patterns which makes them uniquely adapted to a system of inequality, or irrationality, and of disorder. This type of work is indicative of an historically specific type of social organization, linked to the complex characteristics of the system as a whole. These different and flexible roles are needed by a system which is characterized by a very heavy exploitation of the regularly occupied work force, by a centralized and unbalanced territorial structure and by public bureaucratic apparatuses. This system is not one of 'continuous minimal adaptation' or of 'Levantine solutions', as has been said in the CENSIS (Centro Studi Investimenti Sociali) report,[2] but rather one linked to the needs of welfare capitalism. The problem has been under study for several years and it is the CENSIS researches which have documented it.

These researches have underlined the specially Italian aspect of this work phenomenon, characterized by a current phase of 'mediocrity in which adaptation is given priority to development', of degradation and stagnation. All these elements are seen as episodes in a story where 'our process and destiny of development towards becoming an advanced industrial society have not been accomplished'.[3] Against this interpretation, I would suggest another hypothesis, namely, that the Italian case is instead directly linked to the problems of other advanced capitalist countries. The dysfunctions and contradictions are not the product of an interruption in or distortion of the process of development but are intrinsic to the very model of development which these systems embody.

Many developments in current American society – to use the most significant example – can be interpreted in this light. Without entering into the subject I shall merely mention the literature which has developed on the interpretations of the current phase as that of a 'service society'[4] where the increasing weight of the service sector and the relevance of unpaid work in this category have been underlined, with all the consequences for the labour market and the political system. The multiple sociological studies on the organization of life in the 'affluent' sectors as well as in the 'welfare' sectors of American society could yield a useful documentation and description for this interpretation.

There is a need to clarify these problems, to render explicit alternative interpretations and to define a basic level where it is important to examine the context of the reference we are using.

Such a task goes well beyond the purposes of this contribution. Nevertheless, as we have mentioned, all institutions are so interrelated and interdependent that it is impossible to analyse the family (or the labour market, the welfare system and even the political system) without referring to this more complex level of analysis.

How the family functions under welfare capitalism

A preliminary point: the family unit is the locus in which all types of activities and roles are combined and added. It is precisely because resources are maximized inside the family through the interpenetration of roles that the principal goals deemed central in our society can be attained: a state of well-being through an accepted standard of living.

It is important that the family group be internally differentiated, with specialized roles in a society which offers different types of resources to satisfy all needs and where the objective is to seize as many of these resources as possible.

Given these observations, there is a first methodological point which should be raised and which fits in the labour market debate: how does one evaluate the variables linked to the presence on the labour market of different types of persons – youths, adult males, women with families and elderly persons? It would be a too mechanistic and grossly functional answer to say that such a varied presence reflects the most functional division of roles in the family for the maximization of resources. This analysis does suggest, however, that the mechanisms to be reconstructed are more complex than certain interpretations (based on the centrality of the 'offer' and 'supply' factors in the labour market) would suggest. Other elements – such as the ways of using the resources of the state apparatus and the internal organization of the family – appear to be as important in structural terms as those dictated by the logic of the labour market in a welfare-capitalist system.

Another point must also be stressed: it is obvious that these families are not only the centre for biological reproduction and the place for the expression of affection. They are also a centre for 'the compensation of revenues',[5] 'agencies for the production of a composite revenue', 'decision-making centres for expenses', 'decision-making centres for productive and occupational choices'.[6]

Once these aspects are recognized as being central to the functioning of a family, then the apparent differences in family grouping, assigned roles, combination or resources, etc. are seen as differences in organizational models behind a single logic, that of the maximization of resources in a welfare-capitalist society. Different family units develop great capacities of invention and adaptation and there are numerous concrete solutions, but the possibility of real choice is limited to a series of marginal variations around very precise constraints.

In certain situations a solution is found so that women can have remunerated work without diminishing in any way their contribution to domestic work. In other situations, their domestic work 'alone' is seen as a sufficient contribution to the resources of the family. In certain cases retired persons can continue to perform a job, so the family unit keeps them 'inside' and uses them. But once the weight they represent becomes greater than the resources they bring in (when women must use part of their time to take care of them, time which could be used in other tasks), then they are put in old people's homes. School attendance among youths is widespread, but where the opportunity arises for these youths and even youngsters to contribute to the resources of the family they are put to work. In this society of mass education, the work of minors and of youth is still a reality which concerns millions.[7] One must confront these facts if this is the model of family organization for millions of families in Italy. I shall refer later to this point: if it is true that in Italy after the Second World War such a family model has generalized itself, what are the factors which caused it and what do they imply today? I shall briefly consider here what can be fruitfully used for the current debate on the family from the material presented earlier.

Confronted by the multiplicity of roles and by the human solidarity towards a common goal present within the family, some underline its continued validity and its permanence. They claim that the family is not in crisis, that it works very well and that it is necessary that it continues to 'hang on'. It is quite obvious that the family plays an important part in the system as a whole and that it has remarkable capacities of adaptation and modification in relation to the needs of continuity of the system. But such a family is united around a 'puny' accounting of the forces and needs of everyone. It survives at the condition that all conform to it; it cannot tolerate autonomy or diversity.

The need for interdependent and specialized roles inside the family for the maximization of resources implies that there is a very strong pressure which obliges individuals to define themselves and to live in terms of the roles which are assigned to them. In order to function such a family organization must be 'normal' and based on solidarity: i.e. all should accomplish the assigned tasks; all must play by the rules of the game; there must be an authority structure and a common recognition of such an authority. A 'deviant' family – with members who are incapacitated, sick or simply incapable of sustaining the imposed rhythm; or with an 'excessive' number of non-productive members, small children, elderly persons, or invalids; in which the criteria for authority distribution and of family solidarity are questioned – cannot function. Only those who are well, who have a regular family and who conform to the rules survive.

The political implications are clear. This type of society needs a family which functions in this manner, and this type of family generates conditions and controls individuals. The ways might be different. We can only imagine what the daily experience of personal relations, the self-image and the living conditions might be for the women of the Sicilian villages, in the putting-out system of the Marche or in the peripheral neighbourhoods of the big industrial cities; for the children and adolescents in all these contexts where there is no space for their specific needs; for the men in their condition of 'public' life, in their definition of work, in their social relations and in the authority exercised in 'private'. We can only imagine these experiences because they are not conveyed in any type of data. But one can readily apprehend the amount of individual constriction and the mechanism of conformism which underlie all these lives. These problems have been constantly underlined. It is now possible and necessary to go further and to discover how these different contexts work, what lies behind them and how real families function in the Italian society of today.

Laura Balbo

The miracle years and the crisis years: the end of welfare capitalism?

The material and the interpretations presented here refer to the 1960s
and the beginning of the 1970s up to the crisis. By having reconstructed
the preceding situation we can better confront the fundamental problem
behind all these reflections: what is happening today and what can we
expect faced by the crisis of welfare capitalism?

The data we have analysed seem to suggest that the welfare-capitalist
'formula', all things considered, has managed to hold its own in the last
years and that with respect to the demand for change, the resistances
and the choice of conservation of the system will be very strong. I suggest on the contrary that the particular synthesis and model of welfare
capitalism which we have examined is definitively impossible to attain in
Italy. This hypothesis should lead to further extensive research.

The research work, the collection of documents and their interpretation – needs to be entirely carried out, not by dwelling on what is already
understood but by going further. In this context, I suggest three approaches: (1) how to set up a historical research study of welfare capitalism in Italy since 1945; (2) how to set up a comparative analysis; (3) how
to study the actual phase.

One can distinguish three phases in the postwar period: the years of
the 'miracle' in which the objectives of all families were centred on the
development of private consumption; the years in which public intervention extended itself and public expenses expanded (in the second
half on the 1960s), with the particularly Italian characteristic of scarce
investments in collective structures;[8] the actual phase in which it has become clear that welfare capitalism cannot be realized. Already hampered
in its development towards a welfare-capitalist society, Italy is now hit by
the crisis more strongly than other 'advanced' countries.

The term 'crisis' refers to the increase in the cost of living and the
worsening of the financial burden of families; the reduction in revenue
through unemployment or through benefits, or for the young the lack
of access to the labour market; and the reduction or worsening of public
services because of cuts in public expenditures. For family budgets, this
implies that there is less money, that with the same money one can buy
less and that the public sector, which is already inadequate, furnishes
fewer services and of worse quality. It means that the welfare capitalism
of the 1960s and early 1970s does not hold up even to our very modest
standard as a 'welfare consumer society'. But even Great Britain is dismantling her welfare state, and in the United States the growth of welfare benefits in the second half of the 1960s, which had held together a
capitalist system characterized by extreme inequality and deep contra-

200

dictions, has now stopped and has become the object of political clashes. The crisis which has struck the capitalist system has revealed certain structural constraints: there is no returning to the model of the past years, probably for none of the Western societies, and certainly not for Italy where the margin of possibilities is particularly narrow. Therefore an historical and comparative analysis, with references to other welfare countries appears immensely enlightening. The study of the current phase must be linked to the following three levels of analysis, in order not to remain confined to abstractions: (a) territorial organization; (b) the type of formation and structure of revenues; (c) accessibility to the services of the public sector.

Territorial organization

In the last thirty years Italian society has undergone profound transformations in relation to the distribution of productive activities, population and welfare structures in the national territory. Today one must distinguish between metropolitan agglomerates in the industrialized areas of the North, cities like Rome, and the great non-industrialized urban centres of the South. One must also distinguish between 'peripheral' areas of an urban–rural type with the diffusion of decentralized industrial activities, and other areas, rendered different by the types of public services available for the family units. Depending on the territorial situation in which the family finds itself, it will have to adapt and combine different types of resources in its organization. Furthermore, the territorial set-up which determines costs and dysfunctions, leads to new inequalities and therefore to differentiated needs. Health needs, access to information, cultural and recreational services, as well as the living situations of families differ markedly depending on whether they live in the good neighbourhoods of a big city, in the dormitories in the periphery, in the rustic dwellings at the edges of the urban agglomerates, in the villages in areas of exodus or in cities in the provinces. The needs of families change therefore in terms of their territorial location: if in the cities, which cities and in which neighbourhoods. It is at this type of level which an analysis of the family under welfare capitalism should address itself.

Type of formation and revenue structure

The transformation of the productive structure and of the job market since the Second World War can be summarized in the following manner: the percentage of agricultural workers decreased dramatically, while the percentage of the population active in dependent industrial or tertiary work has become the predominant majority. The development of the economy in these two sectors (strictly related to international economic events); the choices of the bourgeoisie and the parties which represent it; the organization of the working-class movement and its trade union force have been elements used in order to explain: the global resources produced by Italian society; which percentage is due to the work factor; with what criteria this percentage is divided among the different work forces.

The essential fact, in terms of family units and the satisfaction of their needs, is that Italy remains a very strongly stratified society in terms of revenue-distribution. Many analyses have brought out the emergence of new mechanisms of inequality. For vast strata of the middle classes as well as of the working class a situation of 'tutelage' developed in terms of work and salary stability: despite the inflationary process, for a fairly long period a relevant percentage of the population registered a constant increase in real wages and an increasing protection (consolidation of trade union rights, especially through the Statuto dei Lavoratori; unemployment benefits; public intervention in situations of crisis in enterprises; privileges for employees of the public sector). Conversely, other categories of the population have experienced, increasingly in these last years, processes of exclusion and marginalization from the labour market (unemployment of youths, female illegal work and the exclusion of the elderly).

Accessibility to services of the public sector

The transferral of public funds, used in part to compensate for these inequalities and also for other reasons which we cannot consider here, increased substantially in the 1960s and became in the 1970s a relevant element in the greater number of family budgets.[9] These services are distributed unequally, however, whether they be transferrals of money (pensions, subsidies or financing of studies), or services and community structures (transportation, hospitals and schools). Different social categories are protected differently by the umbrella of public services. The needs of the beneficiaries also differ in the North and in the South, in the big metropolitan areas, in small and medium-size cities and in the countryside. Since a great portion of public financing is funnelled through local governments, the political 'colour' and choices of the different administrations influence the manner in which these resources are distributed. It is therefore essential that the analysis of the welfare system be carried out at the territorial level. Only in these terms can one apprehend the relationship between family organization and other institutions in this phase of crisis. The last variable in our analysis to be considered is the rigidity of all these elements, which conditions all possible hypotheses of change in Italian society.

This rigidity – which is not an abstract concept but a precise historical fact, as I will show briefly – is the product of two types of conditions. The first, linked intrinsically to the welfare-capitalist formula as we have described it in its different changes, is built on a rigid network of interdependent variables which are used to the utmost of their functioning capacity.[10]

The second condition is the hardest to analyse and cannot be defined in precise terms. It is a 'cultural perception', to use an expression which is not satisfactory. Nevertheless its crucial significance in this period of Italian history must be underlined.

Italian society reached relatively adequate and generalized levels of well-being for the first time after the Second World War. If we compare living standards for the Italian population during the 1960s and the 1970s with those 'before': during Fascism, the war years and reconstruction (to refer only to the second half of the century) there is a marked contrast. From a society with a low consumption, with little access to fundamental goods such as health and education and in a condition of precariousness and insecurity, there has been a shift towards a society in which the majority has job security, consumption above the subsistence level and access to education and health protection. The development of the 1950s and 1960s and the struggles of the working class which obtained guarantees (a cost of living index, unemployment benefits, trade union and pension rights) have profoundly modified the Italian reality.

This process took place in the space of a single generation, the generation consisting of today's adults, with the concrete implication that this experience of change is part of the life of the majority of the population. For the great majority of adults and elderly persons there is, before the shift to the 'Italian miracle', the memory of the autarchic economy of Fascism, of the war and of the first postwar phase. In the life experience of these adults there is no other potential road to well-being beyond the model of the 1960s and 1970s. This fact explains the resistance towards change, the defence of one's living standard, obtained and maintained through hard sacrifices. It is in this light that one should study individual, family and corporative interests in their organization and aggregation. One cannot underestimate the weight of these elements of flux, opposition and fear of change.

These are the factors of rigidity which are undoubtedly present in the

Laura Balbo

current situation. From the opposite end, however, there is another equally precise historical datum, emanating from the younger generations and from those social groups which were kept on the margin of the 'miracle', both of which have now acquired self-consciousness. In a context in which the aspiration towards a better life-style was until recently legitimized and diffused, youths and women in particular, frustrated in their quest for these benefits, are becoming conscious of the fact that this formula no longer produces the well-being which they sought, and they advocate major change. For these groups, not only is it out of the question to turn the clock back but even the current style of life is unacceptable. This is the meaning behind the protests and proposals of movements of the young as well as of women. Their goal of a better life assumes a completely different significance from that proposed by the model of welfare capitalism; indeed it is in opposition to the type of life conditions which were made possible by the current system.

It is precisely the conditions determined by the crisis, which is irreversible, that give an objectively innovative role to these actors and carriers of new demands. In the current phase, therefore, there is a particularly strong confrontation between conservative forces and interests and those advocating change. It is to this struggle that we must look.

I will not go further in these brief reflections. The difficulty and ambition of such a project of analysis is quite obvious. But if we want to understand the developments going on today inside Italian society it is necessary to realize that we are witnessing the end of welfare capitalism and the passage towards a new phase.

Notes

[1] For an analysis in this perspective of American and English society see L. Balbo, 'Stati Uniti, Gran Bretagna e Italia negli anni del benessere' in L. Balbo, *Stato di Famiglia* (Milan 1976).

[2] These terms are used in the *IX Rapporto sulla situazione sociale del paese 1975, Considerazioni Generali*. The data comes from the Ninth Report and from the volume *L'occupazione occulta* (Milan 1976) and also the Tenth Report, 1976.

[3] *IX Rapporto*, p. 25.

[4] I am briefly indicating some of the recent contributions in this current of analysis: V. Fuchs, *The Service Economy* (New York 1969); A. Gartner & F. Riessman, *The Service Society and the Consumer Vanguard* (New York 1974); Manuel Castells, 'The Service Economy and Postindustrial Society. A Sociological Critique', *International Journal of Health Services*, vol. 6, no. 4 (1976), pp. 595–607.

[5] 'The image of the family which emerges from this research is characterized by the summing up of various revenues and services performed by other members of the family (women, youths, elderly) around the central stable revenue generally earned by the adult male (the head of the family) who guarantees

social services to all. The added side revenues are mainly the product of precarious or discontinuous work, often undeclared and therefore deprived of any protection or guarantees. The family therefore presents itself as a "reservoir", as a "compensating chamber for revenues" on the one hand and as the centre of production of services on the other, which enable it to have a determined standard of living . . .'. *Disoccupazione giovanile o piena sottoccupazione?* Atti del Convegno del Consiglio di Zona CGIL–CISL–UIL, Ferrara 1975 (Rome 1977), p. 72.

[6] These terms are all used in the CENSIS report.

[7] In this context the data linked to the prolongation of schooling as well as those which are beginning to emerge on the work activities of the students are highly relevant. These data are the result of a research carried out in Ferrara among high school students in 1975. The finding was that 61 per cent of the boys and 69.7 per cent of the girls had work activities. *Disoccupazione.*

[8] 'Transfers to the families were accentuated with an ever-growing accent on individual monetary redistribution of revenue, at the expense of the satisfaction of the so-called collective consumption; social uses were rapidly translated into investments in telephone and highway networks, in the rise of traditional expensive construction industries, in the astronomical rise in health costs due principally to the rise in hospital fees between 1968 and 1969.' G. Amato, *Economia politica e istituzioni in Italia* (Bologna 1976), p. 26. 'Public expenditure becomes an uncontrollable avalanche. . . . The faults could not be alleviated by the fiscal mechanism, which in other countries could recover the margins lost in transferrals. In Italy revenues were always inferior to the increases of these profit margins.' *Ibid.*, p. 28.

[9] A research on the pattern and distribution of pensions has been carried out at the University of Ancona. The first published data have appeared in Ada Becchi Collidà, 'Donne assistite e controllo del consenso', *Cittaclasse*, no. 11–12 (April–May 1977) and M. A. Cappiello, 'Evoluzioni delle pensioni', *INPS*.

[10] I have tried to provide more precise indications on this matter in another article, 'Le radici profonde del consumismo', *Rinascita*, nos. 17, 34 (29 April 1977).

Editor's note:
Since the appearance of this article the results of this type of research have come out in book form: L. Balbo & R. Zahar, *Interferenze: lo stato, la vita familiare, la vita privata* (Milan 1979); M. Paci, *Famiglia e mercato del lavoro in un'economia periferica* (Milan 1980).

11. Class Structure in Italian Society[*]

Massimo Paci

Class structure in Italian society presents some important specific characteristics in relation to other 'advanced' capitalist countries. I shall deal with these specific characteristics especially, using statistical and descriptive material which has only recently become available, following on new research and studies in this field. Then, as a conclusion to this paper, I shall deal with the problem of interpreting these specific characteristics, asking particularly whether they should be put down to the 'backwardness' (or insufficient development) of Italian capitalism or, whether we should rather see them as the expression of the Italian economy's 'peripheral' position inside the Western capitalist system.

Class structure in the agricultural sector

What strikes us above all in the Italian situation is the persistence of a large agricultural sector. According to the 1971 Census the population active in agriculture was as large as about 3½ million. Furthermore, this number must be considered erroneous because of a defect in the census: it excludes an important part of the population which, because of the precarious nature of its work (agricultural day-labourers or old farmer-owners of tiny plots of land) is not considered part of the 'active' agricultural population. By and large we can estimate this number to be at least one million people; this would take the number of people actively occupied with agriculture up to a good 4½ million.[1] Finally it is very important to bear in mind that in Italy 'part-time farming' is particularly widespread, both at the individual level (as one person's double income) and at the family level (as the presence in the peasant family of a 'guest' member, occupied prevalently in the extra-agricultural sectors). On this phenomenon there do not exist any precise data at a national level: according to a recent sample poll, the people with a 'second job' in agriculture are more than half a million.[2] According to another less recent survey, however, the 'guest' members of peasant families (occupied

[*] First published in *Archives Européennes de Sociologie*, xx (1979), 40–55. Reprinted by permission.

mainly in extra-agricultural sectors) were as many as 1,250,000.[3] The difference between the two numbers can be due to the fact that a large part of the agricultural activity of 'guest' members is not easily ascertainable through surveys on 'second jobs', as this activity is only for family consumption, in most cases being just the looking after a small holding.

Inside the agricultural sector there exist important class differences. There are, above all, 1,200,000 agricultural wageearners, only a part of whom, however, have a stable job all the year round. This part is estimated differently by all the various writers who have occupied themselves with the problem.[4] At the opposite pole of the social stratification of the countryside we find the agricultural upper class, made up of large landowners and the managers of the great farms run on capitalist lines: these, in 1971, did not amount to more than 15,000. It is they, however, who employ the majority of agricultural wageearners, especially the 'stable' ones. Next to these two 'polar' classes, coherent with the Marxist dichotomic model of class structure, there is a large mass of independent farmers, who must be divided into at least three different social strata: the 'capitalist peasants', the 'middle peasants' and the 'poor peasants'. In terms of numbers, taking into consideration the estimations of the various writers in this field, we can estimate the number of 'capitalist peasants' (that is, those who are owners of middle-sized farms which they run by using wageearning labour) at about 350,000; the middle peasants on the other hand (defined as owners of middle and small-sized farms, run mainly or exclusively with family labour) come to about 1½ million; and the poor peasants, last of all owners of small and very small farms, come to about 1,400,000.[5] 'Part-time farming' is widespread among the middle peasants and above all among the poor peasants.[6]

To have a clearer picture of the relative importance of the various social strata identified in this way we must add some more information concerning the agricultural land used by the various social figures. At first sight, one might have the impression of a structure of agricultural property without any clear class 'fractures'. This is not so, however, if we bear in mind that the capitalist farms (whose profits as we have already seen go to no more than 15,000 large landowners or managers of large shareholders' companies) themselves hold about 27 per cent of the national agricultural land. If to this we add the farms of the capitalist peasants (who as we have already said come to 350,000 in 1971) the proportion of used agricultural land is as much as 45 per cent of the national total.[7] The very large majority of the peasant population, made up of almost 3 million middle and poor peasants, holds little more than half of all the available agricultural land.[8]

Another important differentiating element to bear in mind in describing Italian class structure is the difference between the regions of the Centre–North and the South. In the South, in fact, we find by far the largest number of seasonal and day-labourers (estimated by some writers at as many as 900,000) and the greatest part of poor peasants (as many as 600,000 out of the 750,000 peasants to be found in the South).[9]

But to have a better idea of the social stratification in the Southern country areas we must introduce another level especially relevant in these regions: that of the 'emigrant peasant (or farm labourer)'. In fact, over two-thirds of emigration in Italy, which between 1958 and 1970 kept up an average of over 200,000 per year, came from the South.[10] During all these years, furthermore, 65 to 70 per cent of the flow of migrations was made up of people coming from agriculture, either directly or indirectly by the intermediary passage through the building sector.[11] This migration mainly towards European countries is substantially different from the overseas emigration of one time, because of its 'temporary' nature: we can see in fact a change in the immigration policies of European countries, which rather than assimilation prefer more and more the constant changing of foreign labour and a periodical repatriation of immigrants after relatively short periods of permanent residence abroad (from about one to three years). The temporary nature of emigration means that the emigrants do not completely cut off their ties with their own country; many keep tiny plots of land, cultivated only in part by some relative who has stayed on in the village, or they are left completely uncultivated.[12] The little holding remains a fundamental base for the economic subsistence of these families, both for domestic consumption and as a means of obtaining in a politico-electoral way different forms of subsidies and public assistance (Common Market price integration, state contributions in case of hail or bad weather, unemployment indemnities for day-labourers, etc.).[13]

On the whole it is evident that to be able to interpret class differences existent in Italian agriculture we have to refer to an articulated model, built up on the basis of some of the categories worked out by Marx in his analysis of social production relations and the labour market in capitalist society. So it is evident that, as we have already noted, there is a confrontation between the two 'polar' classes of the Marxian dichotomic model, based on the criterion of possession/non-possession of means of production. In relation to this we must emphasize that these two classes, which are the only ones that are really productive for the agricultural consumer market, are increasing in numbers slowly but surely; in fact both the capitalists and the capitalist peasants (favoured as they are by the selective nature of the agricultural policies of the Italian government and the Common Market) and the wageearners are increasing, even though the development of agricultural mechanization puts a limit to the possibility of absorbing the labour force into the capitalist agricultural sector. On the other hand, the fact that the sphere of capitalist production has already covered half of the national agricultural land, and is tending to increase, is sufficient in itself to exclude interpretations of class structure based on the hypothesis of the 'backwardness' of Italian agriculture.

On the other hand it is also true that, side by side with this capitalist sector, there exists the vast proportion of 'poor' peasants' farms, made up of tiny holdings in the mountainous interior and the South of Italy especially, holdings which have absolutely no real productive function. This area has served for many years partly as a kind of 'reserve industrial army', giving away the best of its labour force to internal and international emigration.[14] Today, however, for those who have remained (mainly women and aged people), it has another function. These fringe elements of poor peasants or in the process of pauperization cannot be explained as a class either on the basis of the Marxian dichotomic scheme of the classes inside the 'sphere of production' or on the basis of the principle of the 'reserve industrial army' but need to be described by means of other analytical tools. The hypothesis that can be formulated in this respect is that we have before us one of the aspects assumed, in the contemporary phase of monopolistic capitalism, by the process of consolidation at the edges of productive section of economy, of an ever-growing number of the population on the way to pauperization.[15] In the majority of the more advanced capitalist countries the state takes it upon itself directly to give the necessary 'assistance' to this growing marginal mass of the population; in the Italian situation, a not negligible part of this function is still carried out by subsistence agriculture. This assistential function of agriculture becomes furthermore proportionally more important as emigration to other European countries (and especially Switzerland and Germany) takes on more and more the aspects of short-term and precariousness (referred to above). On the other hand, this large section of peasants has managed to survive up to now also thanks to the policy of subsidies, direct and indirect, carried out by the state in the country areas, by means of the 'client–boss' relationship at local level. This type of policy – whose roots go deep into the Fascist period[16] – if it has not had much success in preventing the deterioration of living conditions in the country and the gradual process of pauperization of wide sections of the peasant community, has had far from insignificant political and ideological consequences, when we consider the moderate, not to say conservative electoral orientation which has up to now continued to be a fundamental characteristic of these strata, which, from this point of view, cannot be transferred in one blow from the peasant petit bourgeoisie to the agricultural proletariat.[17]

Quite a large number of middle and small peasants, mainly spread over the hill and valley areas of Central and Northern Italy, have managed, however, to avoid – at least up to the present day – the family disintegration, social emargination and pauperization which have struck the poor peasants of the mountain regions and the South. This has been mainly thanks to the spreading of 'part-time farming', that is, thanks to the possibility of making up an agricultural income with that coming from an extra-agricultural job, mainly industrial, on the part of one or more members of the family. Inside this social layer characterized by 'part-time farming' we find a wide range of social figures: we go from the peasant family owning an average-size farm, in which the extra-agricultural income of one of the members is only a source of ready cash for the running of the farm (which remains the principal activity of all the family), to the factory worker family which forms a tiny holding or allotment for its own use. Industrial home-work is also very widespread in the peasant family; this kind of work, sometimes procured by an intermediary, sometimes by an actual member of the family who is himself an industrial worker, is usually done by the wife, helped by the very young and the very old of the family.[18] At a hundred years from the beginning of Italian industrial development, the link between industry and agriculture, which was seen immediately to be a specific element in the national economy, has not lost its importance. The function that agriculture has in this case is essentially the basic one of family consumption, and the lowering of costs of reproduction of the industrial labour force.[19] Not by chance, this section of 'part-time' peasants is most widespread in the areas of greatest development of small and medium manufacturing industry, for which, as we shall see later, the compression of the cost of labour is an indispensable condition for its existence.

Class structure in industry and services

Also inside the extra-agricultural sectors a complex social stratification can be discerned. As for the industrial sector, next to the real industrial bourgeoisie, made up of 100,000–150,000 entrepreneurs and managers of big firms, we find a consistent number of petit bourgeoisie, made up of about 750,000 small entrepreneurs and artisans. This wide diffusion of small independent activities in industry is a specific feature of the Italian situation, which is not to be found to the same degree in any other advanced capitalist country (with the possible exception of Japan). As for the industrial proletariat, this seems very large and with important internal stratifications. The estimation of the size of the industrial proletariat varies according to the various authors, not only because of the different definitions adopted by them but also because of the unreliability of official statistics which do not take in the whole population active in the industrial sector, but neglect – as we have seen happen in the case of the agricultural sector – a consistent part of precarious or part-time workers.

However, it can be said that the industrial proletariat is composed of not less than 5½ million,[20] even if according to some investigators this number should be considerably increased.[21] It is important to note that even if we take the more conservative estimate the number of the industrial population in relation to the whole active population of Italy is very high, reaching (in 1971) 33 per cent, a percentage higher than in any other Western country, with the exception of Germany. Furthermore, it must be noted that the territorial concentration of the Italian industrial proletariat is very dense, reaching – in the Northern regions of Italy – about 41 per cent of the total active population, a percentage which makes this one of the areas of highest worker density in Europe. (We must remember that the agricultural proletariat is also very numerous, taking on, especially in the large farms of the Po plain, all the characteristics of the working class.) Without wishing to exaggerate the importance of these purely descriptive figures, it is evident that the diffusion and territorial concentration of the Italian proletariat must be taken into account when explaining why Italy has – in terms of electoral organization and behaviour – the strongest Communist Party in the West.

On the other hand, behind these global figures relating to the industrial proletariat, there hides a quite complex reality. What has been called the 'dualism' of the Italian industry, in fact, is reflected clearly in the composition of the working class. By dualism in Italian industry we refer to various phenomena dealt with by various writers who have occupied themselves with the problem; some have emphasized the territorial aspect and thus the difference between the North and the South of the country; others have emphasized the differences between the 'modern' industries and 'traditional' ones; others still have pointed out the dichotomy between the large and the small industrial firms.[22]

All these aspects undoubtedly describe important differences which exist in the Italian industrial structure and which are then reflected in the internal stratification of the proletariat. However, not all have the same theoretic relevance. The least significant fact is certainly that of territory. In reality the composition of the industrial proletariat takes on specificity in the South only because of the interindustry matrix and size characteristics of Southern industry. Also the differences between 'mod-

211

ern' industrial sectors and 'traditional' must not be exaggerated: on the whole, as we shall see better in our conclusion, we must rather emphasize the substantial homogeneity and specialization of production in the Italian manufacturing industry, as an industry that produces consumer goods destined mainly for export, and in particular, for the markets of advanced capitalist countries.[23] The main difference between industries is that between manufacturing industry as a whole and the building industry; the latter, in fact, which has developed rapidly following on the frenetic process of urbanization which Italy has had in these last thirty years, seems to be characterized by the presence of a vast seasonal and fluctuating proletariat, made up often of ex-peasants or ex-day-labourers, waiting to pass on to the manufacturing industrial sector but often destined to emigrate abroad or to swell the number of unemployed and urban lumpenproletariat.

The most important aspect of industrial 'dualism', is, however, connected with the dichotomy between large and small firms; the structure of the Italian manufacturing industry, in terms of firm size is bottom-heavy, because of the large number of firms with fewer than 100 workers, even though there are a not insignificant number of large firms (with more than 1,000 employees); this is a fact which is not reflected in other advanced industrial countries.[24] We shall see later on what reasons can be given for this particular structure of firm sizes in Italian industry; here we should underline the fact that this structure influences the composition of the working class considerably. In fact, on the one hand, there is a considerable number of workers occupied in the big industrial firms, both private and public, a proletariat which has obtained in the last ten–fifteen years important improvements in wages and conditions, thanks both to trade union action (which is especially strong here) and legislative interventions as regards workers' rights, which cannot very easily be eluded in these firms. (According to some writers,[25] this has resulted in a 'guaranteed' status of occupation for this layer of workers, forming part of what we might define as the 'central' industrial proletariat.) On the other hand, there is the large mass of workers in the small factories, artisan workers and industrial home-workers, often in 'irregular' work conditions, tied to 'part-time farming' situations, hardly ever protected by the trade unions; this 'peripheric' section of the Italian industrial proletariat, much more widespread than in other countries, has received in these last years a new impulse following on the restructuring process going on within large firms themselves, many of which have begun to 'disembody' or 'decentralize' part of their production, and subcontract it to the small firm sector.[26]

In terms of numbers we can say that over half of the Italian industrial proletariat is made up of workers belonging to the 'peripheric' sector.[27] These, however, are always estimated on the basis of official statistics, which are particularly defective in ascertaining this type of occupational strata (industrial home-work, part-time work, etc.).[28]

From the point of view of territory, it is possible to characterize Central Italy and Northeast Italy as the areas of small and 'peripheric' proletariat; the Northwest regions making up the so-called 'industrial triangle' have the largest density of large private firms, even if around them there prospers a thick network of small and very small production units, so that the local working class includes, next to the more important 'central' proletariat nuclei, a vast section of 'peripheric' proletariat. Finally, in the South, we have seen in these last years, on the one hand, the disintegration of the texture of small-artisan and traditional industrial activities (which has fed partly emigration abroad and partly the building industry proletariat, and that underemployment typical of the large metropolitan areas of the South), and, on the other hand, the emergence of important 'central' working-class nuclei, following on the setting-up in the south of large, prevalently public firms.

The size structure of Italian industry, furthermore, does not influence only the composition of the proletariat, but also that of the lower middle classes. In fact, Italy is remarkable for its very low percentage of private white collar workers in the active national total. This percentage is 8.9 (corresponding to 1,759,000) whereas it rises to 19.3 in France, 23.4 in Great Britain, and 24.1 in the United States.[29] Evidently in a production structure dominated by small firms, the lower middle classes are made up rather more of artisans and 'small owners' than of 'white collar' workers.

A social group which is especially developed, on the other hand, is that of public 'white collar' workers, which involves about a million people, to which number must be added about 600,000 school and university teachers. This considerable development of public employment, however, according to many observers, does not mean an expansion of state intervention in support of the production sector but rather expansion of the unproductive and 'parasitic' sectors.[30] Indirect proof of this is the fact that public employment is particularly elevated in the regions of the South, that is, where the development of the production sector is less marked and the intervention of the welfare state is greater. From this point of view a conspicuous part of this public employment layer can be defined, in the same way as before in the case of the poor peasants, by recourse to the category of the 'assisted' surplus population.

Not unsimilar is the appraisal that can be given of the small traders, who make up 1,700,000; by far the majority of these small commercial firms, run generally by old people, obtain from their activities little more than subsistence.[31] The comparison of these with the layer of poor peasants is even more justified here. Also for a consistent part of this 'old' middle class we can say that it is tied – for its own survival – to the favours of political power (in particular to the policy of licence concession). In fact, both for the traders and peasants, it was Fascism that started and tested this policy of protection and assistance which has been followed, with few innovations, by the succeeding governments of the last thirty years.

On the whole it seems possible to point out the scarce utilization of intellectual resources available for productive ends. This fact is shown by the numbers cited in relation to the very low percentage of private employees and the hypertrophy of small-scale trade and 'parasitic' public employment. Finally, in this picture must be inserted the phenomenon of the intellectual unemployment of youth, which is much talked about in Italy today (as in almost all advanced capitalist countries). Following on the expansion of school at the middle and advanced levels, and the difficulties experienced by the young in finding work, a numerous social layer has been formed today composed largely of young students or new graduates in search of their first job. Certainly the process of mass scholarization has thrown the balance between supply and demand of the qualified work force right out. This crisis, furthermore, is particularly serious in Italy because of the antiquated structure of school and above all because of the weakness of the modern production sector. From this point of view the growing youth mass coming out of the higher schools is forming what I defined a few years ago as an 'educated surplus population'.[32]

Nevertheless, according to recent investigations, it appears that quite a high percentage of the students of the higher schools and university already have a job, very often in the manufacturing industries, even if in a precarious or irregular way.[33] On the other hand, research into outwork or 'irregular' work conditions in industry has come again and again upon the use of young people with a diploma or degree, outside any contractual regulation, doing work requiring a certain 'know-how', such as business accountancy, 'design', modelling, even planning. It is true that we still know very little about this irregular utilization of intellectual resources. However, what information has been collected, all over the country, is sufficient to make it clear that the official figures relating to private white collar workers employment underestimate the size of the educated work force needed by the production sector. The present process of restructuring and decentralizing in particular seem to be increasing the demand for educated 'irregular' work, involving in fact the young right from their years in school and university. If the development of studies in this field should verify the persistence of this phenomenon it would demonstrate that the mass of the young and students or new graduates may not entirely be labelled as 'assisted' surplus population. In fact, side by side with the 'peripheric' proletariat there exists, or is in the process of being formed, also a 'peripheric white collar class'.

Economic backwardness or peripheric development?

It is possible at this point to make explicit certain theoretic categories of Marxian derivation used in the preceding pages to describe Italian class structure.

Usually, when one wants to refer to the Marxian model of class analysis, one thinks only and exclusively of the fundamental dichotomy to be found in the 'sphere of production' between those who have the means of production and those who only offer their labour. But the theoretic scheme elaborated by Marx takes in a much wider area than the simple 'sphere of production'. In this context, for an analysis of social stratification, the category of surplus population which Marx conceived as the 'lever and product of accumulation' becomes particularly important; in fact it is possible to describe the numerous social strata exterior to the production sphere by referring to their position as surplus population strata which function as the 'lever' of capitalist accumulation (as for example the peasants and artisans of the past, destined to become wage-earners and enter industry) or which are the 'product' of capitalist accumulation (as the bureaucratic and parasite 'white collar' classes, or the various pauperized social classes directly or indirectly 'assisted' by the state).

During the whole historic phase of its rise as mode of production, capitalism had in all countries a predominance of the first type of relation between surplus population and production sphere: this explains, perhaps, why Marx – who lived in this stage of capitalist development – emphasized above all else the process of proletarization of the 'old' middle class of peasants and artisans. All those who limit the validity of the Marxian schemes to these aspects, however, show themselves to be bad readers of Marx: in more than one place he shows that he has realized the importance of the formation of a new bureaucratic–parasitic middle class 'maintained' substantially by the income produced by the classes involved in the sphere of production, as, also, he emphasizes more than once the relevance of the processes of pauperization which consolidate large areas of society on the edge of the system. The hypothesis which can be formulated as regards this is that – in the present phase of prolonged stagnation if not of incipient decline of capitalism as a mode of production – it is above all the process of formation of the second type of surplus population that dominates the scene.[34]

In the description of Italian class structure offered in the preceding paragraphs we have tried to show how, next to the classes directly involved in capitalist production relations in agriculture and industry, there exists in Italian society a variegated series of social strata whose common denominator today lies mainly in their nature as components or subspecies of the 'assisted' unemployed; a youth mass 'parked' in school; 'parasitic' public employees.

Naturally, between these strata there exist important differences, owing to the fact that the processes of social emargination from the sphere of production are in some cases accepted as a privilege (parasitic bureaucrats); in other cases borne passively (poor peasants and small traders) owing to the cliento-electoral relations with political power on which depends their survival; and finally in other cases (unemployed and students) they seem to cause forms of protest and conflict which are heterodox as compared to those traditionally expressed by the working class.[35] However, in my opinion, it is not only to these strata of surplus population that we should look, if we wish to arrive at the specific features of Italian class structure. These strata, in fact, can be found more or less in all other capitalist countries: perhaps Italy presents a greater number of small peasants and traders on the way to pauperization than other countries. But these strata – made up mainly of the aged – seem to be destined to gradual extinction in Italy too, if only for demographic reasons.

What specifically characterizes the class structure of Italy, instead, is the stratification inside the classes involved in the production sphere, and especially the strong presence of an industrial and artisan petit bourgeoisie and a vast 'peripheric' proletariat.

In other words, the greatest specificity of the Italian situation – and so the element which requires a further effort of interpretation in the application of the Marxian categories referred to before – must be seen in the persistence, beyond all expectation, of a vast area inside the sphere of production in which class relations are based on social figures which – according to a certain orthodox interpretation of the Marxian dichotomic scheme – should have disappeared altogether with the march of capitalist development.

In fact, many Italian investigators interpret these social figures (and especially the small industrial and artisan firm) as an expression of the 'backwardness' of Italian economic development in respect of that of other industrialized countries.[36] But this interpretation is unsatisfactory.

It does not succeed in explaining, in fact, why *after a hundred years of industrial development* – which after all there has been in Italy – our class structure is still so strongly 'unbalanced' in favour of the industrial petit bourgeoisie, the peasant and artisan family concern and the 'peripheric proletariat'. That is, the persistence of these social strata seems *so much a part of Italian development*[37] that it needs a different interpretation. This different interpretation, on the other hand, cannot be that given before for the majority of the strata of the surplus population, that is, their maintenance, direct or indirect, by the state for cliento-electoral or consensual ends.[38] In reality, these strata do not depend exclusively for their survival on the help of political power; they have an important productive function, contributing in a far from irrelevant way to the mechanism of national accumulation. (This is particularly evident in these years of industrial restructuring and decentralization in which we have seen a rebirth in grand style of the small firm and its 'halo' of peripheric proletariat.) So, in the Italian situation, the industrial petit bourgeoisie and the peripheric proletariat appear as a fact of structural importance connected with the productive vitality of the small industrial and artisan firm. It is the productive vitality of this small firm which ultimately we must try to explain.

The explanation, in my opinion, is to be found in the position of the Italian economy inside the Western capitalist system, which has caused a progressive specialization of our industrial apparatus towards certain products, for which the small firm is especially functional.[39] As we have already emphasized above, we can speak of a strong specialization of our manufacturing industry in the production of consumer goods destined mainly to the markets of more advanced countries. This type of manufacturing industry is strongly linked to two factors: the uncertainty of demand, always dependent on the rapid changes in fashion and consumption, and the 'maturity' of the existent technologies which are not susceptible to important labour-saving innovations.[40]

In other words, Italian industry, or by far most of it, has to produce consumer goods from a highly variable demand, with an extremely rigid and a high labour-intensive technology. In these conditions it is not by chance that the size-structure of industry is bottom-heavy, that is, with a great deal of small and very small production units; these units in fact manage to recover important margins of flexibility thanks to their use of 'peripheric proletariat'. (And, in this context, the maintenance of a 'worker–peasant' context tied to subsistence economy constitutes a further element of labour flexibility and of reduction of its costs of production.)

To sum up, the specificity of Italian class structure must be linked to

Massimo Paci

the position of our industrial economy at the periphery of the Western capitalist system. Italy has shared the development of this system in the last hundred years. So it is difficult to accept the idea of 'backwardness' (or of failure to develop) in the Italian economy. It is just the participation – as a peripheric unit – to the development of the whole system that has led to the progressive specialization of our production apparatus in certain manufacturing products, for which the micro-firm, based on the reduction of the cost of labour, seems more functional.

On the theoretical plane this means that the application of the Marxian dichotomic scheme to class relations in the sphere of production must take into account specific features of national history, which are specifically linked to the road taken by capitalist development in the various countries, inside the international division of production and relations of 'dominance–dependence' or 'centrality–periphery' which characterizes it.

Notes

[1] See G. Trigilia, 'Sviluppo, sottosviluppo e classi sociali in Italia', *Rassegna italiana di sociologia*, XVII (1976), 249–95; M. Fonte & M. Furnari, Struttura dell'occupazione precaria in agricoltura: in Italia e nel Mezzogiorno', *Rassegna economica*, XXXIX (1975), 751–80.

[2] Forme e caratteristiche della partecipazione al lavoro-principali risultati di una ricerca ISFOL–DOXA', *Osservatorio sul mercato del lavoro e delle professioni*, I (1975), 15–96.

[3] M. G. Eboli, 'Contributo per l'analisi delle classi in agricoltura', *Community Development*, XXI (1974), 97–118.

[4] See Trigilia, 'Sviluppo . . . in Italia'; Fonte & Furnari, 'Struttura . . . in agricoltura'.

[5] See Trigilia; Eboli, 'Contributo . . . in agricoltura'.

[6] Part-time work involves about 20 per cent of 'middle' peasants, and about 50 per cent of 'poor' peasants, see Eboli. See also C. Daneo, 'Capitalismo e riformismo nelle campagne italiane', *Inchiesta*, II (1972), 10–21; and C. Barberis, *Gli operai contadini* (Bologna 1970).

[7] G. Fabiani & M. Gorgoni, 'Una analisi della struttura dell'agricoltura italiana', *Rivista di Economia Agraria*, XXVIII (1973), 65–118.

[8] Actually, keeping in mind that a part of agricultural land is state-demesne and a part share-cropping, the peasants keep *less* than half of the national agricultural surface. See Fabiani & Gorgoni, 'Una analisi'.

[9] Trigilia, 'Sviluppo . . . in italia'. For analogous estimates see also P. Braghlin, E. Mingione & P. Trivellato, 'Per una analisi della struttura di classe nell'Italia contemporanea', *La critica sociologica*, XVII (1974), 70–116.

[10] G. Mottura & E. Pugliese, 'Mercato del lavoro e caratteristiche dell' emigrazione italiana nell'ultimo quindicennio', *Inchiesta*, II (1972), 2–14.

[11] U. Ascoli & S. Mantovani, 'Riflessi dell'emigrazione sullo sviluppo economico

italiano (1945–70)' in N. Federici (ed.), *L'emigrazione dal bacino mediterraneo verso l'Europa industrializzata* (Milan 1976).

[12] Ascoli & Mantovani.

[13] E. Reyneri, 'Il sistema dei sussidi', *Rinascita*, xxxiii (1976), 15–16.

[14] In connection with this we must remember that the population active in agriculture was cut by half in Italy between 1951 (the year in which it is higher than 8 million) and 1974.

[15] For a brief discussion of the categories of Marxian derivation used in the text, see the third paragraph above. For a limited bibliography of the matter see note 34.

[16] P. Ciocca & G. Toniolo (eds.), *L'Economia italiana nel periodo fascista* (Bologna 1976). See also the observation of V. Castronovo, 'Economia e classi sociali' *in* V. Castronovo (ed.), *L'Italia contemporanea: 1945–1975* (Turin 1976).

[17] The problems connected with the subjective dimension of social stratification or 'class consciousness' are only just touched in the text. However, there is no doubt that in a discussion about the class positioning of certain strata it is very important to keep in mind the role played by ideological and cultural factors on the class 'self-identification' of the strata involved. From this point of view it seems that those people are right who tend to place the majority of Italian peasants among the 'petty bourgeoisie' because of their political orientation, notwithstanding the objective processes of proletarization that they undergo. See P. Sylos Labini, *Saggio sulle classi sociali* (Bari 1974).

[18] On this subject, with reference to a local situation typical of Central Italy, see M. Paci (ed.), *Famiglia e mercato del lavoro in un 'economia periferica: il caso delle Marche* (Bologna 1980).

[19] *Ibid.* Various sources and studies indicate a number of industrial home-workers, mainly women, in Italy as high as two millions.

[20] Sylos Labini, *Saggio sulle classi sociali.*

[21] Trigilia, 'Sviluppo in Italia'; Braghin, Mingione & Trivellato, 'Per una analisi . . .'; see also L. Maitan, *Dinamica delle classi sociali in Italia* (Rome 1975).

[22] The debate over Italian industrial 'dualism' reaches far and wide. Recalling only some of the writers involved, it can be said that they put emphasis above all on the 'territorial' aspects of dualism: C. H. Hildenbrand, *Growth and Structure in the Economy of Modern Italy* (Cambridge, Mass. 1967) and C. P. Kindleberger, *Europe's Postwar Growth – The Role of Labor Supply* (Cambridge, Mass. 1967). The following however underline the interindustrial aspects in particular: A Graziani *et al.*, *Lo sviluppo di una economia aperta* (Naples 1969) and, more recently, M. Salvati, *Sviluppo economico, domanda di lavoro e struttura dell'occupazione* (Bologna 1975). The following, on the other hand, underline the dualism between big and small enterprise: V. Lutz, *Italy: A Study in Economic Development* (London 1962); M. Paci, *Mercato del lavoro e classi sociali in Italia* (Bologna 1973) and G. Fuà, *Occupazione e capacità productive: la realtà italiana* (Bologna 1976).

[23] G. Conti, 'Note sulla posizione relativa dell'Italia dal punto di vista della specializzazione internazionale delle produzioni' in A. Graziani (ed.), *Crisi e ristrutturazione dell'economia italiana* (Turin 1975).

[24] See, finally, the comparative data offered by Fuà, *Occupazione.*

[25] See R. Prodi, *Sistema industriale e sviluppo economico in Italia* (Bologna 1973); L. Gallino, 'Politica dell'occupazione e seconda professione', *Economia e Lavoro.* ix

Massimo Paci

(1975), 81–96. More in general, on the factors of 'rigidity' of the labour force occupied in the 'central' production sector see Paci, *Mercato del lavoro e classi sociali in Italia.*

[26] P. Calza Bini, 'Il dibattito sul mercato del lavoro: dalla caduta del tasso di attività al decentramento produttivo', *La critica sociologica*, XVIII (1975), 49–70; M. Paci, 'Crisi, ristrutturazione e piccola impresa', *Inchiesta,* XX (1975); A. Bagnasco & M. Messori, 'Problematiche dello sviluppo e questione della piccola impresa', *Inchiesta* VI (1976), 64–80.

[27] According to Sylos Labini, for example, the 'precarious' workers in industry came to about 2 million in 1971, and those working in firms of no more than 100 dependent workers were at that date 3,700,000 (of whom 1,600,000 in firms of no more than ten dependent workers). According to Trigilia, the 'precarious' proletariat amounted to 2½ million in the same year. According to Braghin, Mingionne & Trvellato, 'Per una anaisi . . .', the 'marginal' proletariat amounted in 1968 to 3,250,000.

[28] According to a vast poll conducted at national level in 1974, the active employment figures for the Italian population turned out to be 39.6 per cent higher, i.e., by 3.9 in respect to the official statistics. See the inquiry mentioned in note 2. As support for these figures, see also Fuá, *Occupazione.*

[29] These data are taken from Sylos Labini, *Saggio sulle classi sociali.*

[30] *Ibid.*

[31] See the analysis of the process of proletarization of a wide strata of small traders contained in Belloni, M. L. Bianco, A. Luciano, A. Picchieri, *Quaderni di Sociologia*, XXIII (1974), 157–250.

[32] See M. Paci, 'Istruzione e mercato capitalistico del lavoro', *Quaderni Storici*, XXII (1973); English translation: 'Education and the Capitalist Labor Market', *in* J. Karabel & A. H. Halsey (eds.), *Power and Ideology in Education* (New York 1977), pp. 340–55.

[33] *Disoccupazione giovanile e piena sotto-occupazione?* Acts of CGIL–CISL–UIL Congress of Ferrara, 12 Nov. 1976) (Rome 1977).

[34] The hypothesis of an accelerated growth of surplus population and of an intensification of the process of social emargination and pauperization is common in numerous Latin American Marxist investigators; see for example the anthology edited by Turnaturi, *Marginalità e classi sociali* (Rome 1975), and the school of North American neo-Marxists which has its origins in the theoretic work of Baran and Sweezy and the editing group of the *Monthly Review;* see, for all of these, the work of H. Bravermann, *Labor and Monopoly Capital: The Degradation of Work in the Twentieth Century* (New York 1974). In Italy, theoretic enquiries in this direction have been carried out by C. Donolo, 'Sviluppo ineguale e disgregazione sociale nel Mezzogiorno', *Quaderni Piacentini*, XI (1972), 101–29, and M. Paci, 'Teoria e metodo nello studio della mobilità sociale', *Studi di Sociologia*, XIII (1975), 3–29.

[35] For the movement of the 'organized unemployed', see E. Pugliese, 'Sviluppo e problemi attuali nel movimento dei disoccupati organizzati', *Fabbrica e Stato*, III (1976), 79–88.

[36] Among the many supporters of this interpretation, we must include Fuá, *Occupazione.*

[37] See M. Paci, 'Il mercato del lavoro dall'unità d'Italia ad oggi' in N. Tranfaglia (ed.), *Il mondo contemporaneo* (Firenze 1978), I, 629–48.

[38] This interpretation is that offered, for example, by A. Pizzorno, 'I ceti medi

220

del meccanismo del consenso' and by S. Berger, 'Uso politico e sopravvivenza dei ceti in declino', *in* Cavazza Graubard (eds.), *Il caso italiano* (Milan 1974).

[39] See M. Paci, 'Il costo del lavoro non è la variabile determinante', *Inchiesta*, VI (1976), 24–6.

[40] See Conti, 'Note sulle posizione relativa dell'Italia'.

V: Appendix

12. From Sociological Research to the Enquiry*

Vittorio Capecchi

To avoid any misunderstanding, it is important to formulate some premises on the role of the sociologist in Italy. Many of the considerations underlined above were derived from an American context in which the profession of the sociologist as 'expert' has a clearly consolidated role, in the same way as reviews like the *American Sociologist* or associations like 'Radical Sociology' have a clear professional meaning. In Italy the situation is completely different. This is not because of the limited quantity of empirical research published, fragmented in the most disparate fields, nor because of the fleeting professional role attributed to the sociologist (the most pervasive image is that of a distinguished gentleman *passe-partout,* capable of holding forth on topics ranging from football to drugs and whose only hobby is to intersperse his statements with the term 'social classes'); the difference comes from the fact that the number of 'official' sociologists is very small. In such a context the idea of creating an association of radical sociologists can only be a topic for jokes. In reality, the preoccupation with 'sociologists' and 'sociology' as such is somewhat meaningless.

We should calmly stop calling 'sociological' a whole set of legitimate interests on the problems of Italian society and consider instead, in its far wider context, the contradictory role of the intellectual (in Gramsci's sense) inside the class struggle. In such a context, performing an *enquiry* would mean using all types of methodological approaches (it is irrelevant whether these were born or baptised 'economic', 'psychological' 'sociological', 'political' or 'historical', etc.) in order to orient social practice. The purpose of this knowledge is to reach a politically relevant collective analysis in which different intellectual experiences are fused. This goal has nothing in common with the usual appeals for interdisciplinary stud-

* First published in P. Rossi (ed.), *Ricerca sociologica e ruolo del sociologo* (Bologna 1972), pp. 108–20.

ies (which have acted as an alibi to maintain specialized disciplines based on traditional scientific criteria). The search for knowledge with a political intent cannot be carried out by the usual solitary 'expert'. The only solution to the process of fragmentation of political and intellectual experiences is group work.

In order not to fall into the usual utopian 'good intentions' of the Left, it is important to stress the complexity of group work and how generalizations based on individual experiences can be particularly dangerous.[1]

Let us look concretely at the changes in the topics of research and in the role of the researcher brought about by a modified political practice. The professional researcher who has been isolated (i.e. linked to the academic community) will now have to work with a group in whose hands the organization of the enquiry will rest, a group which he can enter. It is one thing to postulate the idea of a group which is ideologically homogeneous and determined to carry out an enquiry (and composed of persons coming from different research and practical backgrounds). It is another matter to realize it.

The discrepancy between the pace of research and the pace of parallel political activity constitutes one of the major difficulties of such group work. There is always the tendency to return to traditional sociological research (even if with some superficial corrections) or to choose the path of political activity detached from a systematic and scientific reflection of the problems treated.

There are, however, encouraging prospects. Both the student movement and the working-class struggles have produced new groups which are fully capable of breaking away from an activism which is too tied to immediate events. They have also been responsible for the creation of local-level groups, especially among social workers and teachers. These groups can be very important starting points for enquiry activities in such areas as the school, social work, etc. Once the group which proposes to carry out an enquiry is constituted, the next key problem is determining who will be the research beneficiary, i.e. the concrete political outcome which the research seeks to attain. To claim that the research will benefit the most conscious and politically mature part of the subordinate classes amounts to little more than an intention. There is no point in reiterating the difficulty of translating a 'mass policy line' into concrete terms.

Let us consider instead the repercussions which different types of research sponsors can have on the unfolding of the enquiry. At least three types of sponsors are possible:

(a) *'A financial sponsor not interested in the political use of the results of the analysis and asking only for 'scientific' guarantees.* The strongest binds in this

224

case (besides those of research topic choice and implementation) are those linked to time delays. The National Research Centre (*CNR*), as well as various foundations, enter into this category; its members are best defined by their belief that the financing of research is an institutional duty and a prestige activity. Given the scarcity of data available at the national level, this type of research sponsor is extremely useful, even if the intense competition for funds makes it difficult to obtain such privileged support. For those interested in pursuing an enquiry, this type of research sponsor presents risks. The research *leader* (who is directly financed) is given a privileged position. Furthermore, since there are 'technical' deadlines for the presentation of the research, it is very easy for a time lag to develop between research activities and the more political action of the group which wishes to pursue the enquiry. The result is often the return to an isolated research leader who *after* having finished his research communicates its politically relevant results to the group to which he is linked.

(*b*) *A financial research sponsor interested in the political use of analysis results,* such as community organizations or trade unions. In this case possible discrepancies can arise between the political objectives of the sponsor and those of the group which pursues the enquiry. Also, the research can be directly commissioned from a research *leader* even if the group aspect is particularly important. Many of Gilli's reflections on this problem are particularly important.[2]

(*c*) *A non-financing research sponsor chosen by the group pursuing the enquiry* because it is necessary for carrying out political action. Of the three this is the newest type of research situation; it presupposes the existence of a self-financed group, i.e. one that carries out enquiry activities outside work or study hours. By using a contact network between various groups this type of research can yield significant intellectual and political results. The importance of such a setting need not be underlined even if research of this kind can run risks similar to those of the most spontaneous political groupings.

Not only are there *different* types of research sponsors, but there are also different *objects* of research. Even if the group which carries out the enquiry defines its pursuits in a very wide political–intellectual perspective there must still be a precise angle of analysis from which to begin (and with which to grasp both the global implications of the problems studied and the various levels of the research). Very schematically, one can note at least four 'objects' of research, each defined by its link to power in relation to the group carrying out the enquiry. The object of research can be:

(*a*) *Enquiries towards the 'top,'* i.e. referring to the power structure and the structures of the dominant classes. For example, these would include enquiries on the management of power in local groups, on the types of strategies of Italian industrialists, on the links between industry and the army, or between national industry and foreign investments, or even on the strategy of state reforms. Those carrying out the enquiry in this case may find themselves obliged to elaborate structural data as well as data obtained through interviews and direct observation. The importance of such an inversion in the direction of the analysis and its relative political implications need hardly be stressed.

(b) *Enquiries at the intermediary level*, i.e. those in which the object to be analysed shares a similar social status to the members who compose the group carrying out the enquiries (enquiries on educational structures carried out by teachers, on social welfare structures carried out by social operators and on the problem of factory work carried out by the working-class avant-gardes, etc.). This type of enquiry is necessary both in order to single out available forces and to strengthen the intentions of the group, which through the enquiry seeks to clarify its goals.

(c) *Enquiries toward the 'bottom'*, under which heading there are at least two wide areas of analysis. First, there are enquiries carried out on people whose social condition is peripheral in relation to that of the researchers (for example the unemployed, the urban or rural lumpenproletariat, deviants, the elderly, the sick, the handicapped, etc.). If one assumes that the enquiries are undertaken by a group which has ties with the working-class avant-gardes and social workers, the problems studied will obviously be set up in a far different manner from those studied by sociologists like Becker. The second type of analysis includes formative processes in which the relationship between the group undertaking the enquiry and the persons analysed is asymmetrical, not only in political terms but also in terms of age. Enquiries carried out in schools, in first job workplaces and in institutions all fall into this category. It is obvious that one cannot have the same type of interaction with an adult as with a minor. The strategy of the enquiry will be strongly conditioned by this difference.

By taking into account these various articulations one can draw up a combined table of the different possible relationships between the research sponsor and the object of the research enquiry.

This table (which must not be interpreted statically because one group can simultaneously conduct several types of enquiries or pass from one type to another in a short span of time) underscores the possibility of many different types of research situations. One can have an enquiry of category 7 in which, for example, a local organization finances research (which can be transformed into an enquiry) on persons seeking jobs; or

	Object of research			
Research sponsor	Towards 'top'	Intermediary	Towards 'bottom' (type 1)	Towards 'bottom' (type 2)
Financial research sponsor not using the results	1	2	3	4
Financial research sponsor using the results	5	6	7	8
Near-financing research sponsor chosen by enquiry group	9	10	11	12

an enquiry of category 9 in which a group without financial research sponsors proposes to delve deeply into local power structures; or an enquiry of category 10 where a group of teachers does an enquiry on other teachers or on school structures; or a situation of category 4 in which the CNR finances research on minors in an institution.

It is therefore impossible to indicate a unilateral strategy for an enquiry. What has been mentioned previously for traditional research strategies can only serve as an *indication*. It must be refined and specified according to the different possible interests of the enquiry group. Depending on the specific problem, one must choose between different sampling and interviewing techniques, while returning in some cases to the use of mathematical models for synthesis of structural analyses, or of ethno-methodological approaches, or symbolic interaction in radical psychiatry.

Enquiries should, however, be specific even if it is dangerous to suggest any major line to be followed. At a general level, the most important themes for discussion still remain the links with power, the difficulty in the formation of an enquiry group and its ties with other potential political forces. As a subset of these problems, two points must be confronted by all types of enquiries: *the necessity of overcoming the imbalances between different levels of analysis;* and *the necessity of specifying the socialist utopia in an Italian context.*

We have already dwelt on the first point at a general level, but it is important to underline it in terms of the Italian context. Many groups which wish to pursue an enquiry at a political level tend to act in terms of a single institution (one need only think of the struggles within schools and the impact of the struggles within psychiatric hospitals). But these groups do not really try to form connections between their specific problems and wider socio-economic developments. For instance, those who do political work in the school or in social welfare institutions often ignore the wider tendencies of the labour market, neglect general legislative aspects and do not even know what the Mansholt Plan is. The risk of closing oneself in a particular perspective and of then being surprised by the consequences of these wider problems in one's own little acre is very high: one need only think in terms of the tensions produced by heavy unemployment or of rural exodus which reaches such a level that the system can no longer tolerate it, and of social welfare legislation which is enacted in sectoral terms, thus bordering on the realm of folly. Conversely, those who tend to analyse problems at a structural level often 'professionalize' themselves (to become pure economists, experts on agricultural problems, the only authority on judicial matters, the specialist immersed in statistics, etc.). The outcome of such a professional analysis is most often completely cut off from the knowledge acquired by those who work at a specific institutional level.

The linking of such different levels of analysis thus becomes a necessary commitment for all groups who want to carry out an enquiry, so that specific struggles can be situated and evaluated in terms of a wider analysis of the tendencies of Italian capitalism (without however falling prey to the myth that there are 'monopolistic' and 'rational' mechanisms of capital, and with an added awareness of the contradictions and discrepancies at the various centres of power). The split between different levels of analysis is not only synchronic but also diachronic in nature, and in this second sense it is very important to use an historical approach which can explain present as well as future tendencies. Groups which are just beginning to perform enquiries often improvise, which can be seen by their lack of awareness of national and international analyses as well as by their ahistorical outlook. Even class analyses can become very abstract, and one touches here the important problem of how subordinate classes can recover their own history.

All these problems are further aggravated by the lack of information at a structural level which characterizes the Italian situation: the researcher who wishes to undertake political work on the countryside discovers that there are no data available on the class structure of agriculture. The same is true for the researcher who wishes to work on welfare assistance in the North. One must often confront the often incredible classifications of the ISTAT (National Statistical Institute). Even if an increase in knowledge does not imply an increase in politicization and class consciousness (one need only think in terms of the USA where there is perhaps a maximum of information available and where the political situation is well known), it is still true that an imprecise, 'foggy' knowledge can only foster class struggles based on slogans or against slogans, while suggesting levels of conflict which are either too backward or too advanced in relation to the reality of the situation.

We have now reached the second problem: how to outline a socialist utopia in an Italian context. The principal function of an enquiry is to generate new contradictions at increasingly deeper qualitative levels. This is the opposite of the rationalizing function which a system such as the American one attributes to traditional sociological research. In other words, the essential goal is to succeed in fostering a greater political maturity of the politically involved groups in an enquiry, while at the same time carrying on 'possible' objectives for struggle. It is important constantly to shift the basis of the struggle towards objectives which can facilitate the formation of a class consciousness which is alternative to the status quo. For example, an enquiry attempting to oppose the existence of differentiated classes in a school should shift its focus, while involving increasingly greater numbers of persons, to the deeper issue of the values transmitted by schooling. In this complex evolution of analysis and praxis the articulation of a socialist image of society must be faced. Such an image should act as an operative tool both in the short and middle term, thus preventing a fall into reformism.

One of the most important points which Baran and Sweezy stress in their *Monopoly Capital* is the necessary ambivalence of the term *surplus*. On the one hand it is defined as 'the difference between what society produces and the necessary costs of producing it', on the other as 'the index of freedom which society disposes of in carrying out the objectives which it can propose for itself'.[3] In other words, two definitions are given simultaneously: one is operative and diagnoses the situation as it *is;* the other is a definition of an *utopian situation* in which *surplus* is only an indicator of *freedom* on which society can reflect in the process of radically modifying its structures (and therefore not only the distribution of the surplus but also the manner in which it is generated). Baran and Sweezy develop the first type of definition. For the second type, one must turn to other contributions on the division of labour, for instance that of B. Beccalli and M. Salvati.[4] An *implicit* framework of values is always present in each diagnosis, either in relation to the current situation (perceived as immutable in its structures) or to a utopian situation (perceived with relative precision and distance from present reality). The social system as a whole, but in particular its intermediary levels where group enquiries take place, must *specify* the utopia and render its distance explicit. In abandoning the traditional principles of scientificity,

229

Vittorio Capecchi

and in entering specific research situations such as schools, factories, hospitals, etc., the researcher often produces strongly critical diagnoses. This critical stance emanates from *within* the structures of the system, because no alternative utopian vision is defined so as to reveal the faults and deficiencies of the intermediary level (institutions, roles performed, etc.). The existing situation strongly conditions all analysis and subsequent action, since the former is not determined by an articulated utopian model but by generic principles such as 'equality', 'antiauthoritarism', 'creativity', 'communal spirit', and so on, all of which lose hermeneutic value by being too generic. The principal problem therefore remains how to articulate a strategy of intervention given current conditioning. In this context 'the crisis of sociological method' must be perceived as one element in a more complex realm.

Notes

[1] From the numerous documents and articles written on the role of the intellectual and the relationship between theory and practice we cite one of the few essays which does not fall into triumphalistic excesses and which can be truly useful for a debate: E. Masi, 'Di alcuni dei molti problemi non differibili', *Quaderni Piacentini,* IX (1970), 19–34.
[2] G. A. Gilli, *Come si fa ricerca* (Milan 1971), pp. 39–45 and concluding section.
[3] P. A. Baran & P. M. Sweezy, *Monopoly Capital – An Essay on the American Economic and Social Order* (New York 1966), p. 10. Translation made from the Italian (*Editor's note*).
[4] M. Salvati & B. Beccalli, 'Divisione del lavoro, capitalismo, socialismo, utopia', *Quaderni Piacentini,* IX (1970), 18–52.

Index

aggregate interests, 6
agriculture: bases of, 4; class structure of, 206-10; rationalization of, 9; Southern, 59ff; workers in Southern, 47-65
artisans: decline of, 5; persistence of, 15

backwardness: and development, 126, 139; and periphery, 215-18

capitalist organization of work: protest against, 14
capitalist sector: in the South, 45-8; relation to working class, 5
Cassa del Mezzogiorno, 8, 10, 48-9, 60
Centre–Left government, 10-13
centre-periphery, 130ff, 215ff
Christian Democracy: Centre–Right coalition, 16; historical compromise with PCI, 169-72; links with interest groups, 24; links with middle strata, 114-18; and power, 13
class structure: in advanced industrial societies, 5; in Italy, 206-22
clientelary interests, 16, 112-21
collective movements: analysis of, 173-94; economic crisis and, 183ff; feminism and, 174, 189ff; human rights and, 22; single issue orientation of, 17; organization of, 13; parties and, 168-9; and politics, 25, 183ff, 190ff; trade unions and, 167-8
consumerism, 12, 111ff, 146

deviant groups, 19
dualism: in industry, 211-18; in the South, 48ff; in welfare state and market economy, 26-7
dysfunction: of lagging sectors, 4; of Southern migrations to the North, 33-46

economic growth: centrality of, 4; dysfunctional consequences of, 7; model of, 4; the state and, 5

economic miracle, 2, 9-10, 200-5
education: in functional theories, 6; hypotheses on, 78-89; individual mobility and, 6; internal migrations and, 90-9; labour market and, 22; the bourgeoisie and, 83-5
entrepreneurs, 11
European Economic Community (EEC): Mansholt Plan and, 47-65; as market for Italian goods, 12; as new reference point, 10

factory: its intellectual role, 24-5; revolutionary ideology and, 102-3
family: economic role of, 6, 26; in functional theories, 6; internal differentiation of, 197ff; nuclear, 6; in welfare capitalism, 195-205
FIAT: reformist role of, 16, 119; immigrant workers and, 41
functionalism: in education, 79-82; its outlook, 4; social model of, 5

gastarbeiters, 1

housing, 22, 69ff
'hot autumn' (of 1969): demands of, 44; origins of, 120; strikes of, 14, 21

immigration: and labour market, 33-46
industrial reserve army, 50, 132-40
intellectuals: and middle classes, 103; and political radicalization, 85ff, and productivist orientation, 102; as functional specialists, 6; status disequilibrium of, 85ff; and trade unions, 161-2
Italian Communist Party (PCI): consolidation of, 13, 211; historic compromise with DC, 18, 169-72; and the middle strata, 23-4, 116; opposition to, 19; terrorism and, 19; political strength of, 17
Italy: Centre–Left Planning in, 10-13; Crisis Years of, 13-20; economic miracle

Index

Italy (*continued*)
of, 2, 9-10; political debates in, 3; postwar reconstruction of, 8-9; specificity of, 2

labour market: dysfunctions of and substitution processes of, 20-2, 33-46; internal migrations and, 33-46; job offers and supply, 42ff; rationalization of, 45; sectoral modification, 36ff; in South, 61ff; unequal development of, 140-3

lumpenproletariat: in Marxism, 75; political action of, 75-7; persistence of, 15

Mansholt Plan, 21, 47-65, 228

marginality: as ideological category, 25; and industrialization in the South, 130-2; historical context of, 138-40; sectors of, 3

marginal workers: and the middle strata, 24; in Reggio Calabria, 15, 21

market economy, 26ff

Marxism: economic reality and, 215-18; its social categories, 132-40; social thought of, 5; theories of development, 2-3

mass society, 12

Mezzogiorno: as agrarian hinterland, 8; capital intensive industry in, 10; dysfunctional integration of in the EEC, 52ff; dysfunctional migrations from, 33-46; internal differentiation of, 59-60; Mansholt Plan and, 47-65; social classes in, 124-58; university students in, 22, 90-9

middle strata: in underdeveloped areas, 148-55; consumer patterns of, 111ff; function in society, 104; links with marginal working class, 24; in the mechanisms of consensus, 101-23; political connotations of, 104-6

migration: to cities, 4; and education, 90-9; internal, 33-46; in Lombardy, 34-8; from South to North, 9

modernization: agricultural in South, 47-65; critique of, 3-4; dreams of, 6-7; failure of, 26; models of, 2

neo-Fascists: elections of 1972 and, 16; middle strata and, 116, 119-21; recomposition of, 15

North–South division: class differences in, 208ff; interpenetration of, 2-3; new aspects of, 128

pauperization: neo-pauperism, 139; in Rome, 71-5; in the South, 136-40

peasants: supposed decline of, 5; persistence of, 15; role in the South, 49

peripheral economy, 14, 27

planning, 2, 10-13, 16

pole of development, 4, 21

political mediation, 26, 114-17

proletariat: agricultural, 61; semi-proletariat in Rome, 68; in the South, 136-40

reconstruction, 4, 110

Reggio Calabria, 15, 22-3, 121, 145

rent: anti-reform forces and, 117-21; landed, 48; urban, 69

Rome: from capital to periphery, 66-77; economic structure of, 71-5; shantytowns in 22, 66-8, 76

school system, levels of, 78-9; open or closed, 81ff

shopkeepers, 5, 15, 116

social actors: limits of, 3, 190-2; politics of, 25-6

social classes, 5, 23-5

sociologists: as intellectuals, 3: methodological positions of, 223-30; political engagement of, 7, 27-9

sociology in Italy: as an academic profession, 3, 28-9; countersociology, 29; journals of, 29; orientation in 1950s and 1960s, 11; originality of, 3; research stances of, 225-30; significant work in, 2; technological change and, 11

South, *see* Mezzogiorno

Southern Question: 'death of,' 24, 124-5; new terms of, 127-8; technical question of, 11; traditional division of, 8

state, 5, 18

terrorism: and collective movements, 185-90; against historical compromise, 10-19; as topic of sociological analysis, 28; weight of, 1, 14

traditional sectors: economic dualisms of, 3; disappearance of, 5; and social classes, 22

trade unions: consolidation of, 13; centralization and decentralization of, 25, 162-6; global strategy of, 25; role in late 1960s, 16; sociologists and, 28-9; shantytowns and, 22; social and economic crisis and, 159-72

unemployment, 1, 15, 21, 43

underdevelopment, 4, 47ff, 128-9

welfare state, 3, 5, 25-7, 195-205

working class militancy, 1, 14, 165ff

working class: advanced industrial, 5; cen-

232

working class (*continued*)
tral vs peripheral, 15, 143-6; consolidation of, 5, 146-8; female, 35-6, 133; highly skilled, 5, 37-40; marginal workers and middle strata, 112-17, 144-6; middle class allies of, 23; older, 36-7; peripheral, 27, 105; privileged vs non-privileged, 19, 105; professional categories of, 14, 37-9; weakness on national scale, 26

81448742R00139

Made in the USA
Middletown, DE
24 July 2018